Beowulf on Film

Beowulf on Film
Adaptations and Variations

NICKOLAS HAYDOCK and
E.L. RISDEN

McFarland & Company, Inc., Publishers
Jefferson, North Carolina, and London

ALSO OF INTEREST
Hollywood in the Holy Land: Essays on Film Depictions of the Crusades and Christian-Muslim Clashes, edited by Nickolas Haydock and E.L. Risden (McFarland, 2009)
Movie Medievalism: The Imaginary Middle Ages, by Nickolas Haydock (McFarland, 2008)

LIBRARY OF CONGRESS CATALOGUING-IN-PUBLICATION DATA

Haydock, Nickolas.
    Beowulf on film : adaptations and variations / Nickolas Haydock and E.L. Risden.
      p.   cm.
    Includes bibliographical references and index.

    ISBN 978-0-7864-6338-1
    softcover : acid free paper ∞

    1. Beowulf—Film adaptations.
  I. Risden, Edward L., 1957–   II. Title.
PR1585.H39 2013
791.43'657—dc23   2013024311

BRITISH LIBRARY CATALOGUING DATA ARE AVAILABLE

© 2013 Nickolas Haydock and E.L. Risden. All rights reserved

No part of this book may be reproduced or transmitted in any form or by any means, electronic or mechanical, including photocopying or recording, or by any information storage and retrieval system, without permission in writing from the publisher.

Front cover image: scene from *Beowulf*, 2007 (Paramount Pictures/Photofest)

Manufactured in the United States of America

McFarland & Company, Inc., Publishers
  Box 611, Jefferson, North Carolina 28640
  www.mcfarlandpub.com

Contents

Acknowledgments	vi
Introduction—A Freud Complex and the Problem of Beowulf *in Film* (E.L. RISDEN)	1
1—Film Theory, the Sister Arts Tradition and the Cinematic *Beowulf* (NICKOLAS HAYDOCK)	27
2—The Cinematic Commoditization of *Beowulf*: The Serial Fetishizing of a Hero (E.L. RISDEN)	66
3—Making Sacrifices (NICKOLAS HAYDOCK)	81
4—The Hero, the Mad Male Id and a Feminist *Beowulf*: The Sexualizing of an Epic (E.L. RISDEN)	119
5—O Dragon, Where Art Thou? "Othering" in *Beowulf* Films (E.L. RISDEN)	132
6—Meat Puzzles: *Beowulf* and the Horror Film (NICKOLAS HAYDOCK)	143
7—Our Man Beowulf: Bowra, Ker and the Contemporary Struggle with Heroism (E.L. RISDEN)	167
Conclusion—The Postmodern Beowulf (NICKOLAS HAYDOCK)	177
Chapter Notes	191
Works Cited	201
Index	205

Acknowledgments

Nickolas Haydock: Thanks are due a number of people who supported and encouraged my work on this project. Dean of the Faculty of Arts Dr. Juan López Garriga and Associate Dean Dr. Miguel Castro generously facilitated my work on the book with release time for the academic year 2012-2013. My department chair, Kevin Carroll, and assistant chair, Rosita Rivera, helped to make the case for reduced course loads in straightened circumstances. Jonathan Wilcox, Tom Shippey, Karl Fugelso, José Irizarry, and E.L. Risden read earlier versions of my chapters and made them stronger. Earlier versions of chapters one and three appear in *Studies in Medievalism* and *Year's Work in Medievalism*. Final thanks, as ever, go to my wife, Socorro Rodríguez Santaliz, *el amor de mi vida*.

E. L. Risden: Parts of my chapters have appeared in earlier versions in the following forms:

"The Cinematic Sexualizing of *Beowulf*." *Essays in Medieval Studies* (2010): 109–15. Presented at the Medieval Association of the Midwest and Illinois Medieval Association Joint Conference, Chicago, February 2010.

"Beowulf Goes Corporate: Epic Medievalism Gets Mod at the Movies." Panel presentation, 47th International Congress on Medieval Studies, Kalamazoo, Michigan, May 2012.

"*No Such Thing* as *Beowulf* Fim." Medieval Association of the Midwest 27th Annual Conference, De Pere, Wisconsin, September 2011.

"Our Man Beowulf: C. M. Bowra and the Cinematic Struggle with Epic Heroism." Northern Plains Conference on Early British Literature, Winona, Minnesota, April 2011.

"Hero, Id, and a Feminist *Beowulf*: Freud Meets Epic Flicks." Invited Honors Lecture at Minnesota State University — Moorhead, March 2011.

"O Dragon, Where Art Thou? Othering in *Beowulf* Films." 28th Conference of the Illinois Medieval Association, Chicago, February 2011.

"From Epic to Heaneywulf to Digital 3-D: *Beowulf* and the Cultural Quantum of Consciousness." 24th Annual Conference of the Medieval Association of the Midwest, Fargo, North Dakota, September 2008.

We both would like to thank José Irizarry for his help with the images reproduced in this book.

Introduction — A Freud Complex and the Problem of *Beowulf* in Film

E. L. RISDEN

This book explores both in terms of theory and practice the growing list of films about or inspired by the Old English epic poem *Beowulf*. Close readings of these films, which no one has yet completed, and a comparative study to note their many and curious variants, both with respect to the poem and to one another, should, we hope, add to aesthetic appreciation and academic consideration of the films and, perhaps more productively, lead audiences back to the original, with all its cultural, linguistic, and inherent visual power.

We are also responding theoretically to Nickolas Haydock's *Movie Medievalism* and the book on the Crusades in film that we co-edited, *Hollywood in the Holy Land*, but with a more specific focus on what in many ways includes an equally provocative but more problematic topic. The difficulty — and the potential — for a study such as this one lies in the fact that most of the films made to date based loosely on *Beowulf* aren't especially good movies. And whatever titles they may bear, they stray quickly from anything that students of the poem would willingly call *Beowulf* — not to say that they don't take interesting directions of their own. Those facts don't mean that critics can't or won't find quite a good number of useful and interesting approaches to them worthy of extended treatment — in some ways bad films or variations on originals can stimulate discussion and study as well as good ones or attempts at faithful reproduction — only that one must treat them as troubled or suasive texts rather than notable aesthetic or traducive accomplishments. We argue that the films derived from or connected by title to *Beowulf* establish an interesting if yet incomplete body of critical variants with specific social commentary: they invariably sway not only from the story, but also from the themes and concerns of the original to those more interesting to the filmmakers and, one may guess they believe, to their audiences. Yet, as the first chapter below demonstrates, these films do sometimes reproduce or evoke the poem's visual strategies with a fidelity and imaginativeness worthy of our attention.

The films we treat include those titled *Beowulf,* but also those that clearly derive from and respond to it, such as *The 13th Warrior* and *No Such Thing.* We also aim to show the persistent power and cinematic permutation of the epic-heroic motif, as represented in *Beowulf* the epic: whether filmmakers choose to treat it directly or to deconstruct it, they almost inevitably return to it because it has had such an overwhelming influence on our art and culture, and the pervasive influence of cinema as a medium inevitably affects the subsequent reception of the literary work.

We direct this book to the same readers who have enjoyed the previous two film books as well as those by Kevin Harty and others on cinematic *medievalism,* but also to readers, students, and teachers of *Beowulf*—not an insignificant number, given that Tom Shippey has called *Beowulf* the most written-upon poem in English literary history. We hope also to appeal to readers and scholars interested in cinematic *heroism,* films based on literary classics, recent film history and technology, and even cultural criticism: as film theorist Robert Stam has argued, as with literature film genre "is also permeable to historical and social tensions" (*Film Theory: An Introduction,* 14). These films, like all others, respond to the *zeitgeist*: they measure the pulse of how we are processing old notions of heroism in contemporary bodies of work, and they teach us more about our own times than about the literary works from which they nominally derive.

We know of no other books currently in print on this subject, but we have heard of other scholars working on it and encourage them to continue: the scholarly community (as well as the more general movie-going public) can find much yet to say and write on a subject we believe will continue to grow and that deserves many voices and approaches. The volume we have found so far that most nearly pertains is *The Medieval Hero on Screen* by Martha Driver, Sid Ray, and Jonathan Rosenbaum; it doesn't treat *Beowulf* at length, but it does address some of the issues we raise, and we believe our readers will benefit from consulting it. We felt moved to assemble this book partly because *Beowulf* provides such a perfect opportunity for cinematic exploitation and exploration. Also, by discussing how filmmakers have invariably swerved from the directions of the poem to make movies that plot their own course often far from that of the original, we believed we could engage in the dialogue about how film both adapts and inflects culture, how it changes our habits and methods of reading and how it may even direct our actions— certainly our understanding.

We also believe that a place exists for a full-length *Beowulf* film that actually sticks pretty closely to the poem; in fact, we wonder that no one has yet avoided the temptation to stray into contemporary polemic, sticking simply to the story that already bears so much cinematographic potential, especially with all that the new technology can do to visualize adventure stories. A brief (just short of twenty-seven minutes) animated version appeared in 1998, written by Murray Watts, directed by Yuri Kulakov, with the estimable Derek Brewer as Advisor; it sticks rather closer to the epic than do most films, but it leaves out a lot, and it, too, occasionally takes its own course (for instance, it casts doubt on the nature of the dragon, whether it is a real dragon or some kind of psychological monster related to the hero's mind). The qualities of the poem, from plot to poetry, have yet to convince a filmmaker of its validity *as is*— it has suffered invasions from a range of other interests, from Freudian thought to video games to contemporary feminism.

The Old English epic poem *Beowulf* has a marvelously simple plot. Beowulf fights Grendel, a monster, and he wins; Beowulf fights Grendel's mother, a monster, and he wins; Beowulf fights a dragon, another monster, and he partly wins. He kills the dragon, and the dragon kills him. That's the end. That's the whole plot. But it makes enough for a powerful if brief epic poem, and it relatively should make enough for great cinema as well.

A great deal of critical material has appeared in response to that seemingly simple story—*Beowulf* generates a perpetual industry of scholarly work all on its own. The few films that have evolved from it have left us critical but interested, irked or impressed. Actually anything that has the *Beowulf* name on it tends *not* to be particularly good, and the best *Beowulf* films actually have other names. One wouldn't necessarily even know from hearing about them that they are *Beowulf* films, which creates an interesting problem for anyone wanting to study how filmmakers have translated epic to screen.

Translation across time as well as language and medium also means translation with respect to culture, intellectual milieu, and artistic taste. For instance, few artistic endeavors of the twentieth century and beyond entirely escape Freud's influence — or that of science or of modern economics. I'm not particularly Freudian myself, but because we live in the twenty-first century, everybody necessarily experiences a Freudian influence on how we perceive ourselves and our relationships to some degree whether we like it or not; Freud has had that great an effect on how we think about art and society and self. His work so enters our discourse, our thought, our *zeitgeist*, and our collective unconscious that we tend toward psychoanalytic readings at some point in nearly any process of criticism (or creation). So to understand what's going on in cinematic representations of *Beowulf*, we do well to gain a little understanding of how our *Freudian* thinking, if not Freud's work itself, inflects products of the medium, and from there, along with some related issues, I will pursue this introduction.

Similarly because of the growth of science as a way of knowing and the enormous increase in technology that has accompanied the expansion of science into nearly all parts of our lives, popular notions of science, science fiction, and the products of our technological boom have also influenced how we recreate classic literature in new media — that fact has affected (and, perhaps, afflicted) *Beowulf* in all its new incarnations. So has economics: while *Beowulf* remains a classic text for classroom study, most younger persons encounter it first (if at all) in its cinematic or artistic renderings rather than in a relatively faithful translation (let alone in its original language). Our society wants *salable* products, not real masterpieces; the former fly from vendors shelves, while the latter tend to linger in the dusty shelves of their largely ignored libraries. Popular taste (or filmmakers' notions of it) redirect what a film will do with story, characters, even what may seem to scholars indispensable ideas and themes from the original.

Below I intend to stray just a little into Freud's thought and to place it amidst the changing intellectual landscape of the twentieth century to help elucidate what I find going on in the films we'll discuss in the following chapters, but also to reflect on how the medium of film has modulated what we do with the epic as we move it from classic text to consumable visual product. *Beowulf* in film has felt the pressure from Freud, from vast changes in cultural expectations and interactions, and from a refiguration of the cultural and intellectual context that produced the original: art of any sort inevitably expresses the tensions of its time, and incarnations of nominally the same text may change into something that would have gone unrecognizable to times past.

Establishing an approach to heroism may also help, since *Beowulf* in film must necessarily deal with heroes, what they do, and how they work, and there I will begin my analysis. The poem deals explicitly and centrally with cultural imperatives of heroism; without understanding their notions and our versions of their notions, we can't begin to think of any adaptation as a *Beowulf* of any sort. But ancient notions of heroism and the modern problem with heroism take rather different directions, and we get the collection of Beowulf films that we have from those very differences.

The word *heros* in Greek really originally just meant *nobleman*. As heroes gradually emerge as more complex characters in more complicated stories, they grow into something much more than that. In our literatures we have tended to vary them pretty rapidly, but what the word means at its inception has affected how our notions have evolved. The heroes such as Achilles and

Odysseus, whom we know from the famous epics, have good and bad qualities, act alternately well and poorly, and can get better or worse. *Heros*, hero, doesn't necessarily imply that that person is a good person, only that that person is a noble person who has performed noteworthy deeds. We start evolving our notion of heroism with the Greeks, not that we didn't have figures we would now term heroic before that — we did — but that the term establishes audience expectations that haven't entirely left us since. Our students may say that their parents and their community or religious leaders are their heroes, but then they read comic books or magazines about media stars, play video games, and go to movies to see someone and something bigger than life. Whatever they may tell us about their tastes for "realism" and the admiration they have for persons who have shown them kindness or courage, they still enjoy stories of larger-than-life characters with special abilities and the desire to strive for excellence beyond typical human achievement.

We also get from the Greeks the term *protagonist*. It breaks down with some pretty easy etymology into *proto agonistes,* which literally means the "first wrestler." The protagonist doesn't have to be any particular kind of character, just the main character in a story, the one who is wrestling with the problem, the primary wrestler of that story. Now we may have other kinds of wrestlers working with that problem or other problems, but the main one, the protagonist, begins — and often ends — as our *hero* for that story. There's an interesting connection with *heros*, hero, and *proto agonistes*, the first wrestler, and it comes in pretty early: protagonist and hero become one and the same, ready to help us wrestle with problems we may be too weak to solve ourselves.

Also, coming into our literature surprisingly early (from Greek tragedies to knightly Romance to picaresque) is the attraction to the anti-hero, and that notion has had a strong influence on *Beowulf* films. As our collective cultural notions of hero gradually fall, our interest in the anti-hero rises. While tragedy kept us among nobles, but nobles who fall by their own errors, the idea of the *picaro,* which comes out of late medieval or early Renaissance Spain, allows us to focus our attention on non-noble protagonists. *Lazarillo de Tormes* is probably the first, unless we would consider the arch-priest in *Libro de Buen Amor* his precursor, and Don Quixote and Sancho Panza follow them into questions of class, madness, and the possibility of truly noble action. We tend to think of the anti-hero as a Modernist turn, a function of twentieth-century tastes for irony and deconstruction; it is, but it isn't exclusively so — it actually goes back a good long way historically and has appeared with nearly the same consistency as the hero.

When we look at *Beowulf* (the poem), we see a traditional, *real* hero — a figure typical of epic as genre, not perfect, but powerful, influential, with traits the time and context viewed as essential to heroism. Beowulf does exactly what a hero is supposed to do. He doesn't really ever fail; he neither requires heroic prophylaxis, nor could anyone in his world provide it. He has great strength and courage, shows devotion to his lord and his duty, undertakes all his tasks with a sense of fair play and even, until the last, a sense of humor. He doesn't suffer from greed, the "deadliest" sin in his context, because it most easily leads to disunity among a people. What may look to a modern audience like pride isn't pride in the Christian sense; for instance, Beowulf will tell beforehand what he is going to do when he plans to enter a fight. Modern readers, when we find him do so, may think him insufficiently humble and therefore bad. But in the Germanic-heroic context, he acts as he should, with confidence and commitment. He must say, "Here is what I am going to do and here is how I'm going to do it." So before Beowulf faces Grendel in the first monster fight, he actually says he will meet Grendel alone and without the aid of weapons. Where we find arrogance, his listeners would find heroism. So Beowulf follows traditional strictures. The hero seeks, as the poem tells us, *lof* and *dom*, "praise and glory." But that's also not a bad thing because he lives in a world that doesn't have any other kind of immortality. Gaining praise and fame serves a significant social function: to have notable heroes in one's troop makes the *dryht* much less likely to be attacked by outsiders. Tribes without famous heroes face a much greater likelihood of regular attack from armies and harrying bands. The hero has great value as a commodity.

So we have this idea of the traditional hero, embodied in Beowulf, and we have also this modern notion of anti-hero that enters very powerfully as we translate the medieval epic into contemporary film; the ideas tend to struggle, mix, and meld. Traditional poetry also gives us some heroic *metaphors* to translate, visual or verbal or even semi- or pseudo-historical images that accompany heroic behaviors in the literature. Medieval narrative follows a specific kind of quest toward what I call the *heart of light*; we may contrast it with the modern psychological descent best exemplified in Joseph Conrad's *The Heart of Darkness*. Probably the single most famous fictional adventure of the Middle Ages, the quest for the Holy Grail, takes us to the heart of light. What do the knights see when they look in the Holy Grail? They see the light of God, the mysteries of Christ. The Grail quest is a very difficult adventure, and it varies greatly among many versions. Depending on the source, maybe nobody gets to it, maybe only one knight gets to it, maybe three knights get to it, but even then they don't all achieve it to the same degree of completion, the full degree of experience, a vision of God sufficient, in today's common parlance, to die for. But that's the quest everybody wants to undertake. Once we learn in the Arthurian tales about the Grail and about the beginning of the quest to find it, all Arthur's knights immediately stand up and say, "We will pursue that quest for at least a year and a day before we come home." Everybody wants to find the heart of light. That quest, in its replacement of the sacred for the profane, best defines the heroism of the Christian Middle Ages. Few of the knights fully realize the difficulty of the quest and what its accomplishment would bring, but they commit to it anyway.

Once we've passed Freud (and absorbed Einstein and Saussure) and got into the twentieth century, we pursue a different kind of quest. It starts *by name* around the same time Freud's work appears in print: Conrad's *The Heart of Darkness* interprets what is beginning in many of the writers and, more generally, thinkers of his time. He anticipates what goes on through much of the twentieth century by turning the old "external" quest for the heart of light into a new "internal" quest for what lies at the dark center of our experience. In the book the nominal external quest, Marlow's journey to find Kurtz, who has lost himself in the "barbaric" practices of the deep, dark jungle, turns into a glimpse of what Kurtz has actually done: thrown himself into the darkest corners of the human spirit. We need a character who searches for the person and finds him, but who can himself reject the descent into the abyss. Marlow finds little more than a disembodied voice because the body, the person, already has descended into that abyss, beyond reclamation. Of course, Conrad urges us to think of Marlow's quest as metaphorical as well as physical. It's not just a quest into someone else's dark jungles, into the Congo far from European "civility." The heart of darkness, Marlow's as well as Kurtz's, is inside — that's where one must go to find it. The deep, dark quest into the deep, dark psyche and all the things we don't know and don't want to know about ourselves lies well below where any normal person feels willing to hunt for it: we need a kind of hero — more exactly, anti-hero — to have the courage to descend so deep. So we move from the quest for the heart of light, the hero's quest, to the quest for the heart of darkness, the anti-hero's quest in the twentieth century. Much of our art, our poetry, and our film then follows in that same quest, so that much of the audience has come to view the quest for the heart of light as maudlin, even childish — we believe we have grown out of it.

Probably more than any others, two metaphors guide twentieth century intellectual and creative life. In addition to Conrad's heart of darkness, the other comes from T.S. Eliot's *The Waste Land*. Particularly after World War I Europe found itself in an expanding wasteland culturally and economically as well as from the lingering effects of the war. The War taught us some things about ourselves as humans: we could no longer hope that *human* implied *humane*. We learned some things about technology, too, that we didn't like, that scared us. We didn't want to know that humans would willingly use machines, poisons, and aircraft to kill one another in vast numbers, but we learned. The War left Europe with a blasted landscape, a wasteland that defied easy repair. All sorts of new doubts arose, and all the things we thought we knew, the things we thought we could trust about ourselves, we lost in that wasteland. The turning inward of the quest comes partly from Freud, but it comes also from the War. It comes most specifically from the introspection into the brutality of human nature, what Conrad called the "fascination of the abomination." The quest for the heart of light remained for many persons an essential part of religious life, but it disappeared as any kind of cultural hope, replaced by a desire to analyze the heart of darkness within each of us.

Around the middle of the twentieth century, in the move from Modernism to Post-Modernism, we did a little bit of the same thing, but we extended the metaphor even further. The quest for the heart of darkness, we found, ultimately leads to nothing. It's a quest into the abyss, into a loss of meaning; with the loss of meaning comes a loss of hope. Hope becomes something quaint, and heroism becomes something for sport and for advertisements, to get us to play or to purchase, not a means to face the real trials of life and international exchange. In the Postmodern world, what do we read?—nothing but the text. As Jacques Derrida, the French deconstructionist and philosopher, would say—there's nothing that isn't text, there's nothing but the text, and even the text falls apart as a construct of our prejudices, expectations, and predilections. No meaning lies within or behind there but the meaning you and I bring to it. And that's one of the big problems that we have even now trying to continue with any kind of quest that we want to believe can lead us to something worth finding. We've taken away *towards*, because we having nothing to move towards: it won't be there when we get there. It will recede indefinitely. There is no heart of light, and even the heart of darkness may at last be illusion. We will find only an abyss, a perpetual *mise en abyme*. We can still suffer loss, but we cannot find something positive at the end of a quest: quest and result disappear like illusions. Postmodernism leaves us in a wasteland of irony.

If we find anything in this quest, the twentieth century teaches us that the reason we pursue anything is simply pleasure. And that idea also goes back to Freud: the pleasure principle lies behind our pursuits. Roland Barthes' *The Pleasure of the Text* (1973, translated into English in 1975) suggests that even the text becomes masturbatory: a text draws us much as does a sexual experience, though privately. Certainly those of us who pursue literature either as our life's work or for leisure do so partly for pleasure, because we love reading, we love good books, we love good stories. But is the pleasure of the text really a sexual pleasure, or does the metaphor simply provide a means of transgression, of turning a gentle pleasure into something naughty to give it a new cachet? Barthes has fun playing with that idea, but it's still a very Freudian turn, and hardly a necessary one, yet it falls into line with what makes the twentieth and twenty-first century literary landscapes so difficult to navigate. If reading is only a sexual pleasure, self-indulgent and self-absorbed, it produces nothing. So we've lost any connection to heroism, we've lost meaning, and we've even lost the safe pleasure of reading that we could once enjoy unabashedly: now we must read in shameful, solitary silence. Sadly, I think movies are taking us in much the same direction: they have less and less the quality of shared public intellectual spectacle and more of the joy-stick private self-gratification. To succeed for that medium in our time, it seems, they must teach us that heroism, the heart of light, the possibility for good, and shared intellectual and artistic experience don't matter.

In the tensions among pleasure, desire, quest, and the sublimation of both creative and "death" drives, we return to Freud. In the 1905 book *Three Essays on the Theory of Sexuality* we find the beginning of many of the ideas we associate with Freud. *Heart of Darkness* appeared in 1899, right at the turn of the twentieth century. The year 1905 proved remarkable on another front of the changing intellectual landscape: Einstein's paper on relativity and the relationship between matter and energy. Relativity turned science in a wonderful new direction, and it entered popular culture and got misinterpreted pretty powerfully and pretty quickly as well. It led to ideas of relativity of meaning and relativity of moral and ethical practice: away went a lot of the old quest for the heart of light. Once everything is relative, we don't really have anything worth finding in the long run (as W.S. Gilbert might say, now everybody's nobody). An intellectually pervasive misinterpretation or a misextension of Einstein's work grades the landscape in which Freud's work on pleasure and sexuality appears. Freud wrote in *Three Essays*—he's writing about aberration and neurosis — that humans have an inherent disposition to perversion. That may not seem like a very nice thing to say about your neighbors, friends and family, but Freud suggested we're stuck with it because perversion is a part of who we are, how we feel and think. In the second essay he developed the idea of infantile sexuality and the Oedipus Complex, though he didn't use those words yet. The term *Oedipus Complex* comes later, but he was developing the idea already in 1905 as we begin doubting the existence of *fact* and fearing ourselves plagued by an internal *heart of darkness*.

Of course everybody was shocked at the idea of infantile sexuality to begin with, but Freud was working towards an idea of pleasure principle—

that's where the work moves more generally. We are not so exclusively sexually driven as more generally pleasure directed. In the third essay he wrote that as we emerge from the infantile stage of our lives, we move gradually towards a consolidating of sexual identity. So what starts as perhaps an inherent predisposition to perversion turns, if we're healthy and move properly into adulthood, towards a reasonable, appropriate sexual relationship with another person, a situation not exclusively self-indulgent, although the goal is still one's individual pleasure.[1]

Beyond the Pleasure Principle (1920) begins with the tensions among movement towards pleasure, the unconscious predisposition towards repetition, and our troubling over the death instinct. We place libido versus patterns of organization and social life versus a death drive or natural tendency towards destructiveness. For Freud, that tension appears naturally in the biological process of anabolism or metabolism. We eat our dinner so we can burn off calories to power our activities. Freud saw also in that movement, the intake of calories, building up and burning off energy, a general metaphor for the way life works, for the way the mind works, the way experience works, the way life develops. We start with a life instinct, a movement towards preservation and a movement towards some kind of advancement. But inevitably things turn the other way: they fail, they atrophy, they break down over the course of time. That's the tension in which we live, the natural mix of anabolism and catabolism.

The libido, Freud said, is not just a sexual energy, but a general creative energy that comes from the build-up of tensions between the desire to create and a recognition of mortality. When we're born, the first big question we have to ask is, "Do I get to live forever?" and the answer is "no." That's actually the big question in the first epic poem that we have, too, perhaps the first lasting piece of literature that human beings created: *The Epic of Gilgamesh*. That is Gilgamesh's great question, when his friend, Enkidu, dies: "Do I get to live forever?" His quest leads him only to the answer that he, like all mortals, must die. "What do I do next, then?" formulates itself as the next question Gilgamesh must ask, and the answer he gets from the gods is "Be nice. Be good to your family, and treat them well. Love your spouse, and love your children. Be good to your friends. Enjoy your life. Enjoy what life allows you." That's it.

Freud is looking at that question, too, and that answer (though through the lens of psychopathology) because that's the tension within which the individual (and the society in which he or she lives) must grow to adulthood. These ideas later become Freud's *eros* and *thanatos*. *Eros* is the erotic, but also the creative energy or impulse. *Thanatos* is the contrary death instinct, though more healthfully we may see it as a recognition of our own mortality, that the life-energy eventually gives out no matter how hard we try to preserve it. No wonder this thought/emotion complex appears as a tension with tendencies to move toward disease. We have the drive to live, and perhaps the drive to produce something immortal that can last beyond us, but we also have a constant awareness of lurking mortality, which Freud is partly working out in *Beyond the Pleasure Principle.* The pleasure principle remains, and it still drives us, but he's looking at other factors behind the pleasure drive that move how we think, how we act, and how we feel in the world of living and struggling with overwhelming power of that recognition.

In 1923 *The Ego and the Id* appeared, and it includes the elements of Freud's thoughts on psychology that remain most influential in popular parlance and popular culture. The *id*, the unstructured intellectual drive, instinctual drive, biological drive, the basic drive that moves most of our normal actions, largely follows the pleasure principle. The *ego*, the part of us that wants to organize things, tries to follow what it perceives as reality: it wants to locate reality and believe in it and stick to it. It tries to please the id in realistic ways, so it's particularly an intellectual drive in that though it feels the pleasure principle, it doesn't feel entirely comfortable with it and tries to direct our desire for pleasure in ways that it considers proper and useful. Beyond id and ego we have a *superego,* literally what stands above the ego: it takes steps towards self-control and morality. Superego includes conscience, but it also involves a kind of narcissistic satisfaction. It aims to direct and to limit our pursuit of pleasure, but also to lead us to the belief that we are doing the right thing socially and personally. It imposes a social limitation on both id and ego. Our problems often come, then, when we the ego, the part we normally think of as personality, gets bombarded from both sides, the id and the superego, which may stand at opposite poles of desire. The id says, "Have fun!" and the superego says, "Listen to what your parents tell you, listen to what the law tells you, and follow the rules." Ego ends up stuck in the middle, working with both of those drives and trying to moderate and resolve them. That's the essence of *The Ego and the Id,* and its ideas have powerfully affected all of our psychology and nearly all of our art and criticism ever since. Nearly all of the attempts to turn Beowulf into film have felt its influence powerfully: if our time can't believe in classical heroism for its own sake, we must find reasons for the heroes' behaviors, and we have gone first to the well of Freud's work to find reasons we believe audiences will accept for the heroes' motivations and actions.

Civilization and Its Discontents (1930) directs our attention to the civil strictures on *eros* that lead to *thanatos*: discontent comes from the tension between drives for personal satisfaction and society's need to temper individuals' innate savage urge for satisfaction for the sake of our ability to live in mutual harmony (or at least an equilibrium short of mutual destruction). Tensions between civilization and the individual (the pressure of social conformity) create repression of urges and of instinctual drives, thus individual discontent that can spread through a society. Religion can provide sublimation, but the pleasure principle persists. And we also aim to avoid displeasure. We seek freedom and gratification, yet we realize the limitations of social reality and communal authority, and so try to avoid the displeasure that would accompany breaking social rules. So civilization necessarily leads to some discontent and even to pathology by its intention to limit freedom and to control us as individuals. The pleasure principle remains, powerfully so, and ego is still working with id and superego on both sides, but civilization provides a medium that informs the superego and keeps the person, ideally, on a safe path, moderated between gratification and destructive excess. Civilization will always displease us in some way because it always places limits. So, Freud suggests, as much as we need civilization to keep us from socially destructive self-indulgence, we always feel unhappy with it because it never allows us the freedom to do exactly what we want to do.

The history of heroism has exhibited many of Freud's tensions. *Beowulf* as epic shows them in Beowulf's drive for the personal status of hero and his culture's drive to make the best use of him in that role. From it he gains lasting fame, a kind of immortality and thus eros in the face of thanatos; the culture reins him in enough so that his heroic acts save his people (or those he serves in any case) from destruction: he lives to fight another day so they may fight to live another day. *Beowulf*, of course, does not begin that idea, but uses an idea as old as human stories, that heroism begins with *eros*, not erotic love, but with the need to create, the need to do something, to achieve something beyond the usual that we can call of value, something of importance that makes one feel fully alive and real and valuable—that's where heroism starts, I think, in our classic texts, and it persists as a cultural as well as personal values system. Pretty quickly, though, even the best of heroes meet the death principle; they meet the thanatos, a desire to destroy and also to confront Death. Beowulf, before he fights Grendel, actually tells a joke that may not seem funny to audiences today, but was probably funny in its original context. First he asks permission from Hroðgar, king of the Danes, to fight the monster; when he gets it, he says he will fight the monster without weapons, since the monster has none, both out of a sense of fair play and to add to his fame should he win. Then comes the joke, as he adds that if he wins, they will have a party, but if he loses, no one will need to look for his body. Why not? Grendel will have eaten it! Beowulf must come to grips early in his heroic career with the constant presence of death: the sacrifice one makes for choosing the heroic life, and perhaps a fascination on the part of the hero with death, its horror and its mystery.

Film versions of *Beowulf* have not seen that kind of traditional heroic (or Freudian) motivation as sufficient to draw the hero into deadly battles: they have found their own fascination in sexual abomination, in the place where the id moves into strange desires, and neither the ego nor the superego can control it.

In the twentieth century generally — and in cinema particularly — we've moved beyond the old *eros* as a life-drive or the Anglo-Saxon *lof* and *dom*, praise and glory, as an ego drive; we've moved beyond thanatos, too, as a desire to confront the reality of our own death and stave it off for a time with memorable actions. In our time the superego has struck us like a right cross in the face: that's where Conrad's *Heart of Darkness* and Eliot's *The Waste Land* have joined Freud to impinge on our old notions of heroism. Our social science says we can't really be heroes any more, not in the old sense — our military tells us otherwise, but it arms us with incredibly technologically sophisticated weapons to face the monstrous Other, an other created by a specific kind of public discourse to encourage young persons to place their lives on the line for the "good" of their societies. We have no heroes of the old sort because we quickly show, once we have used up our willing youth, that no one is really any better than anyone else: political discourse tells the public that because their side tortures, our side must torture, too — no heroism in that. Media sources are eager to prove that we all have our good points, our courage and devotion to country, and we all have our flaws, our brutality, greed, and desire for power and superiority. No hero can stand out for long, because his or her flaws will become public just as his or her heroic actions once did. Today's hero becomes tomorrow's monster. Win today, and the immediate question arises, "So what are you going to do for us tomorrow?"

Freud's psychology makes the same point: that's where *Civilization and Its Discontents* comes in. One has the drive to do something to believe one may be great. As we act heroically, we go to some kind of excess, so society puts a stop to our drives by finding a way to say, "Don't do that: that's excessive, that's dangerous, that's bad." There enters our discontent: we want to continue into greater excesses of heroism, even if it means diving into the heart of darkness or creating a wasteland to get there: the drive becomes self-perpetuating and excess-generating, like an addictive drug. That's what we get with heroes in our time: they're trying to function constantly within that almost-impossible-to-eliminate discontent. *Beowulf* in film takes heroes beyond the point of achievement and satiety to the realm of excess, of failure, of thanatos, of the hero's death-in-life: public failure, which must sooner or later come, or success that still leads to a kind of exile. Our fascination comes not in the success, but in the abomination: the reason Conrad takes Marlow all the way to find a Kurtz who barely has the strength to take his final breaths. He can still, though, express the *fascination of the abomination*. That's one reason Robert Zemeckis's *Beowulf* takes not a chaste hero to a final, fitting, mortal monster fight, but instead a morally weak and sexually indulgent hero to the wasteland of age and decay and finally to battle against his own monstrous son born from a willing tryst with a monster. The film exhorts us to pay for our sexual sins; the epic shows us nothing like that at all. Graham Baker's 1999 version of *Beowulf* makes a similar point: Hrothgar has brought death to his own folk by consorting with a native she-monster who has borne him a monstrous son.

Part of this cinematic vector comes also from the public tensions that developed with the rise of Feminism. The *Beowulf*-poet actually shows feminine sensibilities. We can hardly call it *feminist* because of anachronism: the term applies to a more modern and still contemporary movement, not to thoughts or works of the distant past. We can, though, see that the poem exhibits sympathies for Wealhþeow, Freawaru, Hygd, and even Grendel's Mother: she does no real evil, only avenges her son. *Beowulf* is not, furthermore, simply a pro-male poem: the men sometimes act well and sometimes act badly; we get examples of good kings and bad, good heroes and bad, and bad (and ill-treated) servants. Similarly some women in the poem — most, in fact — act well, and one acts poorly; all arouse audience interest if not outright sympathy for their circumstances. Hroðgar's wife, Wealhþeow, acts prudently and generously in steering her husband's course through the Beowulf adventure. Her name, Wealhþeow, shows us her function in the world of the text: *wealh* means "foreigner" and *þeow* means "slave" or "servant." Even as queen of the Danes she's a special kind of foreign slave: she got married off to Hroðgar, probably by no choice of her own, to end a blood feud between her people and his. Blood feuds can end when somebody wins and one tribe is destroyed, when nobody wins but both tribes are destroyed, or when a noble bride from one family marries a noble husband from the other, so that they become one family, one blood or kin, ending the possibility of blood-vengeance. More often than not, such a marriage didn't work: the soldiers, still angry at one another, would find reasons to fight anyway. That kind of story appears in the lengthy allusion to Hildeburh's marriage to Finn in *Beowulf*. The woman finds herself in a difficult position when she gets married: she must enter a new family, one with which her own has warred, and by her faithfulness convince that family not to fight a blood feud anymore. As the *Beowulf*-poet makes quite clear, that solution is less than foolproof. Hildeburh's family marries her off to a prince from another tribe, and the families meet for a party, but the feud starts up again. Hildeburh's husband gets killed, her sons are killed, and one of her brothers is killed; the remaining members of her family bring her home again, her marital embassage having failed through no fault of her own. And all the poet can say about that story in the end is that Hildeburh found no happiness in what happened — a distinct understatement. No one, woman or man, can solve the problem for tribes who insist on fighting, but the poet thereby shows an awareness of the social strictures that bind the woman to try.

The poet seconds this point when Beowulf returns to Geatland and tells Hygelac his adventures. He mentions that the Danish princess, Freawaru, is also to be married to a foreign prince (Ingeld) to stop a blood-feud. He adds that such matches don't always work, "though the bride be good." Both incidents show that however well women may serve as "peace-weavers," men may (and probably will) unravel the process by the misplaced drawing of a sword.

Wealhþeow, though, is finally one of the most successful characters in the poem. She has borne Hroðgar sons to succeed him, and she properly welcomes visitors to his court and represents that court's hospitality by serving them drink. After Beowulf fights the monsters and wins, Hroðgar is so proud of Beowulf and so happy at what he's done that he says he thinks of Beowulf as if he were a son. The queen must then step in to qualify that the king really means that he admires Beowulf and values his friendship, not that he sees Beowulf, older and more accomplished than his own sons, as his successor. She requests that, should the need come, Beowulf will support her sons as he has defended the king. As queen she makes the intelligent move of specifying that Hroðgar has made a potential *faux pas*, so that everyone may get clear on exactly what comes from Beowulf's heroic actions. Fortunately for everybody involved, Beowulf has no greedy motives. He has gained the heroism and rewards he wanted and has repaid a king who once helped his father in need. He understands what the king meant and what the queen is saying, and he responds immediately to it. He says that Hroðgar is a great king, as everyone knows, and in time to come his sons will be great kings, too. Meanwhile, if he ever wants to foster them out, Beowulf will make sure that his own king, Hygelac, will take them in and foster them worthily. Beowulf understands the queen's message, accepts his position as a vassal or thane, or in this case as a special servant to Hroðgar, and he vows to protect her sons himself if circumstance allows. Wealhþeow negotiates a touchy solution to the problem her husband, the king, has created by an unguarded speech and that Beowulf has created by saving a kingdom from monstrous depredations. The queen's well-placed words carry in this instance more power than does the loving and appreciative if politically incorrect expression of the king's emotional state.

Recent cinematic adventures have made lesser use of Wealhþeow as powerful character than they might, while enhancing (or creating) the roles of other female characters. Both the 1999 and 2007 versions of *Beowulf* re-figure Grendel's Mother as sexy femmes fatales eager to reproduce with human male leaders. The earlier film replaces the scantily-mentioned Freawaru with the scantily-clad Kyra. The 2005 *Beowulf and Grendel* includes a sympathetic sibyl, Selma, who gives birth to a son fathered by the troll Grendel, whose father was pursued and murdered by the Danes. The *13th Warrior* (1999) adds a pre-civilized witch-queen of the Neanderthalish Wendol and Olga, a Norse maiden who treats the wounded warriors. A future Beowulf film, especially one more interested in treating feminist issues, may do well to expand rather than contract the Wealhþeow role, since her character presents a number of important cultural conundrums that the epic itself doesn't fully resolve.

The cinematic expansion and sexualization of Grendel's Mother presents both interesting possibilities and disastrous problems. Until she kills Æschere—in fair vengeance for her son's death, one may add—Grendel's Mother hasn't really caused any trouble at all. Grendel has done that. He attacks the Danish court at night, breaks in, and eats warriors thirty at a time. His mother doesn't do anything like that. She doesn't bother anybody. We must ask, then, in what sense is she a monster? The text tells us that monstrosity comes partly from kin: as a descendant of Cain, she, like her son, bears the stain of kin-slaying. But the movie makers cast that question in a very different way. What does monster mean to them? Beowulf intends to meet Grendel in a fair fight, Beowulf wins, and Grendel dies. According to the laws of blood-feud, if you kill one of my family members, I kill one of your family members: that's the law of feuding, mitigated only by *weregild*, one's paying off the blood-guilt to the satisfaction of the offended family and the society. Grendel's mother goes to Heorot, which she has never done before, and she kills one man in exchange for her son's death. Then she leaves. Grendel would kill thirty at a time; Grendel's mother kills one. Grendel's mother follows, we may say, the law. But since she has killed one of theirs, Hroðgar's folk, proxied by Beowulf, have the right to kill her or one of hers as well. As she is the only one left of her family, her death represents the end of her race. Beowulf does kill her according to law, but one may argue that her circumstance makes her, in context, a sympathetic character. She defends her family, following the law, avenging her son, and in doing so she gets killed, the last of her line. Nobody remains after her, and despite literary history's casting her as "monster," the loss of a race — genocide, in our time — gathers the sympathy of writers and audiences. Not only has her role expanded in cinematic renderings of the story, but she has also acquired powerful sexuality, and in the 2007 *Beowulf*, she not only survives, but may have more to do than anyone else with who rules Denmark in each subsequent generation.

Freud would call that not only a victory of the id, but also a blatant juxtaposition of eros and thanatos, the meeting and blending, even, of life and death drives. The poem exploits that latter notion well enough, too: Beowulf's monster fights represent the juxtaposition, even melding, of life and death drives, though it is nearly if not entirely devoid of sexuality — we don't even know if Beowulf has married.

Hygd, Hygelac's queen, is another potentially interesting figure in the epic who disappears entirely from film versions. Hygelac, her husband, dies in battle, and she offers the young but accomplished hero Beowulf kingship in his stead, since her sons have not yet reached an age sufficient to rule a kingdom. Beowulf doesn't accept, seeing Hygelac's sons as the proper hereditary heirs, and he defends them accordingly. Through no fault of Beowulf's they both die in battle, and Beowulf avenges them and finally, essentially by default, succeeds them. He becomes king by necessity, not because he wants to: he seems to perceive himself as a hero, not as a king (an idea that appears in Baker's film, but not Zemeckis's). But we still have the problem of Hygd, who in a difficult spot tries for an intelligent solution. She finds Beowulf willing to help her, to do what he believes and what she must know is right, rather than to exploit the situation for personal gain and power. Hygd can then help rule the people until her sons come of age, though they come to unfortunate ends: neither she nor Beowulf can stop that. But we have yet another brave female character who knows what she has to do, does her best as queen, and succeeds — for a time, at least — in preserving her realm. Her important contribution to the epic has gone unnoticed by filmmakers, who have found more fascination in the Danish episodes than in the Geats — sadly, perhaps, since Hygd adds an important dimension to the feminist readings encouraged by film.

We come, then, to an interesting problem in gender-based readings of *Beowulf*, one may approach it, for instance through *second-wave feminism*, which resists simplistic resolution in men-are-bad and women-must-look-out-for-them readings. Such readings allow that in general people can be good or bad regardless of gender: writers and readers do well to treat persons as persons rather than to demonize or canonize. There are good and bad men, good and bad women: we must allow each character his or her own range of complexity. While in historically male texts men place women on the proverbial pedestal, sometimes feminist readers have done the same: women are good and oppressed by men, and our stories to be good must show good women evading the clutches of bad men. But that kind of storytelling doesn't allow a woman or a female character to emerge as a real person. Second-wave feminism suggests we must allow a woman to be a person just as we would allow a man to be a person. *Beowulf* does include one "bad woman" story, too, and recognizing her allows for a more complete reading of the poem and understanding of the world — and hints at the means of developing Grendel's Mother such as we have seen in *Beowulf* films. If writers, even those interested in feminist concerns, have only positive female characters, they must leave out the likes of Þryð or Modþryð (scholars still debate on her name, given the ambiguity of the text), and they must miss a significant point about human character as well as the moral range and intensity of the poem. When she's young and a princess, Þryð will have executed any man who dares to look at her. When she grows up and learns better, she repents and becomes generous, forgiving, and a good queen. No male character would get away with such behavior, either, so in Þryð the poet installs the possibility that, just as with male characters, female characters can err and be just as bad as males, but each can learn better and become good in the long run. With the recognition of such a range of character potential, *Beowulf* becomes not an anti-woman poem, not misogynistic; instead, it unveils a world where regardless of gender we have duties, and we may learn and do better at them — though even that may not save us or our folk in the long run. *Beowulf* as poem recognizes the variety of people: good men, bad men, good women, bad women, *monsters*. It says we all can act better if we try, and good action means responsiveness to law and sensitivity to others' concerns. In the poem women play a major role in showing sensitivity to other people's concerns and getting the job of peace-weaving done right; in film that function has extended to allow female characters a greater range of choice yet for doing good — or doing evil. The epic has a broader range of sympathies than traditional criticism has allowed, and *Beowulf* filmmakers have sensed that difficulty and expanded on it — often, sadly, forgetting much of the poem that would translate so well to film without importations of what they may assume to be our contemporary preferences.

Beowulf films have taken particular trouble with (or have fallen under the spell of) our Modern and Postmodern refiguration of heroes and anti-heroes, of the Freudian dynamic of *eros* and *thanatos*, and of our contemporary tensions with the interaction of male and female characters. Those issues quickly overtake traditional notions of heroism, so for filmmakers in our time, the *Beowulf* story, with its weight anchored firmly in the old heroism, no longer holds sufficient interest as is. They seem to see it as requiring doses of the febrile, Freudian, or feminist.

Beyond comic-book remakes or anime — and perhaps not even there — can we accommodate the old hero anymore? We tend instead to believe in the problems of the *heart of darkness* or the *waste land*, with no real heart of light to seek or believe in. Every hero must fail at some point and do something really bad. We foreground that belief about human nature, drawn partly from mistaken understandings of Darwin and from Freud's constant tensions between what the pleasure principle wants to let us do and what civilization wants to make us do. Add an audience that's grown up with the *Xena Factor* (admiring *Xena the Warrior Princess*) and we find ourselves amidst a psychological, artistic, and intellectual context that turns Beowulf from hero to *Other* in derivative films.

Robert Zemeckis's *Beowulf* (2007), with the performance capture technology, aims to introduce an extraordinary technical coup along with the other vectors discussed here. One may even call this film *third-wave feminist*, as it introduces a new and sexually aggressive element that moves from any sense of equal representation to unabashed dominance. Very different than the *Beowulf* of literature or earlier film, Zemeckis's film abrades the old themes to replace them with entirely new ones. The hero comes again to Denmark to fight the monster Grendel, and he does, with the now typical cinematic whiz-bang, but with the phantasmagoric, roller-coasterish whiz bang PCT, which isn't always easy on the eyes. The poem has no fancy Shaw Brothers stunts in this battle: Grendel bursts in the door, and in a gruesomely tense instant he reaches down and grabs a sleeping warrior and eats him whole. He grabs for another one, and for a second course he gets Beowulf. Beowulf merely grabs back: a no fancy holds, no kicks, no locks, no punches. Beowulf simply holds on to Grendel's arm, and Grendel feels in Beowulf's grip a strength such as he had never experienced "in all the days of this life," which is Anglo-Saxon understatement for "no one else had the strength to grip like that." Part of the charm of the poem comes from the offhandedness with which Beowulf faces battles and the near lack of aggressiveness or anger towards humans: he pursues the status of "hero," but not violence for its own sake.

Beowulf's blithe courage contrasts with Grendel's, but it compares pretty well with that of Grendel's Mother. Grendel fails in his encounter with Beowulf because of fear. He gets scared because Beowulf has strength as great as his. The poet makes particular effort to show that the two have a fair fight. Grendel gives in to the terror of facing a fair fight, which he has never before had to do, always vastly superior to his victims. There we find one of the major themes of the poem: the course of events may preserve the undoomed one, if his courage holds, Beowulf says. That simple theme has never sufficiently moved the filmmakers, who inevitably have complicated the battle with devices and psychological (or even genetic) layering. Film versions have relied on cartoonish graphics, fancy fighting, and odd weaponry. The 2007 made-for-TV *Grendel* outfits Beowulf with an enormous crossbow that shoots fiery rockets to fight monsters that look like graphically better versions of claymation beasts from 1960s B-grade horror films. We may not suspect epic poetry of aiming at realism, but the immediacy of the monster battles in the poem disappears in film, replaced by teenager-oriented video-game whiz-bangs.

For the 1999 and 2007 *Beowulf* films, Grendel's Mother is still around, but she's not so easy to identify as a monster. The earlier version casts a voluptuous Playboy bunny who turns into a shape-shifter, her fighting form a cross between the Alien, an enormous spider, and a flexible crustacean. In the later version she is a golden, naked Angelina Jolie with a whip tail. When Beowulf goes looking for her, she seduces him. He gives in. He begets a son on her, and that son emerges as the dragon for the third monster fight. Beowulf then has to kill the dragon, but in doing so he kills his own son. Beowulf dies, and his son dies, but Mother Jolie doesn't grieve for too long: she sets her sights on the survivor, Wiglaf, with the seeming intent of having him beget a monster-king for the next generation. In the Zemeckis version Beowulf gains Denmark: he accepts the kingship in Hrothgar's stead and takes his widow as wife, resulting in an unproductive and apparently mutually unsatisfying relationship: no keeping pace with a sexy beast, apparently, and Beowulf has lost his heroism and becomes a sexually flaccid king. The story turns thoroughly Freudian, a mixture of prohibited desires and disease-ridden results. The film ends not with Beowulf's funeral, as the epic does, but with his successor, Wiglaf's, temptation: he is standing on the shore where Beowulf has died, and out of the water emerges the golden monster-mother, giving the eye to Wiglaf and suggesting he can be the next king, and he too can father a child on her who will make his monstrous mark in the generation thereafter — a sexually vexed version of the story. It no longer deals with knowing one's duty and doing it, but with the evils and horrors of man's libido, which extends even into the realm of the monstrous. It also shows how a strong woman, human or monster, can subdue the male libido and use it for her own purpose, even if someone else will call her a monster for doing it. The films have taken little but the name from the epic and imposed on it a foreign sexuality, a deep doubt of the heroic ethos, a strong fear of desire, and almost a longing to face the moment of death in an extraordinary and chilling way. Interesting in its way, but not anything we have until recently called *Beowulf*...

The 13th Warrior, from Michael Crichton's *The Eaters of the Dead*, which he derived from *Beowulf* and an extant history of a medieval Arab diplomat, is one of the best *Beowulf* films to date, but it doesn't take the approach of the other films discussed in this introduction. It focuses instead on the idea of insiders and outsiders, on whom we identify as Other and why and how *we* treat them — or how they treat *us*. Ahmed Ibn Fahdlan, exiled to the North because he fell in love with the wife of a powerful man, joins a group of Norsemen to complete their troop according to the number a sibyl says they must have to succeed. They travel to fight a "monster" who turns out not to be a single being, but a people. He learns their language, gains their trust, shows his quality, and even falls in love with a Norse woman: he becomes an insider, no longer an Other, though the Norsemen still can't understand his belief in and commitment to only one God. Another good *Beowulf* film, Sturla Gunnarsson's *Beowulf and Grendel,* uses a similar motif, but for a thoroughly different story. This film shows a stronger influence from John Gardner's novel *Grendel* than from the actual *Beowulf*.[2] Grendel begins as the main character, a troll, whom the humans (Danes) have deeply wronged, and for no good reason. Beowulf the hero appears almost unnecessary, other than one sees in him, along with the sibyl Selma, the capacity to value the Other. The film, partly Freudian in its troubling of the experience of desire and in its drawing of the superego back to the ego and id, suggests more fully ideas of racism and a second-wave feminist critique of male-dominated heroic culture. Second-wave feminism is partly about uncovering oppression wherever we can find it, to identify it and root it out. It doesn't strictly or exclusively array women against men; it aims more generally to uncover personal, social, and even international problems that create thoughtless oppression, Othering, to make them clear and show the sources and results of abuse.[3]

Beowulf and Grendel takes that aim exactly, partly with respect to race, but also with respect to how men treat women. Selma suffered sexual abuse from the Danish men until Grendel found her alone and fathered a child on her; afterwards, he protected her from any further abuse, and he never again abused her himself — a curious turn for the Beowulf story to take. The Danes killed Grendel's father for no other reason than, as Hroðgar tells Beowulf, "He crossed our path. He stole a fish." The child Grendel can't save his father, but he does behead the dead body and save the head as an object of reverence and, to some extent, worship — and a reminder to vengeance, which he takes only upon those who have done him wrong.

At first nobody tells Beowulf, who has just come from across the sea to help the Danes and fight their monster, the true story. Grendel won't bother any of Beowulf's folk, and he won't bother most of the Danes. He's only after vengeance on those who killed his father. Beowulf tries desperately to have a fight with Grendel, but he never gets to. Grendel doesn't want to fight him, because Beowulf hasn't done him any harm. With Selma's help Beowulf sorts out enough of what's going on to gain an appreciation and respect for his nominal enemy. The poem has nothing like that, of course, nor does Gardner's Grendel gain that degree of sympathy: as point-of-view character he attracts some, but not because of any kindness or appealing traits — more by his awful loneliness. In *Beowulf and Grendel*, Grendel, caught in chains and so trapped by Beowulf, cuts off his own arm to release himself and causes his own death — the film hints that no one else would have had the strength or wherewithal to kill him.

So why take such a course in the movie? In our time, racism makes a better story than heroism. Traditional heroism isn't enough, because it doesn't make a social point: we find ourselves in the midst of the age of Cultural Criticism. In *Beowulf and Grendel* Beowulf doesn't get to be heroic at all. He does kill Grendel's Mother, a water demon, but he's not really proud of that. She's the nasty one in this story, not Grendel, which makes an interesting turn, too. The film adapts both epic and novel with a goal of understanding and creating reasonable sympathy for Grendel, for the "monster." It diminishes the hero to an afterthought. The movie makers plot a new course to find something that works in our social context and with our contemporary concerns: we fear being identified as haters of the Other far more than we fear the Other, at least in our art, if not in our politics. We're dealing partly, too, with a question of power. The *eros* and *thanatos* come into play all the way through the film in the immediate impingement of the death drive on the life drive, with the life drive sneaking through just enough to leave a next generation to deal with the problems of Othering.

I will treat one more film in this introduction, but we will revisit these films and address others in the chapters to come. If you look up *No Such Thing* (Hal Hartley, 2001) on the Rotten Tomatoes or IMDB websites, you'll find that it gets pretty low ratings, largely, I think, because no one has recognized it for what it does as a *Beowulf* film: without identifying marks in the title, the film weaves motifs and ideas from the epic with dark humor, a deceptively calm pacing, and wrenching ironies from our time to highlight some really interesting ideas about courage, heroism, and one's duty and place in the world — with the obligatory nod to Othering as well. I think the movie makers understood exactly what they were doing. Though Hartley didn't call the film *Beowulf*, he did capture and recast the poem's tensions and images without the intention to capitalize on the name: the film represents a true and honest artistic endeavor with appreciative but humorous bows to its antecedents.

No Such Thing begins in New York and moves later to Iceland. The "no such thing" is a monster that turns out to be such a thing indeed, though one can read the no such thing as the young female hero as well: someone really heroic in an age that no longer believes in heroism any more than it does in monsters. A crew of young filmmakers had gone to find the monster, and they have disappeared. The main character, Beatrice (in a nod, perhaps to Dante, but also because of her name, "blessed one"), was the girlfriend of one of the lost filmmakers. She goes looking for him, replacing Beowulf as seeker-of-monsters. In the meantime, early in the film we have already met the real monster of this story, "The Boss," the director of a TV news agency: she places no value on life, decency, or even accuracy; she simply wants glitzy stories to attract attention and money.

The Beatrice character looks mousy and inoffensive, even cute: pretty, but not too pretty, says The Boss. She has pigtails, wears a long, nondescript dress and a blank expression. She looks entirely inoffensive, as though she couldn't and wouldn't harm anyone and probably wouldn't be brave enough to try. But she proves incredibly brave. When she meets the fire-breathing monster, fully capable of murder out of boredom or disgust with humans in general, she has no fear of him whatever: she has already been through the worst suffering a human can experience. The news director, by contrast, willingly sends a young woman to her likely death for the sake of a fleeting news story. While The Monster is definitely a monster, for the most part he doesn't really bother anybody: he doesn't seek trouble and exploit others for gratification, but he suffers terribly. He's certainly neurotic, almost psychotic; he's a drunk, and he's been around for a very, very, very long time, much longer than people. Meanwhile, people have gotten really noisy and troublesome and have spread all over the planet, leaving him no respite. As the only one of his kind, he has nobody to love, nobody with whom to reproduce, no one for whom to care, and he has nothing to do but live in an entirely purposeless and increasingly silly world. He's tired, disgusted with life, and can't stand living anymore. Ironically, he would welcome Beatrice's killing him: he would welcome a monster slayer. He knows of only one means by which he can die: a "mad scientist" knows how to do it, and he asks Beatrice to help him find that man.

So Beatrice as Beowulf must kill The Monster, but she grows more troubled with the whole idea because she gets attached to him. She understands that he suffers horribly all the time, and she doesn't want him to suffer anymore. She makes the mistake of taking him back to New York, partly to satisfy The Boss and partly because of the fame she gains thereby, and The Boss leads him into all sorts of trouble as he experiences some kind of torture from everyone he meets. Finally Beatrice helps him escape and takes him back to Iceland to meet the scientist, Dr. Artaud, whom she has found for him to keep her promise. The name refers to Antonin Artaud and The Theatre of Cruelty, the idea that good theatre must deal with the true, painful, horrifying edges of existence. Dr. Artaud, of all persons, has the kindness and the means to kill The Monster. The device Artaud uses to destroy The Monster visually recalls the one on which surgeons suspend Beatrice to perform the surgery that painfully saves her life. The compassion framed by realism that the Icelandic doctors show Beatrice foreshadows the relationship Beatrice develops with The Monster: not one of sexuality or desire, but instead a sense of company in suffering. As the scientist prepares to destroy The Monster on his miraculous machine, he, Beatrice, and the others present wear dark glasses so light given off by the machine won't hurt them. In the final instants of the film, and of The Monster's life, Beatrice takes the glasses off so she can face death with The Monster. In a curious twist of casting, Sarah Polley, who plays Beatrice here, also plays Selma the Sybil in *Beowulf and Grendel*. I think the filmmaker is saying that in our time the true heroic face is the face of compassion. In *No Such Thing* even The Monster's face is a heroic face at last because he faces death squarely having developed a kind of love for at least one of his enemies, the one who has shown him kindness and who understands him.

No Such Thing is a notably second-wave feminist *Beowulf*, a powerful revision of the story that makes no claim on *Beowulf* and yet rewrites it in a way that makes important points for a contemporary audience. It says that the life drive and the death drive, the *eros* and the *thanatos*, remain always contiguous. They interchange and interweave. If we want to find heroes, we may best seek them where the two drives meet most forcefully. This film, unlike other *Beowulf* films, exploits a surprisingly muted sense of desire: The Boss desires lurid stories partly out of a sense of amoral but tenacious commitment to her job, but partly from an apparent personal gratification in feeding the diseased imagination of a violent and uncaring public.

The movement of heroic desire in our own time — at least as we find it exhibited in the films we've considered above — relies probably more on *eros* than on *thanatos*, but a different kind of *eros* than we normally understand from Freud. We desire of our heroes, and our heroes themselves seek, an *eros* of creativity and kindness instead of martial success. Cinema typically has, when it has treated *Beowulf*, diminished the hero, at least according to the traditional notion of hero such as we find in the epic. The idea of *hero* still implies desire and performance, but a different kind of desire and a different kind of performance. We have our superhero films, but because of their roots in comic books and video games they tend to mix desire with destruction —

massive destruction given the current love of special effects. Their financial success suggests they feed an audience's desire for the power to destroy (in villains as well as heroes). I don't think filmmakers exploit it cynically or satirically, but that they use that desire and even revel in what through technology they can do with it. *Beowulf on Film* has on one hand reveled in the technology and on the other turned its human heroes toward the recognition of the Dark Side of The Force: it has always been there and always will be there, but now our heroes ask more questions about which is the Dark and which the Light side, how anyone knows, and on which side they actually find themselves. They push questions of gender, race, and courage, and they look for their epiphanies at different boundaries of human experience. I think the best of the *Beowulf* films, rather than simply exploiting that dark side, try to direct our attention to how we perceive it. We can recognize it, they suggest, without feeling a need to eradicate it: it may, like Kurtz's heart of darkness, lie more inside than out. We can accept it without attacking it, learning to see it as something humanely productive that may lead us to understand and to learn compassion — a generation ago such approaches would generally, in our culture, have produced claims of sentimentality.

Film has, though, helped accomplish a kind of recovery of Beowulfian heroism: though the poet only once tells us what Beowulf *feels*, he never pursues wanton violence and often acts with restraint, consideration, and self-sacrifice. Grendel, a figure of *nachtmere,* nightmare, the beast, embodies the chaos from which the "beast" comes and to which it would return us. Heorot is the *hart,* the male deer, a symbol of Oðin in the ancient world, but also implies the heart in the body and the heart of a society. Grendel implies everything that resists the heart, whatever destroys life, compassion, civilization. He breaks it up and creates chaos in its place. His *thanatos,* destruction, responds to human *eros,* creativity, the desire to have order, place, continuity, freedom of artistic creation. But in film he has come instead to represent the wronged Other; the courage applied in our pursuit against chaos hasn't the same implications when we direct it against a wronged Other: it produces rather than releases from oppression, the demon of our time, as second-wave feminism would point out. Beowulf, too, isn't so far from beast: his name means *bear,* and he likes to confront enemies as a bear does: close in his grasp, free of other than natural weapons. He can be dangerous, too, but chooses not to do wanton harm; in a thoroughly non-erotic epic, he supports but does not contribute himself to *eros*: he preserves life as he can, but creates none of his own, and he can't stand in for his fellow humans indefinitely.

I'd still like to see, though, a real *Beowulf* film. The old heroism has value as does the new. The epic still has the potential in its narrative directness, spiritual expansiveness, and visual sweep to inspire a brilliant and beautiful film. In the meantime, *The 13th Warrior*, *Beowulf and Grendel*, and *No Such Thing* particularly have an equally valid approach to the issues of heroism at the borderland of human experience. They ask us to confront complex questions of desire, human performance, and our relationship with whatever we choose to consider the monstrous — useful questions given our current public struggles with genocide, corporate and personal greed, and sexual abuse. Those issues have little to nothing to do with *Beowulf*, but *Beowulf* in epic or on film can help us reconsider how we view heroism and so teach us to confront and fight such problems. Beowulf goes to the heart of darkness not to revel in forbidden desires, but to bring it out into the light and neutralize its destructiveness; any art that does so accomplishes a grand epic result indeed.[4]

The following chapters deal not only with *Beowulf* on film, but with related films that deal with medieval Germanic or Northern European culture (or with medievalism) to establish a cinematic context for what's going on in the conversion of epic-heroic from poetry to cinema. Though J. R. R. Tolkien drew great inspiration from *Beowulf* and alluded to it regularly, we won't be dealing with the *Lord of the Rings* films in this book, not with any intent to neglect them, but because they are receiving a good deal of treatment elsewhere, while *Beowulf* movies have yet (understandably) to achieve a scholarly following. We hope to open critical space (both in this subject and in movie medievalism more generally) that will encourage further artistic endeavors as well as continued dialogue on why and how the movies do what they do: *Beowulf* on film yet has far to go.

1

Film Theory, the Sister Arts Tradition and the Cinematic *Beowulf*

NICKOLAS HAYDOCK

This first chapter contributes to a larger conversation about the relationship between medieval studies and medievalism that has occupied an increasing number of scholars in recent years.[1] Concerning the sub-field of movie medievalism, how can we put into productive relation the all-too-obviously disparate projects of writing a critical essay on *Beowulf* and adapting the poem for the silver screen? This chapter revisits the question of homologies between scholarly and cinematic approaches to *Beowulf* by posing the question in another register — that of inter-media relationships as informed by what is commonly known as "the Sister Arts Tradition." My working thesis is simply this: inter-arts comparisons occupy the borderland between these two different realms, where crossovers and continuities between traditional scholarship and filmic adaptations are most readily apparent. Such a project offers an example of how scholars of medievalism might begin to move beyond the parochial tendencies of a sub-discipline — one that typically over-emphasizes medievalism's exotic, egregious departures from original sources — into a more open, level field of play. Specifically, I provide evidence of interactions between scholarship and popular culture that are anything but one-sided or unidirectional; rather, scholarship can be seen taking its cues from cinema and cinema decoding scholarly approaches to texts and then encoding them in nuanced, subtle ways. Such filiations between scholarship and popular filmmaking have not always registered with academics who tend to focus on dialogue and plot to the virtual exclusion of any concern with how images and their collocations function in film.[2]

Comparisons among different media are perhaps as old as criticism itself: Aristotle's anatomy of tragic drama and its interrelationships with epic, lyric, music, dance, and mime; Horace's famous comparison *ut pictura poesis*; Lessing's influential discussion of plastic and poetic arts in depictions of Laocoön; down through recent film, media and cultural theory in which the translations across an increasing array of media platforms have become an emergent, if not the dominant paradigm. The sister arts tradition also informed the development of film theory from Sergei Eisenstein and the Russian formalists down through thinkers as diverse as Erwin Panofsky, André Bazin, Siegfried Kracauer and Giles Deleuze. Inter-art comparisons and analogies have likewise served as the basis for a number of now classic essays on *Beowulf* by Alain Renoir, John Leyerle, Fred C. Robinson, and Gillian R. Overing, among numerous others. In particular, I survey the role of sister arts comparisons in the work of J. R. R. Tolkien and Alain Renoir, highlighting some issues in what W. T. J. Mitchell has recently called the "pictorial turn" in postmodern culture, before returning to the mutually implicated topics of *Beowulf* as an object of cinematic analysis and as a product of recent films.[3]

Alain Renoir's inter-arts criticism on *Beowulf* seems almost genetically determined. He was the grandson of the impressionist painter Pierre-Auguste Renoir and the son of the *auteur* Jean Renoir, on whose films Alain worked as an apprentice and assistant cinematographer between 1938 and 1941. During these years his father Jean directed two films often mentioned in reverent terms by film scholars and cineastes alike, *The Human Beast* (1938; Apprentice Cameraman: Alain Renoir) and *The Rules of the Game* (1939; Second Assistant Cameraman: Alain Renoir). These films are celebrated for a realistic style that allows meaning to emerge within a single take, as a function of *mise en scène*, deep focus, and, especially, the spatial relationships and movements of actors within and through the frame, rather than chiefly as the production of montage. These years saw a crucial break with the tenets of classical cinema toward a modernist form, perhaps most evident in the work of Renoir and a young Orson Welles. For these influential directors — and for the French New Wave and Italian Neorealism more generally — the shot, not the image or the cut, constitutes the chief element of film composition.

The son of Jean Renoir became a professor of comparative literature at Berkeley, and his work deserves recognition as an important, though unacknowledged forerunner of media- and cultural studies. The younger Renoir *compared* not only texts written in different languages, but he also made numerous, sustained and richly elaborated inter-media comparisons as well. The scholarship for which he is best known applied oral-formulaic theory to poems written in medieval Germanic languages, like *Beowulf* and *The Nibelungenlied*, down through the survivals of oral formulism in works of the alliterative revival such as *Sir Gawain and the Green Knight*. To simplify somewhat,

Renoir worked within traditional comparisons between painting and poetry, greatly influenced by Lessing's preference for poetry's greater capacity to express movement and change, while also tapping into vibrant debates in film theory that sought to situate the new art form in relation to painting and written language. The result was a revolutionary thesis about oral-formulaic texts and their acute visualization of specific details and perspectives, which compared alliterative poetry to cinematic montage. Renoir's revolution, however, was premature. The outlandishness of his claims provoked little more than a ripple in Anglo-Saxon studies,[4] which was more accepting of less anachronistic sister-arts comparisons, such as those of John Leyerle, Fred C. Robinson, and Gillian R. Overing. Leyerle observed a "parallel" in the intricately woven designs of plastic arts in the north of Britain, as evidenced in productions such as the Lindisfarne Gospels or Franks Casket, which he dubbed the "interlace style" of *Beowulf*. Robinson stressed the poem's "appositive style," linking its paratactic diction to larger juxtapositions of imagery, episodes, and over-all structure. More recently, Overing turned to Charles Sanders Peirce's semiotic categories to compare swords in the poem with surviving weapons of the period, noting that the final significance of such objects in *Beowulf* is never established but rather deferred, met again in later contexts and interwoven with different themes.

The work of these scholars — as they themselves were happy to affirm — can be seen as attempts to elaborate on Tolkien's magisterial, elegiac argument about the essence of the poem: "It is essentially a balance, an opposition of ends and beginnings [...] a contrasted description of two moments in a great life, rising and setting; an elaboration of the ancient and intensely moving contrast between youth and age, first achievement and final death" (Tolkien 2006, 28). If we look at Tolkien's essay with something like the loving stewardship he lavished on the Anglo-Saxon poem (following his practice of moving to the center what has traditionally seemed marginal or unworthy of attention) what we find is an argument buttressed at every stage by inter-arts comparisons. For Tolkien, the diction of the poem should not be confused with the subtle harmonies of quantitative verse favored in southern climes; rather, it is "more like masonry than music;" in fact, its "verse-kind approaches rather to sculpture or painting. It is a composition not a tune" (Tolkien 2006, 30). In the famous allegory of the poem's composition and reception, he likens *Beowulf* to a tower, with stone quarried from an older ruin, from the top of which its owner could look out upon the sea. Generations of historians and archeologists have toppled the tower, scrambling over the chaotic ruin they themselves created, attempting to reconstruct the older building from which its stones derive, and even digging beneath it for clues to even earlier civilizations. So goes perhaps the most famous demolition of a scholarly orthodoxy in the history of medieval studies.

Yet if Tolkien insisted upon restoring the balanced architecture of the poem, the way in which this famous allegory is developed throughout the essay has received considerably less attention. The more extensive critical allegory at work concerns not simply architecture but artistic perspective — a focus that chastises modern critical views for their failure to respect that of the poet, whose panoramic vistas we can learn to appreciate though never fully share. The dominant analogy throughout the essay is with painting — modern, not Anglo-Saxon painting — urging us toward recognition of a three-point perspective in which depth of field and point of view allegorize historical differences. The "scene" of the poem, as Tolkien repeatedly calls it, resembles nothing so much as a romantic landscape painting, with a distant figure in a tower amidst the ruins, rapt in contemplation of a horizon that recedes from his view, even as he recedes from ours.[5] Tolkien encourages an elegiac response similar to that of the poet toward the world represented in the poem, wherein we are urged to sympathize with the poet's sense of loss from an even more distant point of view. The poem is designed to "give that sense of perspective, of antiquity with a greater and yet darker antiquity behind." What Tolkien calls "this impression of depth" results — like three-point perspective — from an "illusion," that of "surveying a past, pagan but noble and fraught with deep significance — a past that itself had depth and reached backward into a dark antiquity of sorrow [...] mostly darker, more pagan, and desperate than the foreground" (2006, 27).[6] While from this perspective *Beowulf* does not present an "actual picture" of fifth-century Scandinavia, it is "on a general view a self-consistent picture, a construction bearing clearly the marks of design and thought" (2006, 27). The repetition of the word *picture* in different senses — photograph and painting — is typical of Tolkien's style of argument; it juxtaposes documentary with aesthetic approaches, even as it insists upon the deliberate construction of a deep and progressively more obscure perspective.[7]

Of course, this "impression of depth" is also richly evident in Tolkien's fiction and his paintings. Many of the most oft-reproduced drawings and watercolors recede from the viewer into intricate depths of tantalizing complexity. Numerous examples of this style might be adduced, such as the painting of *Rivendell III* seen only as a distant prospect at the end of a long crevice.[8] Nearer rock formations and vegetation are sharply delineated, while the ostensible topic of the painting, Rivendell, sits tucked away behind trees on a plateau between a sheer rock face and the bending river Bruinen, with Lonely Mountain as an even more distant prospect. Indeed, one of the many pleasant surprises of *The Lord of the Rings* film trilogy was to find Tolkien's picture of

Rivendell rather carefully rendered via CGI in a painterly shot within *The Fellowship of the Ring*.⁹

As has been often remarked, the technology of computer graphics imaging (CGI) brings movies into a more intimate relation with painting than ever before. Frodo's distant perspective of Mount Doom in the film version of *The Return of the King* seems similarly inspired by Tolkien's artistic and intellectual style. Frodo looks up from the dangerous position of Shelob's cave through a deep crevice to the tower in the distance, shining with the searchlight eye. The distant light thus represents at once a beacon, lighting the way to his goal, and the sign of a malevolence that continues its unblinking search for *him*. Jackson also employs a shot Hitchcock invented for *Vertigo*, produced by a lens zooming in mounted on a camera tracking backwards, to represent the vertiginous feelings provoked by such gazes. In *The Fellowship of the Ring*, Frodo feels before he sees the approach of Ringwraiths. As he looks back, the deserted road telescopes in a *Vertigo* shot, as though the threat were propelled toward his gaze. Such shots objectify fears of the unknown: we gaze into the abyss and it looks back at us — as Nietzsche warned it would. The unsettling visual effect combines in a distinctly Lacanian way the combination of aversion and attraction in the gaze, the means through which objects of the gaze interpolate the viewer.¹⁰

Tolkien's impressionistic pictures in pencil, crayon and watercolors, such as *The Front* Gate (16), *The Doors of Durin and Moria Gate I* (22), *Helm's Deep and the Hornburg* (26), *Dunharrow* (29), or *Gondolin and the Vale of Tumladen* (35), illustrate what he christened "*ishness*," a quality that seems at least partially a function of recessive compositions. Paradigmatic in this regard is the drawing *The Elvenking's Gate II* (12), in which the ostensible topic of the composition is merely a tiny square placed at the center, though the picture itself is dominated by the curving tree-lined path in the foreground that leads (our gaze) to the gate. Likewise, in the crayon drawing *The Doors of Durin and Moria Gate I* (22) the doors comprise a tiny, fingernail-size center of a picture featuring enormous rock faces and the intervening lake. Even Tolkien's interiors, such as the drawings *Beorn's Hall* (10) or *The Hall at Bag End, Residence of B. Baggins Esquire* (20) share this extreme depth of field. *The Hall at Bag End* has at its center Bilbo's open portal, leading the viewer's gaze ever onward to the outside world and the long road that awaits an initially reluctant traveler. Further evidence of this style exists even when the artist intentionally breaks with his own conventions, as in *Glaurung Sets Forth to Seek Túrin* (38), where the dark and pale mountains open at a tunnel — reminiscent of Three Cliffs Bay in Swansea, Wales — from which a dragon lunges in lurid colors beyond the borders of the painting to confront its viewers head on.

Tom Shippey's *J. R. R. Tolkien: Author of the Century* proffers the intriguing suggestion that the painting described in *Leaf by Niggle* may well serve to allegorize Tolkien's own career, and that the *ekphrasis* of "this great picture" in the story can be seen as the gradual unfurling of Tolkien's imagined worlds:

> How good a painter is he (Niggle)? This is one of the two main questions raised in paragraphs two to five of the story, and the answer is fairly complex. He is certainly "Not a very successful one," partly because "He was the sort of painter who can paint leaves better than trees." But the "one picture in particular which bothered him," while it started as a leaf caught in the wind," soon became a "tree" indeed a "Tree," while behind it "a country began to open out; and there were glimpses of a forest marching over the land, and of mountains tipped with snow." If one translates this from Niggle to Tolkien, it makes good sense. Tolkien began with short poems like the 1914 "Lay of Earendel" (leaves, so to speak); they grew into explanatory narratives [...] as he wrote "a country began to open out" ... and there were indeed glimpses in it of a "forest marching" (the Ents) [...] Niggle's "great picture," existing only in the mind, was something like a completely finished and integrated version of the whole history of Arda from Creation to the end of the Third Age [268–269].

What emerges across Tolkien's art, his fiction, and his scholarship, then, is a remarkably abiding concern with perspectives in depth, attentive to spatial and temporal relationships, as any moment a single image or ancient object becomes the leaf from which a mighty "Tree" (and an even mightier world) can spring abundantly forth. This philosophy of deep perspectives informs Tolkien's art and his fiction, just as it informs his philology and his appreciation of *Beowulf*—in all of which spatial depth figures historical distance. Indeed, one might call "the impression of depth" the key to Tolkien's perspective in his paintings, in his fascination with Fairy Tales, and in his approach to *Beowulf*. At the dead center of such concerns is often that furthest from view; his sublime is a function of this rule of depth, but it is also a standing invitation to close distances and penetrate obscurities, like the door in *Bag End* that opens onto the road beyond, or the painting of a leaf that burgeons into a world. In similar fashion, what emerges in the *Beowulf* essay is not simply an allegory of poetic and critical perspectives, but the *ekphrasis* of an imagined picture like that described in *Leaf by Niggle*, which — had Tolkien painted it in watercolors rather than in words — would have necessitated a style in close accord with Niggle's greatest creation.[11]

Tolkien also utilized the analogy of painting to distinguish *Beowulf* from the musical hexameters of ancient epic verse like that of Virgil's *Aeneid*, with which the Old English poem had often been unfavorably compared. Not only a picture, *Beowulf* is a painting of a specific kind, promoting the illusion of depth and employing chiaroscuro effects which cast the heroic age of Germanic paganism in semi-darkness. Tolkien's distinction between Greco-Roman and Anglo-Saxon resembles that made by Erich Auerbach in *Mimesis*: Homer like the sun shines on everything alike, while the Book of Genesis is rather more like a searchlight, illuminating certain details yet leaving so much else in shadow and inscrutable.[12]

It is only with Alain Renoir, however, that sister-arts comparisons are fully marshaled to distinguish the different styles of visualization in ancient and Old English epic. Renoir's essays read like a calculated response to Tolkien's *ut pictura poesis* comparisons, drawing the distinction between the visual poetics of Old English and Latin just as definitively as Auerbach did for Greek and Hebrew. Renoir contrasts Virgil's static, painterly style with what might be called the *cinematic Beowulf*, characterized by "a mobility of point of view" and shifts in scale — techniques of visualization that Renoir contends are central to oral-formulaic poetry (1974, 155).[13] Traditional source study had attempted to relate the descriptions of the underworld in the *Aeneid* and *Beowulf* through the identification of similar details. Renoir's work moves in the opposite direction — a truly critical and comparative mode — which attends to contrasting styles of visualization, and leaves little doubt which of the two styles he finds the most effective.

In "The Terror of the Dark Waters," Renoir makes a rather direct reply to Tolkien's insistence that the poem resembles not a photograph but a painting. Instead, he judges Virgil's description of Avernus akin to "a simple photograph" and calls the similar scene in *Beowulf* "a motion picture" (1974, 154). The approach to Grendel's mere for Renoir features a "quasi-cinematic motion" by which means "the audience ... is irresistibly swept toward the mounting terror of the scene," just as a tracking camera mounted on a plane might film the shot (1974, 159). The visual style of *Beowulf* manipulates our perspective upon arrival at the banks of this other world, drawing the gaze of the audience steadily upward, from the tarn seething with swamp-gas fires, to the hunted stag frozen motionless on its banks, to the waves vaulting toward the darkening heavens. In particular note that Renoir's analysis of the description of the tarn reads like a shot schedule: an establishing shot of the "general area" followed by a tracking shot approaching the pond, "a close up of the stag on the shore," panning down again to the frightening water and then tilting to follow the arc of its waves heavenward (1974, 154).

Another essay, "Point of View and Design for Terror in *Beowulf*," analyzes Grendel's approach to Heorot, in which Renoir discovers a tour de force of subjective camera and *mise en scène*, whereby, as the night-stalker glides ever nearer, he takes up ever more of the frame, until the whole shot is composed only of "two dots of fire against a veil of blackness" (1968, 164). These tightening shots also function to increase the monster's imagined proximity to the *audience* of the poem, allowing us to share the mounting tension within the scene by aligning our point of view with that of Grendel's potential victims. When Grendel finally arrives at the doorway, a radical shift in perspective makes the audience share the point of view of the monster as he touches open the door and approaches the sleeping thanes within. Finally, as the monster bolts the flesh of Handscio, our perspective shifts for a third time as we observe the ugly light from his eyes glowing like fire in the dark hall through the half-open eyes of Beowulf, whose viewpoint both combines and reverses that of the potential victims and the stealthy hunter in the night. Thus, Renoir concludes, "the terror which the scene so powerfully evokes in the audience is entirely the result of masterfully selected visual details consistently presented from the most immediately effective point of view" (1968, 166).

Certainly Renoir's inter-arts essays deserve more attention from scholars of film medievalism than they have received, but it is also necessary to point out an unexpected limitation of his approach. I mentioned earlier his work as a cameraman on some of his father's most important films, such as *The Human Beast* (1938) and *The Rules of the Game* (1939). The long takes in deep focus with people moving in and out of the frame that characterize the cinematography of these films opened auteur cinema and film theory to an approach that was in stark contrast to the intellectual montage championed in the films and theory of Sergei Eisenstein. As Jean Renoir's greatest champion, Andre Bazin, would maintain, it is the shot not the cut that is the central compositional element in film: the relationships, contrasts and tensions between actors and objects in an expansive environment moves film art out of the cutting room into a sustained engagement with the movements and rhythms of the world. Hence, the threshold of the film frame is not an artificial barrier but rather points beyond itself; in this beyond reside not only cinema's connection to reality, but also its access to the sublime. The meaning of film is composed on location in real time, a function of the continuous relation of elements within and beyond the film frame.[14]

However, Alain Renoir's cinematic analyses of *Beowulf* are chiefly informed by the montage theory of Eisenstein (whom he cites repeatedly) rather than by his father's revolutionary conception of a cinema made out of inclusive long takes, staging in depth, moving camera and depth of field. The reasons are not far to seek. Stark juxtapositions and the intercalating of radically different times and places *is* a distinctive feature of the poem's narrative style. If one sought to champion oral poetry as an art form that did not preclude complex design and a high degree of artistic self-consciousness, what better analogy for this than the auteurist cinema as theorized by Eisenstein? Nevertheless, a markedly dissimilar style of visualization does occur periodically in the poem, a style of the cinematic shot, not the cut, to which we should also attend. Take, for instance, the feast after the defeat of Grendel. Here the emotional and political complexities of the scene produce a style of visualization analogous to a long take in deep focus, as Wealhtheow circulates among the gleeful warriors, pouring mead into their cups, speaking privately to Beowulf about her son, and then addressing more formally the whole assembly. Just as in the layered, textured shots staged and shot in depth in Jean Renoir's *The Rules of the Game*, competing agendas — collegiality and suspicion, present joy and apprehensions about the future — compete for our attention within a single frame, as Wealhtheow sits down between Hrothgar and Hrothwulf, who are for the moment at least still faithful to one another, while the kin-killer Unferth reclines, part dog and part snake, at their feet. Within the festive celebration lurks a dynastic controversy simmering just beneath the surface. Wealhtheow's initial place seated between the king and Hrothwulf correlates with her insistence that the succession of her sons under the protection of Hrothwulf be maintained, despite the rumor that Hrothgar has decided to name Beowulf his heir. Next, she carries the cup of friendship over to the bench upon which Beowulf sits between her sons, Hrethric and Hrothmund. The hero's position is likewise correlative with the danger he represents in Wealhtheow's eyes. Ever the subtle politician, Wealhtheow publicly interprets Beowulf's situation as an expression of his support for her two sons. The torque she bestows is explicitly tied to the version of the fostering relationship between Beowulf and the boys that Wealhtheow is taking elaborate pains to establish: "Cen ðec mid cræfte, ond þissum cnyhtum wes/lara liðe" ("Prove yourself with skill, and to these boys be/kind in giving instruction" 1219–1220a). Her instructions, couched in imperatives, are careful to distinguish what Beowulf's triumph means from what it does not: he has won everlasting fame, not the right of succession. The imperatives are draped in dignified, regal discourse, but they fail to hide her evident anxiety about the danger Beowulf's victory poses for her sons' future:

                Wes, þenden þu lifige,
æþeling, eadig!   Ic þe on tela
sincgestreona.   Beo þu suna minum
dædum gedefe,   dreamhealdende!
Her is æghwylc eorl   oþrum getrywe,
modes milde,   mandrihtne hold;
þegnas syndon gehwære,   þeod ealgearo,
druncne dryhtguman   doð swa ic bidde [1224b–1231].

>   Be, while you live,
> noble one, happy.   I properly grant you
> the wealth of treasure.   Be to my sons
> gracious in deeds,   protective of happiness.
> Here each man is   true to the others,
> mild of heart,   loyal to the lord of men.
> The thanes are united   the nation quite ready;
> having drunk, the retainers   will do as I bid.

The scene is thus about places — physical space and the power relationships of individuals occupying that space — which Wealhtheow, with elaborate politeness and subtle implication, struggles to fix and contain. Obliquely she groups Beowulf among the loyal retainers to whom she passes the cup, enjoining the hero to be like them and do as she bids. Of course, further complexities also shadow the scene for audiences aware of the later history of these Danes. The Queen negotiates this political minefield with a graceful majesty, and the poet's camera-stylus tracks her throughout the scene as she attempts to weave peace in a hall rife with dangers only reawakened by the death of Grendel.

Indeed the hall and its *unheimlich* reflection at the bottom of the tarn offer contrasting styles of visualization to the rapid cuts and shifts in point of view which Renoir highlights in Grendel's approach to Heorot and in Hrothgar's short subject film of the tarn. Taking our cue from Renoir's work, it should be possible to chart differences in styles of representation across a major episode, noting shifts in perspectives and techniques of visualization in a version of a shot schedule. What such a strategy discloses, as we shall see, is neither the over-ingenuousness of an analogy pushed to the breaking point nor an anachronistic celebration of the proto-cinematic *Beowulf*. Instead, we discover that a critical methodology from film studies, which is no more or less anachronistic than psychoanalytic, semiotic or deconstructive approaches, can indeed make contributions to and work in concert with philology-based readings. Film terminology, such as *deep focus*, *objective* or *subjective camera*, *montage*, *cross-cutting*, *zoom*, *pan*, or *tracking shot*, will thus be employed unapologetically to characterize changes in perspective and point of view, which the language of the poem specifies or suggests.

In Beowulf's *catabasis* at the center of the poem, point of view (what film critics call *subjective camera*) remains an integral feature, but such shots are mixed with an *objective camera* (not bound by any single character's perspective). The intricate warp of apposite visual perspectives (in conjunction with the weft of changes in light, colors, or objects within a particular frame) makes complex contributions to the texture of the episode. If one marks off Beowulf's *catabasis* as a more or less self-contained passage from lines 1492–1631, beginning with his dive into the lake and concluding with his triumphal return, the deft coordination of changes in perspective and within the *mise en scène* emerges quite distinctly. Such changes are organized in the complex patterns familiar from Leyerle's comparison of the poem to interlace, Robinson's to grammatical apposition, or the more widespread recognition of envelope and ring structures in the poem.[15] Repetitions of visual perspectives occur with sometimes subtle and sometimes glaring variations. It is this interlacing or apposition or montage of *visual perspectives* that my method seeks to make more readily apparent. While the following fourteen segmentations of the episode are not airtight, neither are they arbitrary; rather, they are based upon two similar but distinct linguistic cues. Some segments routinely begin with adverbs of time (*ða* or *sona*) coupled with verbs of visual perception (e.g., *ongitan* or *onfindan*) to signal a change to a subjective point of view (POV). While other segments employ the same adverbs of time coupled with action verbs to mark the change to objective camera, sometimes accompanied by changes in depth of field.[16] The first three segments are given below:

Segment 1
æfter þæm wordum   Wedergeata leod
efste mid elne,   nalas ondsware
bidan wolde;   brimwylm onfeng
hilderince   [1492–1495a].

Segment 2
    ða wæs hwil dæges
ær he þone grundwong   *ongytan mehte* [1495b–1496].

Segment 3
Sona þæt onfunde   se ðe floda begong
heorogifre beheold   hund missera,
grim ond grædig,   þæt þær gumena sum
ælwihta eard   ufan cunnode [1497–1505].

After those words   the man of the weather-Geats
hastened eagerly—   not at all did he wish
to await an answer.   The surging lake received
the battle-warrior.   Then it was a time
before he could   descry the bottom.
Soon she found out,   who fiercely ravenous guarded
the expanse of the flood   for half a hundred years,
grim and greedy,   that there a certain man
explored from above   that home of alien creatures.[17]

Admittedly, what I have identified as Segment 1 contains neither of the cues just specified; the formulaic signs of alterations in perspective begin, unsurprisingly, with the first change in perspective. Segment 1 takes place just after Beowulf's brave last words and focuses on the hero's hasty departure, when, pre-empting any reply from the assembled warriors, he quickly plunges into the tarn. In film terminology this would be an establishing (or master) shot. The emphasis on silence is paradigmatic, for, as we shall see, the otherworldly quality of the adventure depends in part upon the eerie quiet of the sub-aquatic adventure. We watch from the perspective of the assembled Geats and Danes on shore as the waves take Beowulf (*onfeng*, 1494b) — recalling in its subtle personification, perhaps, the final voyage of Scyld in the prologue (*on flodes æhte*, 41a). Beowulf, like Scyld, journeys into the unknown: there is no telling what awaits him. The echo of the watery grave of that earlier savior of the Danes contributes significantly to the gloomy fatalism of the scene — the audience *within the poem* will grow increasingly convinced that they have witnessed Beowulf's death.[18] The *mise en scène* of the watchers by the shore also provides a stark contrast with the earlier fight in Heorot only observed by the Geats (because their weapons were useless) and heard far away in the outbuildings by the Danes, as thuds and screams resounded through the hall. Now here again they can only stand and watch, awaiting the outcome of a battle they neither see nor hear. Still, the shots of those who can only stand and wait serve to punctuate stages in the episode as a whole, when the scene changes strikingly from the fast-paced action beneath the waves to the misprisions and disillusions of those above on shore.

A marked change in perspective occurs in segment 2, which also establishes the leitmotif signaling a change in perspective via an adverb of time + a verb of visual/intellectual apprehension: "ða wæs hwil dæges/ær he þone grundwong *ongytan mehte*" (1495b–1496, emphasis added). The short phrase records the long while Beowulf spends trying to find the bottom of what for less powerful swimmers would no doubt be a bottomless lake. Segment 3, in turn, presents a counter-shot POV, employing a similar cue ("sona ... onfunde," 1497), from the look out of the loch-woman who watches from beneath the arrival of this stranger in a strange world. The verb *beheold* (1498) usually translated "guarded," also permits the sense of "observed" or "was on the look-out," the same word used to describe Beowulf's covert surveillance of Grendel in Heorot (736). The echo encourages the inference that she is waiting for him, plotting an ambush, just as he ambushed her son. In both episodes, *beholding* is a prelude to *holding*: the creature seeks to entrap Beowulf in her hall just as he had Grendel, because charms and chainmail forestall more conventional assaults. The episode in the tarn-hall, however, contains more than the thematic echoes so often remarked by readers of the poem; it carefully duplicates in reverse — like a mirror image — the deft interweaving of visual perspectives and points of view that Renoir detailed in the scene of Grendel's approach to Heorot.

The beginning of the attack is visualized in segment 4 from an objective angle of view from outside the struggle. Twice a rack focus[19] tightens in onto the body parts of the combatants, closing in on the specific details of Beowulf's chainmail and the talons and tusks that seek to rend it.

Segment 4
Grap þa togeanes, guðrinc gefeng
atolan clommum. No þy ær in gescod
halan lice; hring utan ymbbearh,
þæt heo þone fyrdhom ðurhfon ne mihte,
locene leoðosyrcan laþan fingrum.
Bær þa seo brimwylf, þa heo to botme com,
hringa þengel to hofe sinum,
swa he ne mihte, no he þæs modig wæs,
wæpna gewealdan, ac hine wundra þæs fela
swencte on sunde, sædeor monig
hildetuxum heresyrcan bræc,
ehton aglæcan [1501–1512a; emphasis added].

She grasped then towards him seized the battle-warrior
in horrible grips, none the sooner injured
the healthy body; the rings outside protected him,
so that she could not puncture with hostile fingers
the war-covering, interlocked mail-coat.
When she came to the bottom the sea wolf
Then bore the prince of rings to her dwelling
so that he could not, no matter how brave he was,
wield weapons, but many of the monsters
in the lake harassed him, many sea-beasts
with war-like tusks broke the war-shirt,
pursued the giant one.

Formally, this segment is divided into two parallel actions, each initiated by an action verb (*Grap*, 1501 and *Bær*, 1506), followed by the familiar *þa* ("then," "thereafter") used to demarcate successive events. Though it is described in two stages, neither the *mise en scène* nor the perspective alters, we watch as in a *single take* as the "sea wolf" pulls Beowulf down to the door of her hall, aided in her attack by the swarming "sea-beasts." Cinematically speaking, both portions of the segment feature an identical pulled focus from long shots of the two figures struggling within the frame to extreme close ups, highlighting in visual synecdoche the attack of claws and tusks on the interwoven rings of a mail-shirt. Beowulf begins as a "guðrinc" and is denominated at the beginning of the second stage "the lord of the rings" ("hringa þengel"), but in both stages of the segment his chainmail seems to be doing all the fighting, to the point of becoming a personified combatant: "hring utan ymbbearh." The effect of this zooming technique is not unlike the personified mail coat in riddle 33, who, born from the cold, wet womb of mother earth, remains preternaturally impervious to arrowheads. Each of the two stages in the *Beowulf* segment concludes with an opposition across the caesura of the resistant mail-shirt and the sharp points that seek to rend it: "locene leoðosyrcan" beset by "laþan fingrum" (1505) and the "heresyrcan" finally breached by "hildetuxum" (1511) of the swarming sea-monsters. The zooming effect in these attacks reflects (again, like an image in a mirror) the synecdochic shots in the first fight where Grendel's claws met unexpected resistance in Beowulf's handshake. In that earlier scene, the close-ups on hand and claw were a prelude to Grendel's dismemberment. The personifications of Beowulf's armor and the zooming effect down onto the claws and burnie suggest an attenuation or suspension of Beowulf's volition — perhaps even his humanity — cinched by the final word of the segment denominating the human hero by the word typically used throughout the poem to describe the monsters: *aglæca*.[20] The word is used repeatedly of Grendel and the dragon, while Grendel's mother is an *aglæcwif* (1259). In line 2592, both Beowulf and the dragon are characterized together as *aglæcean*. Klaeber's glossary offers two possibilities for *aglæcan* in line 1512: a genitive singular with the verb *ehton*— as the quoted translation by Edward Risden takes it — or, as a nominative plural including Grendel's mother, her allied sea monsters, *and* the hero. The latter option is attractive because it makes neater sense. It allows us to treat the phrase as a conclusion to the segment as a whole, rather than a stale restatement of what has already been described in detail. Beowulf has pursued the *mere-wif*, and she him. This plural, encompassing and collapsing Beowulf with Grendel's mother, would be in exact parallel with the only other plural usage of the word in the poem, which unites Beowulf and the dragon under a single rubric ("aglæcean," 2592). There, as here, each antagonist rushes toward his opponent. In both cases the reason why Beowulf becomes indistinguishable from monsters may be a function of visual elements within the scene working to obscure such distinctions: in the former, the dark sea; in the latter, a cave-mouth billowing with flames.

Yet, in this frenzied whirl of claws, teeth and rings, the suspension of subjective perspective also helps to suggest Beowulf's confusion at this point — no doubt short on oxygen, ambushed from below, prevented from actively defending himself and then attacked on all sides, his bearings and perhaps even his intellection are stymied by the rabid swirl of enemies all around him. He is momentarily reduced to the armor that safeguards his life, a shell of his former self, the self who waited unarmed for Grendel in the dark. The suggestion that Beowulf is disoriented (or even loses consciousness at this juncture) is reinforced by another distinct alteration of perspective:

Segment 5
>   ða se eorl ongeat
> þæt he in niðsele   nathwylcum wæs,
> þær him nænig wæter   wihte ne scepede,
> ne him for hrofsele   hrinan ne mehte
> færgripe flodes;   fyrleoht geseah,
> blacne leoman,   beorhte scinan [1512b–1516; emphasis added].
>   Then the man perceived
> that he was in an enemy hall,   he knew not what sort,
> where none of the water   in any way harmed him,
> nor could it touch him,   sudden rush of the flood,
> because of the roofed-hall.   He saw fire-lights,
> gleaming flames   shining brightly.

Segment five elides intervening actions the way a jump cut does in film. The return to Beowulf's POV is markedly *subjective*; it highlights his dazzled response to new surroundings. Some time has elapsed; the hero (it seems) has been dragged through a pressure-lock, leaving the lady's marine guard dogs outside on the porch. The "niðsele nathwylcum" is a masterstroke — truly, a "where am I?" moment. That is, the language here registers Beowulf's dazed reaction to his new surroundings, like a film noir detective waking after a Mickey Finn or a working over, whose POV was conventionally represented by a blurred focus. Weirdly, what first seizes Beowulf's attention is that the water no longer presents a threat to him. The negatives pile up (*natwhylcum, nænig, ne, ne, ne*— all the space of two and a half lines), suggesting perhaps that the most real and present danger he has survived is drowning. When last we left our hero, his body armor had been breached and he was locked in the lethal embrace of a she-troll. He wakes, left for dead in front of a fire, which is envisioned from a subjective point of view that makes the flames seem bright indeed.[21]

Certainly the *mere-wif* believes him dead or unconscious, why else would she have released him and moved so far away that he can finally draw his borrowed sword and mount a battle rush in her direction ("mægenræs," 1519)? After looking around for the absent water, scanning the hall and the roof, and dazzled by the fire, Beowulf finally discovers his target again:

> Segment 6
> *Ongeat þa se goda*   grundwyrgenne,
> merewif mihtig;   mægenræs forgeaf
> hildebille,   hond sweng ne ofteah,
> þæt hire on hafelan   hringmæl agol
> grædig guðleoð.   ða se gist onfand
> þæt se beadoleoma   bitan nolde,
> aldre sceþðan,   ac seo ecg *geswac*
> ðeodne æt þearfe   [1518–1525a; emphasis added].

> Then the good man eyed   the earth-cursed one,
> mighty mere-woman.   A mighty rush he gave
> with his sword,   did not withhold hand-swing
> so that on her head   the ring-adorned blade rang out
> a greedy war-song.   Then the guest found
> that the battle-light   would not bite,
> injure the vitals,   but the edge failed
> The nobleman at need.

The collocation of *ongeat* + *þa* once again works to mark a shift, though here not in POV but in the object viewed. The passage also suggests a tracking shot following Beowulf's perspective as he rushes toward the hag, and then, as in segment 4, the focus zooms down to the weapon and its target (the tarn-hag's head), as the two come into contact. Point-of-view camera picks up the sword where it meets and fails to penetrate her head, and the resounding blow ("guðleoð") punctuates the narrowing of focus with the only sound described in the whole episode. The parallel techniques of visualization in segments 4 and 6 are important, helping to emphasize the image-in-the mirror relationship of the two attacks — both of which fail to hit home when they are foiled by tightly woven mail and an incredibly hard head. Like segment 4 as well, the sixth segment contains two actions, the second of which begins with the ironical "ða se gist onfand." The guest's discovery, of course, looks back to the first fight, to Grendel's own discovery ("onfunde," 750) of an unexpectedly powerful hand and to the spell that made him impervious to weapons. Yet it also looks forward to the failures of the sword Nægling in the dragon fight, which twice employs the verb used here to describe that weapon's treasonous failure (*geswac*, 2584, and 2681).

The extended focus on the sword is both detailed and digressive. It gleams in the firelight ("beadoleoma," 1523) and the poet suspends narration of the action to relate its former reliability in battle (lines 1525b–1528). The language here continues the subtle personification of weapons that has characterized the episode throughout: we are told, "this was the first time for the beloved treasure that his reputation failed" ("his dom alæg"). In the only other use of the verb in the poem, Wiglaf employs it to describe the shame incurred by Beowulf's cowardly retainers. Both Beowulf and the poet seem eager to dissociate the hero from the shame-laden sword: as its fame wanes, Beowulf, *mærða gemyndig* (1530), grows even more resolute and flings it aside:

Segment 7
Wearp ða wundenmæl   wrættum gebunden
yrre oretta,   þæt hit on eorðan læg,
stið ond stylecg;   strenge getruwode,
mundgripe mægenes.   Swa sceal man don,
þonne he æt guðe   gegan þenceð
longsumne lof,   na ymb his lif cearað [1531–1536; emphasis added].

> (The wrathful warrior   then discarded the patterned-sword
> bound with serpent-figures   so it lay on the ground,
> strong and steel-edged;   He trusted in the strength
> of his mighty hand-grip —   so must a man do
> when in battle he   thinks to win
> enduring fame,   cares not at all about his life.

As I have maintained throughout this analysis, the action verb + an adverb of time (*Wearp ða*) signals a perspective akin to objective camera, a view from outside the scene. Beowulf throws the sword away, but our gaze follows it sliding to rest on the floor. We linger there to note its ornamental, serpentine pattern, its strength and sheer edge, before the camera pans or racks focus back to Beowulf, who, perhaps clenching his massive hands, has decided to trust in his own strength. The phrase "wundenmæl wrættum gebunden," as Tolkien remarks of the "poetic class" of kennings more generally, "flashes a picture before us, often the more clear and bright for its brevity, instead of unrolling it in a simile" (*Essays* 59). Here the flashing image allows us to register the intricate beauty of the discarded sword even as it confirms the weapon's uselessness, the glimmering snake-patterns hinting perhaps at something malevolent woven into Unferth's gift. (Later, with the description of the melting of the giants' sword, the poet will pause more elaborately, quite deliberately "unrolling it in a simile.") The gnomic statement that concludes segment 7 helps to confirm our sense of an objective, admiring distance in the shot: a portrait in resolute, empty-handed courage. In fact the poet's interruption at this point disrupts the intense concentration on the visualization of action that has dominated the whole episode. Obviously, this proverbial editorializing cannot be subsumed in our cinematic shot schedule, yet — to stretch a point — it functions in a way comparable to a filmic voice-over, drawing the contrast between the slack sword and the steely hero.

Segment 8 continues the action verb + adverb of time pattern from an objective point of view to describe the irresolute grappling that ensues:

> *Gefeng þa* be eaxle   (nalas for fæhðe mearn)
> Guðgeata leod   Grendles modor;
> brægd þa beadwe heard,   þa he gebolgen wæs,
> feorhgeniðlan,   þæt heo on flet gebeah.
> *Heo him eft hraþe*   *andlean forgeald*
> grimman grapum   ond him togeanes feng;
> oferwearp þa werigmod   wigena strengest,
> feþecempa,   þæt he on fylle wearð.
> *Ofsæt þa* þone selegyst   ond hyre seax geteah,
> brad ond brunecg,   wolde hire bearn wrecan,
> angan eaferan.   Him on eaxle læg
> breostnet broden;   þæt gebearh feore,

wið ord ond wið ecge   ingang forstod.
Hæfde ða forsiðod   sunu Ecgþeowes
under gynne grund,   Geata cempa,
nemne him heaðobyrne   helpe gefremede,
herenet hearde,   ond halig god
geweold wigsigor;   witig drihten,
rodera rædend,   hit on ryht gesced
yðelice,   *syþðan he eft astod* [1537–1556; emphasis added].
The man of the war-Geats   then seized by the shoulder
Grendel's mother —   he did not mourn for that feud
the strong one flung into the fight   the mortal foe
when he was enraged,   so that she fell on the hall-floor.
She quickly after   paid him requital
with fierce grips   and seized him against her.
The strongest of men   then stumbled disheartened
so that he fell,   foot-warrior.
Then she sat on her hall-guest[22]   and drew her knife,
broad and bright-edged;   she wished to avenge her son,
her only progeny.   On his shoulder lay
the woven breast-net: that saved his life —
it withstood entry   against point and edge.
Then Ecgtheow's son   had perished
under the earth   he champion of the Geats,
but the battle-burnie   provided help,
hard war net,   and holy god
brought him the battle-victory —   the wise lord,
ruler of the heavens,   decided it rightly,
quite easily,   once he again stood up.

This sequence visualizes in rich detail an elaborately choreographed fight scene, the three stages of which are signaled by the now familiar combination of action verb + adverb of time. The objective POV does not change throughout these lines. The sequence also repeats the established pattern of irresolute conflict in a similar image-in-the-mirror structure. Beowulf's inability to injure her is followed by the mother having another go at his burnie, this time with a *seax*. Beowulf knocks or throws her down by the shoulder, apparently in some variation of the wrestling hold he used on her son ("be eaxle," 1537). She rallies, grabbing him in a way similar to the initial attack in the lake ("gefeng, 1501; "feng," 1542). She then sits on his torso, produces the thoroughly unexpected *seax* and begins hacking away at the burnie, but has no better luck with knife than claws. The same racking focus effect we saw in segment 4 recurs here, produced by the tightening focus on the burnie ("breostnet broden") and the weapon ("seax ... brad ond brunecg"). We perhaps remember that while her claws could not breach the armor, the tusks of the sea-beasts did pierce it. The series of attacks and countermoves within an extended take has shifted back and forth, each movement definitively marked by the formula for objective camera: 1. "*Gefeng þa* be eaxle" (1537a); 2. "Heo him *eft ... forgeald*" (1541); 3. "*Ofsæt þa* þone selegyst" (1545). But here the topsy-turvyness comes to a halt. A fourth formulaic signal follows the pattern, but alters it subtly too, relating the death of Beowulf in an optative: "Hæfde ða forsiðod sunu Ecgþeowes" ("Then had the son of Ecgtheow made his final journey..." 1550). Again, if pressed, we should have to hedge a bit and insist that this glance into a non-existent future functions like a voice over, though in a film the music track or facial expressions can easily convey the sense of heightened danger. In any event, such interruptions remind us of how deliberately the narrator is constructing the scene, introducing his own perspective just as auteurist cinema often does. Two things prevent this actually being Beowulf's final journey: the oft-mentioned chainmail and almighty God, who sets about making things right — as he can easily do — when, in another clear iteration of the objective formulaic signal, Beowulf "syþðan he eft astod" (1556b).

Exactly how God comes into it is never fully explained, though the presence of the divine is palpable in the episode from this point onward. Like cinema, God is light and, as Galadriel would no doubt remind us, this quintessence of the divine can be a beacon for us even in the darkest of places. The firelight within the hall allows Beowulf to discover the sword of giants:

Segment 9
Geseah ða on searwum   sigeeadig bil,
eald sweord eotenisc,   ecgum þyhtig,
wigena weorðmynd;   þæt wæs wæpna cyst,
buton hit wæs mare   ðonne ænig mon oðer
to beadulace   ætberan meahte,
god ond geatolic,   giganta geweorc [1557–1562; emphasis added].

He saw then among the armor   a victory-blessed blade,
an old, monstrous sword   with firm edges,
honor-memorial of men;   that was the best of weapons,
though it was larger   than any other man
could carry   into battle-play,
good and noble   the work of giants.

Once again, what we have designated a formulaic signal (*Geseah ða*) for changes in perspective describes a shift back to subjective, POV camera, as Beowulf catches a glimpse of the giant sword amidst the enormous hoard. Hardly a needle in a haystack, admittedly, but having just been informed that God is at work even in this darksome lair, we may well conclude that light glancing off the gigantic, "victory-blessed blade" within the hoard has caught Beowulf's attention.[23]

In segment 10 the return to objective camera widens our perspective as the hero takes hold of the sword and decapitates the she-troll, but it also bears witness to a miraculous transformation within the visual frame:

> *He gefeng* þa fetelhilt,   freca Scyldinga
> hreoh ond heorogrim   hringmæl gebrægd,
> aldres orwena,   yrringa sloh,
> þæt hire wið halse   heard grapode,
> banhringas bræc.   Bil eal ðurhwod
> fægne flæschoman;   heo on flet gecrong.
> Sweord wæs swatig,   secg weorce gefeh.
> *Lixte se leoma,   leoht inne stod,
> efne swa of hefene   hadre scineð
> rodores candel*   [1563–1572a; emphasis added].
>
> He grasped the ring-hilt,   adventurer of the Scyldings,
> fierce and battle-grim,   drew the ring-decorated one,
> despairing of life,   and angrily struck
> so that it grievously gripped   against her neck.
> Bone-rings broke;   the blade passed entirely through
> the death-fated flesh-home.   She crashed on the floor.
> The sword was bloody;   the soldier rejoiced in the deed.
> *The spark gleamed;   a light issued within,
> Even as from heaven   the candle of the sky
> Shines brightly.*

The cut decapitating the *mere-wif* cues what can only be called a supernatural suffusion of light, compared in the simile to the sun in the sky.[24] No montage occurs; rather, a new light from an unidentified source floods the *mise en scène*, allowing Beowulf to go off in search of Grendel. In an analogue of this scene in the eighth book of the *Aeneid*, Hercules dislodges a jagged rock-formation and plunges it into the cave from above. The effect, also described in a simile, compares the result to an earthquake that exposes the trembling inhabitants of Dis to sudden, unexpected sunlight (*trepident immisso lumine Manes*, 8. 247).[25] Whether or not one concludes that the passage in the *Aeneid* is a likely source for the episode in *Beowulf*, glaring differences persist. However supernaturally achieved, the flooding of sunlight into the subterranean home of the cannibal Cacus is thoroughly naturalistic — earthquakes do expose buried places to sunlight. Yet in the Old English episode, what causes a similar light like the sun to shine through the hall in the mere, permitting an extensive search of its contents by Beowulf? The answer may be hinted at within the simile itself, which metaphorically calls the sun "the candle of the sky." Soaked in the lake-hag's blood and sparked, perhaps, by the sword striking flint-hard flesh, the sword itself has become a bright candle, slowly diminishing, being melted down by the hot blood — as we are later told — into "battle-icicles."

Klaeber, mistakenly in my view, reads the line "lixte se leoma" (1570a) as referring to the firelight mentioned in line 1517 (188n1570). The same half line occurs in the description of Heorot, where the light shining from the hall radiates over many lands ("lixte se leoma ofer landa fela," 311). The only other use of the word in *Beowulf* describes a sunrise ("þonne dæge lixte," 485). In the description of light in the cave-hall, the parallel construction in the next half line "leoht inne stod" would also seem to support my reading because the verb here emphasizes directionality: not, "the light stood within;" but, "the light issued forth within (the hall)." A similar use of the verb *standan* in a similar context gives an identical sense, where light, most like a flame, shoots forth from the eyes of Grendel: "him of eagum *stod*/ligge gelicost leoht unfæger" (726b–727; emphasis added). Even more similar in form are the lines describing flames issuing from the mouth of the dragon: "bryneleoma stod" (2313b). It seems reasonable to suggest, then, that Beowulf— with God's help — ignites a candle (though *torch* or *beacon* would be better words for an object so enormous) on the spine of the tarn-hag, which illuminates his reconnaissance for Grendel's remains.[26]

The next segment, which narrates the search, introduces complications in perspective that challenge the distinction maintained thus far between objective and subjective camera:

Segment 11

He æfter recede wlat;
hwearf þa be wealle,   wæpen hafenade
heard be hiltum   Higelaces ðegn,
yrre ond anræd.   Næs seo ecg fracod
hilderince,   ac he hraþe wolde
Grendle forgyldan   guðræsa fela
ðara þe he geworhte   to Westdenum
oftor micle   ðonne on ænne sið,
þonne he Hroðgares   heorðgeneatas
sloh on sweofote,   slæpende fræt
folces Denigea   fyftyne men
ond oðer swylc   ut offerede,
laðlicu lac.   He him þæs lean forgeald
reþe cempa,   to ðæs þe he on ræste geseah
guðwerigne   Grendel licgan
aldorleasne,   swa him ær gescod
hild æt Heorote.   Hra wide sprong,
syþðan he æfter deaðe   drepe þrowade,
heorosweng heardne,   ond hine þa heafde becearf
[1572b–1509; emphasis added].

(He afterwards gazed at the hall,
went along the wall,   raised the weapon,
hard in its hilts,   Hygelac's thane,

wrathful and resolute. Nor was the blade worthless
to the battle-warrior, but he quickly wished
to repay Grendel for the many war-rushes
that he wrought on the west-Danes,
much more often than on one venture,
when he slew as they dreamt
Hrothgar's hearth-companions, devoured sleeping ones,
fifteen men of the people of the Danes
and carried off a second fifteen likewise,
loathsome booty. He gave him a requital for that,
fierce champion, when he saw Grendel lying
battle-weary in his resting place,
lifeless, as he had previously harmed him
in battle at Heorot. The corpse sprang wide open
when after death it suffered a blow,
stern sword-stroke, and the head was hewed off.)

The division between objective and subjective camera would seem to be vitiated here by the first two half lines, the first of which ("He æfter recede wlat") assumes Beowulf's POV, while the second ("hwearf þa") takes the form we have assigned to objective perspective. In cinematic vocabulary such a texturing of viewpoints would be termed a "following shot," which tracks an actor's movements from behind, filming both the looker and what he sees. Thus we are made to assume Beowulf's perspective as he searches along the wall, even as we watch him search, via a staple of cinematic suture called "an eye-line match," wherein the angle of audience's viewpoint duplicates that of the protagonist, seeing what he sees from the angle at which he sees it. The fact that Beowulf raises up the sword ("wæpen hafenade") as he looks for Grendel lends further support to the notion that the bloody sword now serves a kind of torch or candle, lighting the way. Lines 1578–1584 relating Grendel's crimes would also seem to violate the pattern of action verb + adverb of time= objective camera, because what is being narrated occurred at a different time and place. Though digressions are ubiquitous in the poem, this particular inset — with its detailed remembrance of Grendel's former depredations — functions in ways analogous to a flashback, neatly filling the time between the onset of Beowulf's search and his/our discovery of the corpse. The psychological effect of this flashback, this detailed evocation of past horrors, serves to motivate the desire for revenge and to justify Beowulf's desecration of the corpse — it seems designed to encourage our identification with Beowulf's fury.

Thus far we have observed the subtle interlacing of visual styles, subjective and objective camera, perhaps knotted together in segment 11 with the combination of perspectives, as we followed Beowulf's search for Grendel's carcass through the hall. The next segment (12) anticipates the montage of many a self-conscious chiller by "cutting on the cut." In the final half line of segment 11, Beowulf hacks off Grendel's head ("þa heafde becearf"). This is followed immediately by a jump cut to a very different scene, back to the warriors (about whom we had perhaps quite forgotten) waiting on shore:

> Segment 12
> *Sona þæt gesawon* snottre ceorlas,
> þa ðe mid Hroðgare on holm wliton,
> þæt wæs yðgeblond eal gemenged,
> brim blode fah. Blondenfeaxe,
> gomele ymb godne, ongeador spræcon
> þæt hig þæs æðelinges eft ne wendon
> þæt he sigehreðig secean come
> mærne þeoden; þa ðæs monige gewearð
> þæt hine seo brimwylf abroten hæfde.
> ða com non dæges. Næs ofgeafon
> hwate Scyldingas; gewat him ham þonon
> goldwine gumena. Gistas setan
> modes seoce ond on mere staredon,
> wiston ond ne wendon þæt hie heora winedrihten
> selfne gesawon [1591–1605a].
>
> Soon the wise men saw,
> those who with Hrothgar gazed on the water,
> that the wave-turmoil was all mingled,
> the lake stained with blood. The gray-haired
> old ones spoke together concerning the good man
> that they did not expect again that nobleman,
> triumphing in victory, to come seeking
> the famous king. Then it seemed certain to many
> that the she-wolf had slain him.
> Then came the ninth hour of the day; the brave Scyldings
> abandoned the headlands. The gold-friend of men
> departed thence home. The guests sat
> sick at heart and stared at the mere.
> They wished but did not expect that they would see him,
> their friend-lord.

This cross-cutting from the tarn bottom to the shore side represents a master stroke, so formidably brilliant in its strained continuities with the prior segment, so plangent in its elegiac tone, so ironic in its undercutting of this tone, and, finally, so decisive in introducing a series of distinctions. Those on shore misinterpret the sign of blood, a mistake emphasizing the difference between their perceptions and reality. Yet the old Danes and young Geats also respond differently to what they see: the latter return home muttering to themselves, while the former stay on desperately trying to keep hope alive. Subjective camera makes the audience assume the POV of the "snottre ceorlas," but as in the previous sequence, we seem to look over their shoulders in a long shot at the churning waves. Gore oozes in the surf as dusk settles in, but we also understand how short-sighted are the understandings of these "wise" and "brave" gray-beards who give up and go home. Knowing what we know, the extended vigil of the youthful Geats testifies to their perseverance, though we will also come to understand that these same Geats — or others like them — will flock to the forest fifty years hence when Beowulf is finally in desperate need of their support. Indeed, such cross-cuttings from intense physical combat to the restricted, compromised perspectives of the internal audience is crucial to the style of the poem: the Danes quivering in terror from the relative security of the outbuildings during the first fight (783b–788a); the differing reactions of Danes and Geats at the apparent sign of Beowulf's death in the middle episode; down to the last episode's band of *hand-gesteallan* (2696) cowering in the woods when their failing lord finally does need a hand.

Twice- and even thrice-told tales comprise a hallmark of the poem, so much so that the depiction of momentous, violent action from multiple perspectives must be said to be a distinctive feature of its recursive style. All three of the monster fights are narrated directly and then retold — and sometimes retold again, as is the case with the Grendel episode, which is first narrated, then woven into the riding scop's song including the comparison with Sigemund, then chillingly recalled as the hero searches for Grendel's corpse in the Tarn, and then retold again as part of a larger story upon Beowulf's return to Gotland. Note as well how the swimming match with Breca is twice recounted, first by Unferth and then retold by Beowulf in a way which uncovers the hidden proof of strength and endurance that Unferth's account glossed over. Something similar is at work in the second episode, where the Danes in general likewise mistake a triumph for a failure, because they, like Unferth, are mislead by superficial appearances, while the truth of what has occurred in the subaqueous hall is unfathomable to them.

This segment from line 1591 occupies the exact midpoint of the 3182 lines of the text in modern editions; the uncertainties and ambivalence of the scene tie it inextricably to the funerals that begin and end the poem. James W. Earl suggests that "*Beowulf* is an act of cultural mourning" (133), "a literary form invented as the culture's way of mourning the recent loss of its past" (134). Earl's insight also allows us to remember that the first half of the poem is more about renewals, unexpected resurgences, metaphorical and metaphysical rebirths, than it is about mourning a lost past. The past continues to be prologue, and that motivates the poem's intricate structure as well as its apocalyptic closure. Premature reports of Beowulf's death are both immediately funny and ultimately tragic — as Mark Twain's quip recognizes — but in Earl's terms such proleptic ironies also contain a shadow of the future, so that we can begin mourning Beowulf long before he dies, throughout the final half of the poem.

A second radical jump cut returns us at midline to the hall in the mere, but to a starkly different *mise en scène*— an extreme close up on the marvel of the melting sword:

> Segment 13
>   þa þæt sweord ongan
> æfter heaþoswate   hildegicelum,
> wigbil *wanian*.   þæt wæs wundra sum,
> þæt hit eal gemealt   ise gelicost,
> ðonne forstes bend   fæder onlæteð,
> onwindeð wælrapas,   se geweald hafað
> sæla ond mæla;   þæt is soð metod.
> Ne nom he in þæm wicum,   Wedergeata leod,
> maðmæhta ma,   þeh he þær monige geseah,
> buton þone hafelan   ond þa hilt somod
> since fage.   Sweord ær gemealt,
> forbarn brodenmæl;   wæs þæt blod to þæs hat,
> ættren ellorgæst   se þær inne swealt [1605b–1617; emphasis added].
>
>   Then that sword began,
> from the battle-blood, the war-blade to dissolve
> into battle-icicles; that was a certain wonder
> that it all melted most like ice
> when the father loosens the bond of frost,
> unwinds winter-fetters, who has the power
> over season and time: that is the true god.
> Nor took he from that place, man of the weather-Geats,
> more precious possessions, though he saw many there,
> than the head and the hilt together,
> adorned treasure; the sword had melted before,
> the wave-patterned blade burnt up. Too hot was the blood
> of the poisonous alien-spirit who died therein.

Continuity editing in film tends to place fewer demands upon an audience than disorienting, jump cuts like those in segments 12 and 13. The suspense of Beowulf's fight with the tarn-hag was driven along by seamless manipulations of perspective, requiring little in the way of interpretation in order to be appreciated. These "invisible cuts," as they are sometimes called, work to stitch the viewer into the scene and to encourage our vicarious participation in the action, thoroughly in keeping with the Hollywood style of films made to be watched rather than looked at. Once the fight concludes, however, radical montage and the deep-focus texturing of shots more commonly associated with auteurist cinema work to complicate appreciably the meaning of this central episode in the poem. In segment 12, the cut from the beheading of Grendel to the warriors' view of the gore-plashed whitecaps troubles continuities even as it affirms them. For Eisenstein, intellectual montage creates an idea out of the juxtaposition of images, such as when shots of strikebreaking in *Strike* are counterpoised with insets of a bull being butchered in a slaughterhouse. For Renoir, meaningful juxtapositions can also be achieved more realistically within a single, extended take. In *The Rules of the Game*, a wife watches through binoculars her husband's passionate conversation with another woman. (The husband has decided that he loves his wife and must break off the affair, which he is in fact doing, as his wife watches from afar.) Yet the wife imagines that she is witnessing the beginning of a seduction, the intensity of which suggests that her husband cannot love her, and she quickly demands a divorce.[27] Segments 11–13 of the Old English poem function in analogous ways, deploying both "intellectual" montage as well as emotionally charged but ironically textured shots in deep focus. The light shining from the giant sword and the blood-stained waters juxtapose hope and despair, a lord who shows the way even in the dark places of the world to those who do his work, over against those in no danger giving into gloom and doom at the garish signs of a bloodbath. Though equally misled by what they have seen, the Danes and the Geats go their separate ways, and the tone and meaning of the scene modulates from ironic distance to a trenchant focus on loyalty and its opposite, pride.

As Beowulf's Danish support melts away, the second radical cut in segment 13 presents an extreme close up of the liquefying sword: "þa þæt sweord ongan/æfter heaþoswate hildegicelum, /wigbil wanian." The shot of the shrinking blade thus serves as an objective correlative for the waning of hope above the tarn. Yet, with the simile of the spring thaw (in film terminology this would be called a match cut inset, juxtaposing the melting blade and icicles), the meaning of the image is transformed as well. Beowulf's victory, however doubtful it may have seemed to those on the bluffs, was — because God willed it — as inevitable as the coming of spring. The simile, in distancing the poem's audience for a moment both physically and emotionally from the carnage in the tarn-hall, provides a much broader context and a glimpse of transcendence. However, the wider meanings of this composite image have only begun to accrue, arguably becoming complete only when Hrothgar glosses the sword-hilt for Beowulf in his famous speech. The hilt memorializes the obliteration of the race of giants who broke faith with God; he destroyed them with a flood and his power can still be seen in the changing seasons, freeing the world from freezing cold (as from the frost giants) and opening the seas to men. The hilt then functions with something like the deadpan irony of Piers the Plowman's pardon: it is neither a curse nor a magic talisman; rather, it serves as a remarkably durable assurance that God will destroy those whose pride makes them break their troth — a terrible fate to which by the end of the poem both Geats and Danes will have fallen victim.

The final segment (14) may appear anti-climactic, but it closes the circle adeptly and also contains tantalizing enigmas worthy of consideration:

> *Sona wæs on sunde*   se þe ær æt sæcce gebad
> wighryre wraðra,   wæter up þurhdeaf.
> Wæron yðgebland   eal gefælsod,
> eacne eardas,   þa se ellorgast
> oflet lifdagas   ond þas lænan gesceaft.
> *Com þa* to lande   lidmanna helm
> swiðmod swymman;   sælace gefeah,
> mægenbyrþenne   þara þe he him mid hæfde.
> *Eodon him þa togeanes*,   gode þancodon,
> ðryðlic þegna heap,   þeodnes gefegon,
> þæs þe hi hyne gesundne   geseon moston.
> ða wæs of þæm hroran   helm ond byrne
> lungre alysed.   Lagu drusade,
> wæter under wolcnum,   wældreore fag [1618–1631; emphasis added].

> Soon was he swimming; he who had known in struggle
> the fall of the enemy quickly swam up through the water.
> The surging waves were all cleansed,
> a vast area, since the alien-spirit
> relinquished life-days and this transitory world.
> The protector of seafarers then came to land,
> swimming stout-hearted, rejoiced in sea-plunder,
> in the might-burden of that which he had with him.
> They went to him together, gave thanks to god;
> the trusty troop of thanes rejoiced for their leader
> because they were able to see him sound.
> Then from the strong one helmet and byrnie
> were quickly loosened. The lake grew still,
> water under the clouds, stained with slaughter-blood.

With this final *mise en scène* we return to the establishing shot of Beowulf's departure in segment one. The stages of his return to shore are carefully demarcated in three racked focus increments: from the long swim ("Sona wæs on sunde [...] wæter up þurhdeaf"), to the hero's arrival on shore ("Com þa to lande") and his reception by the Geats ("Eodon him þa togeanes"). Nevertheless, the joyous welcome of the retainers is sharply undercut by a caustic reminder of those no longer there: "þæs þe hi hyne gesundne geseon moston."

Moreover, though stained with gore in the prior segment, the whitecaps have now been thoroughly cleansed ("eal gefælsod," 1620). Beowulf had used this word when he promised Hrothgar he would "Heorot fælsian" (433). Twice after he made good this boast, the cleansing was confirmed in the same terms ("Hæfde þa gefælsod [...] sele Hroðgares," 825–826, and "Heorot is gefælsod," 1176b)—but that was before Grendel's mother emerged to resume the feud. The lapse into contamination is about to recur yet again—in very literal terms. Beowulf is quickly disarmed with the help of his retainers, yet the camera lingers at the scene for a final glimpse at the tarn. Two changes have taken place in a brief span. The waves have ceased churning; instead, the lake seems to drowse ("drusade"), and the waters cleansed by Beowulf's victory are once again awash with gore ("wældreore fag") beneath an overcast sky.[28] The perspective and direction of the shot has not changed; rather, the location has itself been transformed (for a second time). A recurrent *topos* in the poem, that of danger lurking on the outskirts of peace, has been subtly reiterated. Our first sight of these gore-plashed waters occurred on the morning after the first fight, when the warriors followed Grendel's bloody tracks back to the tarn. Then too there was cause for celebration, though blood called out for blood, and that same night Grendel's mother took her revenge. This final, eerie transformation within a scene celebrating the monster-slayer's glorious return functions much as the stereotyped open endings in horror films—it threatens a sequel, which of course the third part of the poem provides, albeit in a different locale. Has the evil hosted by the tarn really and truly passed away, or is it only sleeping ("drusade"), waiting like the monsters that woke after the flood ("onwocon," 111) to be born again?

We can draw a number of salient conclusions from this analysis of visual styles, especially as regards deliberate manipulations of light sources and changes within the *mise en scène*. The first three segments establish all three alternatives: an objective shot portraying an action (Beowulf diving into the mere) and subjective shots from the POV of the hero and Grendel's mother. Parallel zoom or rack focused shots in the objective camera of segment 4, which describes the attack of the sea-troll and assorted sea-beasts, work to personify Beowulf's armor, but these tight shots also suggest that his powers of resistance have been so diminished that only the armor forestalls his death. The return of Beowulf's POV in segment 5 after an indeterminate interval expresses a marked change; not only has the sea-troll released him but his confused reaction to the literally *unheimlich* hall implies that he has been dazed or rendered unconscious, half-drowned by the struggle deep below the surface. The first light source mentioned—from Beowulf's perspective an extremely bright fire ("blacne leoman, breohte scinan," 1516)—spurs a halting, incredulous recognition that he is no longer in dark waters but rather in a dry, illuminated hall. Light will repeatedly take his side in the struggles to come. In segment 6 the firelight allows Beowulf to re-discover his antagonist, only to find that Hrunting, Unferth's battle-light, is insufficient to the task at hand. Beowulf throws away the sword, which like all conventional swords proves no match for his powerful grip. The cine-stylus pans to follow the sword and pauses there to admire its design, perhaps rendering the ornamentation suspicious, before returning to the matter at hand. The wrestling match in segment 8 also proves indecisive, and, though he is very close to death, the tide turns in the richly symbolic movement at the very end of this segment when Beowulf stands up again ("syþðan he eft astod," 1556b). We are told that God, the ruler of the heavens, easily decided the conflict on the side of right ("hyt on ryht geced," 1555b) after Beowulf stood up. Fair enough, but exactly how did God accomplish this and what did that have to do with Beowulf getting up off of the floor? Generally speaking, we could perhaps agree that God, like *wyrd*, favors the resolute. Yet Beowulf's POV also alters markedly once he gets out from underneath the *mere-wif*, thereby extricating himself from a perhaps morally but certainly optically compromised position — and stands up again. The change in angle of vision allows him to discern amidst a large cache of booty the choicest of weapons ("wæpena cyst," 1559). The word used to describe what God did ("geced") literally means to separate, set apart, or distinguish one thing from other things. God has used light to decide the battle, by permitting Beowulf to distinguish this weapon in a large cache treasure.[29] What did Beowulf see hanging there on the wall? Perhaps what caught his eye was the light playing off the images on the hilt of God destroying the giants. If so, what we have here (though specified only later) is indeed a proto-cinematic moment, a tiny film in two shots, depicting: a. the origin of "fyrn-gewinnes" (1689a) and b. God's exaction of revenge with the whelming waves ("þurh wæteres wylm," 1693a). When Beowulf leaves the mere, the hilt is all he takes out of the many treasures he saw there — in stark contrast to the wholescale plundering of the hoard at the end of the poem. Perhaps these monsters had discovered a hoard in a hall after the flood, just as the dragon finds an abandoned hoard at the end of the poem. Treasure is of no more use to the Grendel-kin than to the dragon; both hoard rather than distributing it, as men are supposed to do, but these piles of wealth contain the seeds of their destruction: the sword of giants and the cup of the thief.

From segment 10 to the end of the episode, the styles of visualization become more complicated and the use of symbolic imagery grows increasingly dense. The spine of the tarn-hag serves as a flint to kindle her flammable blood on the sword, which then radiates with a brilliance like the sun. We follow Beowulf, holding this sword-torch on high, on his search for the *hra* of Grendel.[30] As the flashback to Grendel's grisly haunting of Heorot is interposed, we seem to view this flashback — just as we do the search — through Beowulf's eyes, though — just as in many film flashbacks — what Beowulf "sees," he has not witnessed — though poem's audience has. The sharpest, most radical cut in the episode comes at the precise moment when Grendel's head is struck off, transporting the audience back up to the shore, where an audience within the poem sees the waves churning blood, which they mistakenly conclude is the hero's. A subtle irony is contained in this juxtaposition of external and internal audiences. As readers/viewers we identify with the validity of Beowulf's perspective and scornfully dismiss the skittish old Danes who succumb so readily to despair. The next jump cut juxtaposes the shot in depth of the blood-streaked waves and the Danes abandoning the watch with a tight shot on the melting sword. The effect of the cut is highly surreal, but the resultant concatenation of images represents a dense interweaving of metonymic and metaphoric images of blood. The synecdoche of the blood in the water is misinterpreted as a sign of Beowulf's death in segment 12. The blood on the sword in segment 13 signifies his victory in the tarn, while the melting of the sword down to the hilt figures the melting away of support on shore down to the faithful stub of Geats. Of course it also reveals that there is something supernatural about the creatures' blood. They are hell fiends and reside in a hellish hole many fathoms beneath the earth, but their corrosive, flammable blood suggests that hell is also within them. The simile juxtaposing the images of the melting sword and melting ice widens the context of Beowulf's achievement still farther, re-mixing, as it were, the blood and waves of the earlier image in the tenor and vehicle of a simile. Just as the burning blood dissolves the sword, God melts the ice, opening up the waterways for mankind, as the blood apparently does for Beowulf, who meets no further resistance from sea monsters on his return swim. Beowulf's victory is thus also God's, but the watery images within segment 14 juxtapose cleansed waves (like those in the simile) with the final transformation of the lake into a stagnant, gore-choked pool — a metaphor that seems at once to glance backward to God's rout of the giants and forward toward the tenuous and brief nature of Beowulf's achievements in Denmark and later among the Geats.

However, we should be cautious in interpreting so dense and fascinating a concatenation of images. Manichean readings of the poem as an irresolute battle between good and evil, light and darkness, or heavenly vs. hellish halls must still be placed within the larger context of less heretical Christian theology, as the remaining portion of the first half of the poem is careful to achieve. Darkness may well be the absence of light, but there is no darkness so absolute that God cannot see into it or from which his light is absent. God destroyed the giants with a flood (though races of aquatic monsters like Grendel and avian monsters like dragons apparently survived), but even this hiding place deep beneath the sea contains the instrument of their destruction, which itself contains an image of the giants' destruction. The water demons are beheaded with a fiery sword, the dragon, his fire spent, consigned to the waves. That no final defeat of evil manifests itself in the poem does not mean, *pace* Niles, Overing, Frantzen, *et al.*, that none is forthcoming, or that the battle between good and evil is "aporetic," or that the giants of the Eddas may indeed return to destroy heaven and middle-earth. The sword boils down to a quintessential message, a pattern established at the beginning of time, which recurs throughout time: God will overwhelm evil no matter how, where, or in whatever form it rears its head. The final victory is postponed, but never in doubt. The fundamental mistake, made by a number of recent critics and a number of characters in the poem to greater and lesser degrees — but never by the poet — assumes that any earthly king — Scyld, Hrothgar, or Beowulf— might through his own force destroy evil forever. Their failures to do so demonstrate the ultimate weakness of human power — however impressive its achievements — not any essential challenge to God's ultimate power. This may be the final significance of the melting sword, which winnows down from a divine power Beowulf is allowed momentarily to wield, to an enduring *sign* of that power, which is no longer a serviceable weapon. And yet something like a Manichean conflict *is staged within human souls*, and that is why Hrothgar's sermonizing gloss on the sword hilt resonates so profoundly through the second half of the poem. God can easily defeat his enemies and so (with his help) can heroes, but the war in the mind is never really won in this loaned life. Pride can be defeated, but it cannot be destroyed. It is always on the prowl, hoping to surprise the hall's guardian, asleep at the watch.

If we turn now from the cinematographic styles of *Beowulf* to films adapted from the poem, we find not only the predictable lack of fidelity to the story, which has been widely adulterated with ideas drawn from novels by John Gardner and Michael Crichton, but also (and more egregiously in my view) a lack of attention to styles of visualization already extant in the poem itself.[31] Yet one does catch glimpses, even in popular action-adventure cinema, of shot compositions and editing strategies that arguably descend from the poem's visual poetics. The purpose of this third section is to demonstrate specific examples of films *adapting*, not plot elements or dialogue from the original poem, but rather the very same visual strategies identified by scholars such as Tolkien and Renoir elaborated above.

A sterling example of the latter comes from Graham Baker's 1999 film, *Beowulf*. Set in a futuristic world, starring Christopher Lambert as an undead Beowulf, and featuring the Playboy centerfold Layla Roberts as Grendel's mother, no one has ever mistaken the film for a faithful adaptation of the poem. At the level of plot, the film's relationship to its source is tenuous at best, a kind of reverie we might imagine inspired by the distant memory of a text finding expression in a genre film. Yet the visual strategies of the poem receive much more faithful translation. I discussed above the radical montage in the second monster fight where the poet "cuts on the cut," jumping from the hall within the mere to those waiting on shore and back again. Though it conceives the monster fights very differently, the 1999 *Beowulf* cleverly and rather exactly reproduces this sequence of jump cuts. Beowulf's second fight in the film is a rematch with Grendel, which the hero contrives to stage within a flooded basement. He employs a spring-loaded, purpose-built hand blade, which multiplies the power of his punches manifold. As his uppercuts drive the wedged blade into Grendel's armpit, a radical cut takes us to Hrothgar and his Danes assembled in the dining room, who misinterpret the screams resounding through the castle and conclude that Beowulf is being slaughtered. The collocation of shots thus combines the internal audiences of the first two fights in the poem: those who hear the screams of Grendel from the outbuildings and those who see the blood rising to the surface of the tarn in the second fight. A second jump cut returns us to the flooded basement with no apparent lapse of time — in fact, just in time to catch the severed arm splashing into the water on the floor. The corresponding passage in *Beowulf* masterfully employs a simile at this point comparing the melting sword to melting ice, a comparison we likened to a form cut which juxtaposes similar objects in different frames. An analogous form cut occurs in the film at this point: the shot of Grendel's arm falling horizontally into water is juxtaposed with a second shot of the arm, still soaking wet, falling horizontally onto the dining room floor, where Beowulf has unceremoniously dumped it. The crash surprises the internal audience who remain clustered along the wall listening for the some sign of the outcome of the fight. Hopefully, there is no need at this point to insert the usual disclaimers: this is not a good film nor a faithful adaptation. However, it does contain a rigorously detailed and clever imitation of one of the poem's most complex visual strategies, a citation that reveals a remarkable appreciation of the poem's appositive style and what we might call its proto-cinematic use of radical montage.

Another, more subtle and complex interrogation of the poem's visual strategies occurs in the last sequence of Hal Hartley's *No Such Thing*. As Renoir first argued, one of the poem's most striking visual effects is the manipulation of POV in action scenes. In the fight with Grendel, we see prospective victims through the eyes of the monster and view the monster through the POV of Beowulf, who has a plan and the advantage of surprise. The success of such strategies in yielding suspense, horror, and irony is even more pronounced in the second fight, with Grendel's mother. For instance, even after Beowulf beheads the she-troll, the outcome of the fight remains ambiguous for those on shore. Hartley's *No Such Thing* revels in such limited perspectives to end the film in a sublime ontological ambiguity. As the anti-matter machine works to obliterate the troll, a rapid series of cuts flashes rapidly from the monster, his "slayer" Beatrice, and those watching the miracle behind protective glass. The final series of shots from the monster's POV are of a seemingly beatified Beatrice, who flashes before his eyes in a series of close ups. But the monster is most probably no longer *there*, having been turned into *nothing*. So from where are we (and he) viewing this beatific vision of the divine Sarah Polley? Obviously from somewhere beyond the abandoned missile silo in Iceland where the sequence began. Polley's Beatrice is most likely no longer there, as well, since she was in the anti-matter chamber along with the monster. In so far as she and the monster still exist on some other ontological plane, we have joined her there, followed this vision of her there, in a glimpse of transcendence, because in aligning our gaze with the subjective POV of the monster Hartley has transported us along with him into the beyond.[32]

One can also find in popular cinema significant uses of depth of field of the kind Tolkien valorized in his *Beowulf* essay. Take, for example, *The 13th Warrior*. Early in the film we have a long shot in deep focus, with that deepening of perspective that is crucial to the cinema of Jean Renoir, as well as to Tolkien's championing of the poem's darker background and its "impression of depth." The scene takes place on a riverbank at night and depicts the ship burial of Buliwyf's king. An undulating procession of mourners bearing torches shoulders the king to a ship loaded with treasure and sets it ablaze. Through the smoke and the gloaming we watch from a considerable distance as a young woman dressed in white is raised three times into the air. She and the mourners chant the prayer: "Lo there do I see my father, Lo there do I see my sisters and brothers, Lo there do I see the line of my people back to the beginning. Lo, they do call to me. They bid me take my place among them in the halls of Valhalla where the brave may live forever." These depth-of-field shots are intercut with eye-line matching counter-shots from the POV of the Arabs, Ahmed ibn Fadlan and his interpreter, and the Viking, Herger. The latter glosses the ritual for the Arab foreigners in increasingly tighter shots, as the camera zeros in on the reactions of ibn Fadlan. The final shot in extreme close-up registers the reaction of this Arab ambassador, played by

Antonio Banderas, as Herger comments: "She will travel with him. You will not see this again, it is the old way." The alternation between tight and long shots in deep focus (in harmony with the simultaneous translation by Omar Sherif's Melchisidek of Herger's Latin) works to establish the obscurity, the incomprehensibility of a pagan culture even now receding from view. This scene, in its mysterious, bleak perspectives, while not at all faithful to the ship burial which begins the Old English poem, is remarkably close to the poem's negotiation of Germanic paganism as Tolkien conceived it: "a past that itself had depth and reached back into a dark antiquity of sorrow" (2006, 27).

It would be misleading to suggest that either Michael Crichton's novel or its film adaptation pursues anything akin to Tolkien's insistence upon the depths of *Beowulf* or his aesthetics of "sub-creation," wherein richly imagined worlds are both internally self-consistent and philologically derived. Instead, Crichton invests in an imaginative response to evolutionary biology — to which, of course, the development of comparative philology owes a great deal — in its euhemeristic rationalizations of myths and monsters. The film version directed by John McTiernan rather adroitly evokes visual parallels between the funeral scene, just discussed and the fight with the "dragon." First glimpsed by Edgetho through the branches of the tree he has made his look-out post, the *fyr-wyrm* glows like a red worm on the mist-shrouded mountain in the distance — a shot thoroughly in keeping Tolkien's perspectival style in his art and his criticism. Ahmed ibn Fadlan catches sight of a lost child wandering in a valley between the mountain and the fortress. As he rides out to rescue her, he sees that the "fire-worm" is actually a line of a torch-bearing cavalry, snaking its way down the mountain and across the plain in tight formation. As ibn Fadlan reports the truth of this illusion to Herger, the Viking wistfully comments: "I rather prefer a dragon"— thereby giving voice to a sentiment shared by many in the film's audience. But while the shots of the undulating faux dragon clearly quote the earlier funeral procession, itself the vestige of a custom said to be dying out, the perspective of those within the film is here revealed as an illusion, a visual trick orchestrated by fog, night, and hundreds of remarkably well-drilled Neanderthal horsemen! (Later they organize their cavalry into the silhouette of a dragon in a remarkably intricate formation that would tax even the most accomplished marching band.) The thirteenth warrior thus serves as a rational stand-in and middleman, bridging modern and mythological perspectives. (He also discovers that the cannibals are men, not monsters, as well as the location of their lair in the Thunder Caves.) Crichton's reimagining of the poem is in essence a fictionalization of the scholarly approaches Tolkien had so thoroughly routed in his essay: archeology and anthropology (however gerrymandered) uncover the realities beneath or behind the poem, and, in doing so, destroy its carefully modulated view of the past.

The difference between an "illusion of depth" and depth as productive of illusions is an enormous one. Crichton's ibn Fadlan exposes the illusoriness of superstitions just as thoroughly as his counterpart Hank in Twain's *A Connecticut Yankee in King Arthur's Court*. In fact, commonplaces in the scholarly history of the poem — oral transmission, "Christian coloring," the bear's son folktales, analogues from *Grettis Saga* and *Hrolfs Saga Kraki*, etc.— are leveraged in order to recast Tolkien's "perspective of antiquity with a greater and yet darker antiquity behind" on an evolutionary scale. The fight between monsters and men becomes a battle between competing sub-species of *genus homo* — a difference within phenotypic history that underlies ibn Fadlan's vacillation about their classification: "They are men, They are men!" (when he first examines a Wendol corpse); "I was wrong, these are not men" (later, when the extent of their cannibalism is appallingly revealed). He also reasons about the furtive strategies of these creatures of the mist, slowly recognizing that "They want us to think they are bears," thereby glossing the Neanderthal bear costumes as attempts to fool human beings into thinking they are under attack by a wholly different species. This inter-species masquerade later aids the cause of the Vikings when one strolls up to the guarded cave mouth disguised as a Wendol in disguise as a bear.

The genealogies in the Old English poem that help to create its sense of depth are replaced in Crichton's novel by the immeasurably vaster time schemes of evolutionary genealogy. Neanderthals were once apex predators atop the food chain; they shared an evolutionary — and for perhaps 10,000 years in Europe a physical — boundary as well with physically less powerful human beings.[33] The inference that *homo sapiens* contributed to the extinction of *homo neaderthalensis* in Europe some 30,000 years ago is only conjecture. Another speculation erected atop this conjecture is that the fear of "monsters" living at the borders of human settlements might have originated from a war of natural selection fought between humans and their shorter but significantly stronger "relatives," descended from a common ancestor — a form of fictional anthropology familiar from the Eloi and Morlocks in H. G. Wells' *The Time Machine*.[34] Thus Crichton rationalizes (if that is the right word for it) the descent of monsters from Cain, as well as tracing the origin of the feud to that first murder and the divergence of two parallel species sharing a common ancestry in Adam and Eve.[35]

Until critical reappraisals of the Old English poem's central episode beginning some 40 years ago, Beowulf's fight with the tarn-woman was largely overshadowed by those against Grendel and the dragon. Films such as the 1999 and 2007 free adaptations of the poem, as well as *The 13th Warrior*—in their different ways—make the *æglacwif* the star of the monsters and her lair the showpiece of the film. The Thunder Caves in *The 13th Warrior* can thus serve as a way out of this chapter and as a way into many of the topics that will come up in later chapters, such as the twin specters of cannibalism and human sacrifice, or the filmic re-coding of monstrosity in terms of racial and cultural otherness.

In *The 13th Warrior* the recursivity of feud in the poem is recast: "Slaughter them until you rot, you'll accomplish nothing. Find the root; strike the will. This is the mother of the Wendol, she they revere ... she is the earth, seek her in the earth."[36] The implicit assumption that Neanderthals were matriarchal is impossible to prove, but if one accepts Crichton's premise about the parallel existence of *homines neaderthalensis et sapiens* in Denmark, then the inference that Neanderthal societies retained matriarchal organization even after it died out among European *homo sapiens* is plausible in terms of Tolkien's rules for sub-creation. Yet this inference also transforms the battle from a Wellsian inter-species war of survival to something much more on the order of a Manichean conflict between feminine and masculine principles. Recent *Beowulf* films in general are no more faithful to movements in recent scholarship than they are to the poem, but one can easily find analogies to feminist and gender studies of *Beowulf* in these films. That, of course, is another reason why many scholars find such films so abhorrent, not because they ignore advances in scholarship but because of how they reflect them: we feel misunderstood and misappropriated.

The matriarchal womb of monsters—even of the "dragon"—in *The 13th Warrior* is the Thunder Caves, ultimately given, as are most marvels in the film, a thoroughly rational explanation. But the idea of a cave beneath the earth pregnant with forces of destruction set loose upon the world by an undying feminine malevolence also finds an echo in the paradigmatic first scene of *Aeneid*. There Juno bribes Aeolus (with sex, what else?) to release the teeming winds that destroy the fleet of Aeneas and cast him upon Dido's shores. Though the Thunder Caves scene is set near the middle of the film, it is paradigmatic of the film in the same way the opening scene in *Aeneid* is paradigmatic.[37] It is the source of a feminine chaos that threatens to obliterate the Danes, just as Juno's "undying hate" sought to expunge forever the fugitive Trojans. As the "mother of the Wendol" and as a formidable warrior in her own right, as a sign of supernatural fertility and the equally fecund destructiveness of war, the film's earth mother is both the source and the root of monstrous evil in all its incarnations.

Earlier I suggested that the ancient sword-torch in *Beowulf* was protocinematic, initially as a source of light that determines a view and later when the metalwork on the hilt is (arguably) said to depict stages in story of the flood — the rebellion of the giants and God's revenge. I also suggested that *The 13th Warrior* employs an analogous strategy of painting with (torch)light, when torches illuminate the dying ritual of human sacrifice or are choreographed to produce the illusion of a dragon snaking its way down a mountainside. In the *catabasis* into the Thunder Caves, torches light the way for a team of explorers bent on finding the feminine "root" of evil, just as Beowulf sought the bed of Grendel's corpse in the poem. Their spelunking adventure thus translates Beowulf's journey into terms easily recognizable from lexicon of action-adventure cinema. The scene stretches out the dialectics of the seer and the seen, as Viking SWAT team launches a covert raid on the Wendol. Eye-line matches from the POV of the invaders survey pockets of Wendol warriors gathered around campfires.

The descent, then, is staged as a journey back in time to an earlier point in human development when men too lived like bears in caves and competed with bears for control of this precious bulwark against enemies and the cold. Cinematically speaking, the most striking shots in the film depict the Wendol at home in their caves, their elaborately painted bodies blending into the backdrop of similarly painted cave walls. They seem to disappear chameleon-like into their surroundings, emerging from and fading into the cave paintings, just as they appear and disappear with the mists in the world above. The torch-bearing spelunkers quickly discover the still point of this nether world, a kind of altar overseen by an enormous, headless fertility statue with bulbous breasts and an enormous womb. Awe-struck, they raise their torches high to scan this impressive monument, but then — in a shift familiar from other action-adventures such as the *Raiders of the Lost Arc* franchise — they finally lower the torches to view the horror of what lies beneath. Piles of skulls and assorted bones pave the floor and have been fashioned into columns and dividing walls — an architectural feature not drawn from archeology of the Neanderthals but from Christian churches! Yet the idea that this is a shadow world fertile with death rather than life is, within the context of the film, what differentiates the species that must be utterly destroyed from that which must survive.[38] Fadlan at this late juncture finally concludes: "I was wrong, these are not men." The headless feminine statue, like the headless figurines found throughout the film and the soon-to-be-beheaded mother of the Wendol signify a world not ruled by masculine reason.

Mixing elements from *Grettir's Saga* and *Beowulf*, the spelunkers next cross through a waterfall and then swim further toward the center of this cave, where who-knows-what-kind of a religious service is in progress, including chants and ritualized dancing. The Vikings emerge from the water to ambush the Neanderthal shamans giving thanks, perhaps, for the earth mother's favor in their war against humankind. They do not pray to demons like the back-sliding Danes in the poem; rather they are themselves the race of demons whose *wig-weorþung* (war-like sacrifice to idols, 176) stacks human bones on the altar of a female god. The next shot staged in depth but with a wide lens shows the band of species warriors standing up silently behind the Neanderthal congregants, rising to their feet as Beowulf does in the poem to turn the tide in his fight with the troll wife. This objective shot also encapsulates the evolutionary approach of Crichton and McTiernan to the matter of *Beowulf*.

Like the ubiquitous textbook illustrations charting the descent of man from apes across generations of distinct species and sub-species, this shot parses differences and similarities in a group portrait containing both Neanderthals and Northmen. The Neanderthals are more physically powerful, but human beings are taller, stealthier, and more adept in the use of weapons. Those still illustrations of genetic relationships and the slow process of natural selection thus become a moving picture of one species overtaking another. When, at the end of the film, Beowulf has killed the Grendel-like military leader of the Wendol, we get a final long shot in deep focus in which the remnant of the Wendol army quite literally disappears at the crest of a hill into the mist. This is not simply the fog of war; it is the wedding of visual strategies we have identified in the poem with a cinematic style that, in its fashion, is considerably more faithful to these visual strategies than to the plot of the poem. The Wendol evaporate, as Grendel once materialized, in the distance beneath mist-covered hills ("under misthleoþum," 710). Indeed, as Hugh Magennis avers, the *mises en scène* of the film are characterized by "muted colors and an atmospheric use of the perpetual mixture of mist, darkness, and rain" (37). In a sympathetic discussion of the film's genetic and commercial adventures, Elizabeth S. Sklar similarly notes its "gloomy, dark-hued *mis-en-scène*" (*sic*, 127). Yet these tentative observations on the look of the film leave too much unclear, obscuring the function of obscurity in the film through approaches that fail to strike a balance between dialogue and moving pictures. What troubles the word-heavy approaches of Magennis and Sklar is precisely their difficulty in accounting for why they, as scholars of the original poem, still find the film so compelling. I suggest that the answer lies chiefly with visual strategies in *The 13th Warrior* that resonate both with our experience of the poem and its scholarly tradition.

Jas Elsner has recently suggested that the discipline of art history is essentially a form of *ekphrasis* (that is, the description of an artwork), which translates plastic forms into words. The approach has much to recommend it.[39] Obviously, film criticism represents a more complex instance of ekphrastic discourse than writing on painting or sculpture, not only because films are made of images that appear to move, but also because they are composed of words, music, sound-effects, and, increasingly, many other things as well. Yet with reservations and *mutatis mutandi*, the insight still holds true for film adaptation, and it encourages us to explore the interrelationships between words designed to evoke visual images in the minds of readers/listeners, and films attempting to translate such word-pictures into the mixed media of moving and talking pictures. On the one hand, we can say that film adaptations of written texts, especially with the new resources provided by CGI and other techniques, can (and perhaps should) respond more assiduously to visual cues within their source texts. If filmmakers pursued such a strategy, their adaptations might well meet with less resistance from audiences already familiar with the poem, play, or novel, however much they truncate or consolidate plot elements or tack on happy endings. Brief examples of this kind of attention to visual cues in Jackson's *The Lord of the Rings*, Graham Baker's *Beowulf*, Hal Hartley's *No Such Thing*, and McTiernan's *The 13th Warrior* were described in this chapter. On the other hand (and closer to home), scholars of movie medievalism cannot simply reduce the sources of a film to language or plot elements in their work on films adaptations. Their work is chiefly a form of *ekphrasis* which should account for how the visual styles of source texts are rendered in films. This constitutes more than a call for authentic period costumes, wooden instead of metal shields, or leather scabbards, however. It is a call to recognize that sister-arts comparisons have been an integral part of things like *Beowulf* studies for a long time now and that by placing interrelationships between media more toward the center of our concerns, we thereby situate ourselves at a nexus where medieval studies, medievalism, and film studies can productively interact.

2

The Cinematic Commoditization of *Beowulf*: The Serial Fetishizing of a Hero

E. L. RISDEN

Seamus Heaney's 2001 "translation" turned the Old English epic *Beowulf* into an internationally marketable and colonizable product; subsequent film adaptations have built on the poem's new cachet to reach the expanding audience for visual adventure with a thematically variable but attractively packaged product with plenty of visual excitement. While "*Beowulf* films" treat the poem loosely, they borrow its traditions and postmodernize them so that each incarnation, successful or unsuccessful in itself as a film, retextures what we receive and understand as "*Beowulf*" to broaden its salability as commodity. The notion of commodity, however, doesn't ring as entirely foreign even in the original poem. While most *Beowulf* films enter the market as salable commodities aiming, in a sense, to defeat competition, Beowulf the character readily accepts, even seeks, a position as a commodity: the martial and political hero necessary in the context of his world.

The significance of *commodification* and *commoditization* marked medieval Germanic culture as much as it does ours, and the concepts apply usefully to a consideration of Beowulf as a character, both in his original and contemporary incarnations. From his childhood days as a *kolbìtr* (a Norse term for a "male Cinderella") to his funeral and beyond, Beowulf actively seeks to fill a role that his culture values and rewards: hero. The Anglo-Saxon culture lived and thrived on notions of heroic courage[1] and even more so of gift-giving, each gift strengthening bonds of leadership and service, much as a monetary economy does on manufacture and exchange, each purchase deepening the assumption that a culture must exchange goods to survive. The hero gives and receives gifts, but also in a strong sense lives as a gift, one which in the world of the text his king may employ or which the king or hero himself may lend as an applicable commodity.[2] Later incarnations of the Beowulf story may also exploit the idea and name of the hero either for thematic purpose or simply for the sake of name recognition to contribute to the salability of a product: thus they to some degree modify and re-commoditize an old commodity, since especially today audiences may, for instance, see the films before they read the poem, changing how they will read. The name *Beowulf* itself acquires a "magical," value-added status and power, not only within the poem for the hero but for producers in new media who co-opt the name for its salability.

Traditionally the term *commodification* has signified the process by which we assign something monetary value, by which it becomes no longer exclusively or in a limited sense itself, but more socially or at least publicly a commodity for sale or acquisition. *Commoditization*—sometimes applied interchangeably with commodification and probably a better word to use to denote the circumstances by which we turn objects, ideas, and persons into salable/buyable commodities—has instead referred to the process by which related objects with distinguishable value at one point become simple, indistinguishable possessables. Both terms imply a shift in the object's capability to inspire an audience with a sense of its increased value, the adjustment occurring as a result of a culture's shifting perspectives on what it desires or sellers' abilities to redefine or reposition their products. Recently the Old English epic *Beowulf*, once Seamus Heaney's iricization had modified the poem to represent not an "oppressive" but an "oppressed" culture, acquired new status as marketable commodity: for an epic poem that scared away generations of high school readers, it sold not just remarkably, but almost unbelievably well. *Beowulf* (as poem, as name, as intellectually and artistically plastic item, available at Barnes and Noble and other fine booksellers near you) acquired new cultural capital for the status it represented rather than because audiences came suddenly to find it an inherently valuable and pleasurable tool for practical use. Heaney's rendering found its way to the *New York Times* bestseller list—perhaps America's best test for a book as successful sales item, and soon *Beowulf* as commodifiable and commoditizable notion began generating movies that tumbled one after another as unflinchingly as Chinese gymnasts after gold medals.

Film producers, finding an unexpected bestseller, sought to adopt and adapt the freshly commoditized hero for a more lucrative medium than the printed book. No longer in popular critical parlance simply a tool of dead, white poets or irrelevant, out-of-date professors of medieval English literature, the name *Beowulf* has re-gained cultural currency. Even more than the story and the sense of ancient hero contemporized, even more than the poem itself as cultural artifact, nearly as much as the poem (manuscript) as museum treasure, the salable *idea* of Beowulf has acquired new relevance as usable tender, an attraction for a new age and range of sellers and buyers.

Beowulf-at-the-movies has suffered both commodification and commoditization: *Beowulf*, or what users extracted from it, became a re-fetishized commodity for cinematic exploitation, something beyond its existence as priceless, untouchable manuscript or its erstwhile life as scop's magical utterance. A refreshed public desire focused on the exploitability of name and notion, not on the hero as we find him in the poem (the poem as story or treasure). The films, then, as the hero had willingly done, became, at least for a time, possessables, pop-culture "cool" because critical and creative practice have made in-corporating said hero and his story potentially fiscally productive. We have made a smart business move, a commodification in the modern sense, because we didn't adopt the poem or the hero for their substance, but for the power of the name to make deals, to strut the cinematic runway until the inevitable cultural *auf viedersehen*. The films need not even be *good* if they catch some of the magic of fetishization: the means by which the product adds value beyond its content. At what point market saturation may come we may guess, but at present *Beowulf* still bears cultural if not intellectual capital far beyond what it could command fifteen years ago despite the poem's continuing appearance in college and university syllabi through several preceding generations. Those of us who enjoy great literature may hope it keeps the additional value for some time, since it may lead viewers to become readers. We may also examine the films for the value they draw from the poem or that they achieve, relatively, on their own.

One result of the commoditization that we have seen (the process by which an idea becomes a commodity) is commodification as *co-modification*: films and the original poem are co-modified by their subsequent cultural intertextuality. Filmmakers have by no means felt compelled to remain faithful to the poem; they have in fact used it only as a point of departure, sometimes hardly more than a name, from which to address their own concerns. Audiences who first meet a cinematic *Beowulf* will come to the original text, if at all, with predispositions about its contents and meaning distant from anything the poet (or poets) created—films will thereby have modified text in some ways more fully than the text influenced the contents of the films. Written text and films modify but remain independent of one another, but with the continual exploitability of the name; products become, in an environment of variable marketing strategies, interchangeable but unequal alternatives for purchase. One may, for instance, go online and with a credit card purchase either book or film.

Subsequently in this chapter I will use the term *commoditization* to denote our act of reducing living experience to the exchange of goods and *commodification* as the process by which both goods and those who exchange them evolve as a result of their establishment as commodities. Through fetishization (in Marx's sense) a commodity can change value remarkably. It can rapidly gain recognizability and salability, or it can drop precipitously from public view — even as for scholars or readers (if not collectors) it retains a relatively constant value with respect to emotional attachment and its capability for personal influence. It can also return later with greater (or lesser) value, depending on how hard it proves to get and who if anyone wants to find and purchase it.

But Beowulf as hero is of course, as I have mentioned, already a commodity in his own culture, one based on the exchange of gifts as commodities of peace and honor[3]: heroes have great value, and kings feel loath to share them. Hygelac makes this point clear to Beowulf by asking him not to go to help the Danes with their monster to begin with and then by wondering if Beowulf has returned more Hroðgar's hero than his own. One needs not just a hero, but a loyal hero: the independent hero has a different fetishistic power than does the one entirely associated with one lord. So contemporary culture isn't doing something that the epic's own culture didn't already do: we re-do that voodoo that they did so well, adding festishistic value, but according to our own sense of commodity. We hoard the hero, as a Germanic king might try to do, then copyright our versions of him, then make him available on the hero market, then immolate him culturally once his value has declined. The process expands to new media and to conform to a wider range of preferences for what audience members want the hero to do or be; sellers seek a new magic that transforms the subject to fit amidst additional "similar" products, so that marketing dollars can cross-fertilize.[4] We co-modify to re-commoditize: more careful study of the old poem may lead new writers and directors to attempt "new and better" versions in contemporary media, while those who confront the new media first may seek the original with expectations and preconceived notions of what it should be or do — thus they read it from a perspective earlier generations could not, already commodified several times over. We re-fetishize to move the product fractally to and through new markets until the concept reaches financial entropy — then the poem will return to the literary scholars once more, and films good and bad will attract slowing royalties, disappear, enter archives, or persist as subjects for film scholars. Thoroughly successful films, either in a financial or an artistic sense, may even modify their culture — one may note for instance the continuing cultural capital of the *Star Wars* franchise. Something like an ancient epic poem has a harder time (but not an impossible one: we may consider the Renaissance) modifying a new culture as it did its own.

Yet, again, the process of commoditization — and commodification — begins in the poem. Beowulf and his own culture co-modify each other on the way to and through his heroic status and his kingship, and his death shows the necessary and ultimate failure of what Marx called "commodity fetishism," the replacement of the person by the commodity.[5] Even the best of heroes can't stay young and strong, essentially invincible, like Beowulf, forever. The treasure that Beowulf wins by killing the dragon — another valuable literary commodity and a practical one for his survivors — hardly replaces the man, though he leaves it for that purpose, and no hero will appear sufficient to keep away enemies from the Geats as Beowulf once could. With Beowulf's funeral the Geats dispose of both hero and fetish.[6] They shove the corpse of the dragon over a cliff into the sea, place the treasures on the funeral pyre with their lord, and dump the remnant into his burial mound, "where it now yet dwells,/ just as useless to me as it was before" (lines 3167–68[7]). Beowulf has lost his "magic" — his folk lie open to attack — and the treasure has lost its value to his folk, a demystified, devalued mass of metal drained of its fetishistic power by the death of the only hero who could have protected it.[8]

The poet, too, aims to commodify with the culture: cultural taste dictates the audience for the poem and thus to a large extent the content of the poem, the subject matter and the method the poet may employ. The poem's didactic quality — inherent and foregrounded in all medieval literature — directs its audience to behave bravely, avoid greed, jealousy, and perhaps excessive pride, and to remember its mortality. Whether they improve their character or not, if the audience feels moved by the poem and its message — and those of us who believe in literature still claim and value its capacity to do so — the audience will change in some way by the hearing (in the experience of pleasure or in the attachment to the values the hero displays). Poets may modify their fortunes — or be so modified by their audiences — by making a living from the product.[9] The poem's capability to survive depends on its fetishistic power: does it embody the power that brings audiences to it and back to it, and does it continue to draw new audiences as time passes and cultural expectations and media change. *Beowulf*, though it survived in a single manuscript, has done so, if in fits and starts, from Nowell's library to Thorkelin's copy to novelized extensions of the story to new translations (in many languages) to loose cinematic renderings. J. R. R. Tolkien once wrote that in his youth he had a profound desire that dragons be real,[10] and the hero motif goes back to the first human stories of which we have records. The number of dragons actually to appear in medieval literature is relatively small; the number of dragons and heroes in more recent literatures has increased, I suspect, arithmetically and exponentially, respectively, as we've moved into modern and postmodern ages. With the expansion of "children's literature" in our time and the (faulty) assumption on many parts that fairy stories are for children, common fairy-tale motifs have appeared with increased frequency — not to mention the importance of new technology that can render such figures as dragons more convincingly.

As Beowulf, a good and honest hero, sells himself— in the sense of the modern job-seeker — to the king of the Danes, similarly writers and producers have sold him to publishers and investors with the hope of heroic results. The element of desire drives both the producer and the consumer, and the power of the commodity lies in both: to modify oneself or one's product to fit the market or to induce the market to find the magic to produce and spread the marketable commodity. Both producers and consumers seek the treasure as an external good, as both may hope to find within it either immediate capital or investment potential, but either or both may end up finding intrinsic good there as well. Art can have the power to change attitudes and lives.

In our post–Heaney world, films, ranging from the distantly connected 1999 film *The 13th Warrior* to the John Gardner–inspired 2005 *Beowulf and Grendel* to the computer-generated 2007 *Beowulf* to the misguided made-for-TV 2007 *Grendel* to the quirky and artsy 2001 joint American and Icelandic production *No Such Thing*, borrow on that old commodity of *Beowulf as treasure*, though they stray quickly into their own agendas with barely a nod to the poem. They trade on the fetishistic power of the name, not on the substance of the poem, though they may choose to do that as well. All also exploit, as did Gardner in his novel, the *monster as fetish*. They clearly show distinct and distinctive commoditizations, as does the original. In that sense the Anglo-Saxon culture differed not so completely from our own: they kept commoditization central to their social interaction, as do we, though with different purposes and conceptions of its importance. Beowulf fights Grendel partly to repay a debt to King Hroðgar, who once paid a weregild for the hero's father, but also because the monster serves as a commodity necessary to one's establishing a reputation as hero. Beowulf tests his chops against the monster, and no less grand a test will do for one who seeks fame, reputation, and useful influence: outsiders will less likely attack such a king as Hygelac if he has, in addition to his own powers, such a hero as Beowulf.

The Anglo-Saxon consciousness of commoditization lies in the idea of the gift as honorific. The gift — heirloom sword, torque, weregild, remnant appendage of a defeated monster — given by and to, as Shakespeare might say, honorificabilitudinatatibusly established heroes, represents not only social and military bond, but also its human antecedent. The person who made it, who owned it, whom it replaces, from whom it was taken has added human, historical, or familial value to the physical usefulness or beauty of the object. The fact that swords bear names shows their value; that Beowulf praises Hrunting, even though it does him no good in battle, establishes friendly relations with Hunferð, sealing the wound of whatever rift may have come from their flyting and clarifying that no animosity need exist between him and any the Danes. Weregild specifically replaces human with commodity: money in exchange for a life, the payback for an untimely death. Thus a life is also a commodity with a specific social and monetary value.

In our world commodity implies commerce, exchange of goods to keep an enormous and deeply internationally interlaced economy going; we sell stuff to get money to get better stuff to show off our money and so that the people who sell us stuff have money to buy other stuff that brings greater status than that offered by the stuff they sold. Consciousness of status still accompanies commodity, but where in the Anglo-Saxon literary world heroism served as currency to win the reward of status-solidifying gifts, we replace heroic acts with money as the intermediate step to reach the commodity. Possession of the money and the commodity wins status, regardless of how one acquired it: in one generation a voting public can forget the means by which its leaders gained the fortunes that allow them to run for office. Beowulf's world intended to remember deeds, and those deeds became the means to other deeds: material-free commodities.

In the early Middle Ages the commoditization of heroism lay at the essence of the culture; in *Beowulf* the Danes, lacking a hero sufficient to fight their monster, must acquire or borrow one; the Geats, growing a new hero in recognition that their old one (King Hygelac) cannot last forever, loathe to risk or lend him for fear that he has not yet grown sufficient to the task. In our time the money or the means to the money — for example, the movie as commodity — drives the conscious shaping of our culture persistently, on a daily basis: many persons believe, or at least will say so, that the buying and selling of commodities represents the only "real world." In the Middle Ages the creation of heroes in consumable form represents a means to acquisition or a hope to protect the process of acquisition (by selling a proven product or protecting a creation with copyright). Our popular entertainments will change how we think just as much as how we think shapes our entertainments, and the name that we give to a commodity reshapes all commodities that bear that or a similar name. We call something *Beowulf* because the name itself, for a time, sells heroism as an idea around which one can build a product. Audiences may care little about the thought-complex of ideas and ideals that the name implied to the poem's first audience — unless the product stimulates us to seek it in the world of the original. For some persons that process becomes an avocation and for some few a vocation — thus it still serves as a potentially powerful modifying agent.

So when a movie — for example, Zemeckis's 2007 *Beowulf*— appears, the name recognition initializes the commoditization process from seller to buyer. Fetishization of the hero stirs the pulse of the market. The remarkable quality of *No Such Thing* (written and directed by Hal Hartley) in this context comes from the way it adapts *Beowulf* without using the name, without supplying the denomination of the currency, not allowing the audience its usual fetish — though it does provide another common turn, monster as fetish, more fully than has any other product since *Beowulf* itself.[11] Without the public fetishization that the name *Beowulf* allows, critics and audience fail to bring to consciousness its cultural capital, and, as Bernard Shaw might say, they have stayed away in droves. Yet the film critiques and satirizes commoditization even as the epic poem does: like the American TV news director who encourages her young employee boldly to seek the Monster, the no-such-thing that doesn't and nominally can't exist (but does), we the audience insist on commoditizing the monster, the only choice contemporary consciousness allows us. What else would we do with a monster once we've found it but splay it as quickly as possible across radio and TV worldwide? But, as the film shows us, in destroying the monster we destroy ourselves: we live by the commodity; the commodity predates us, and we depend on it; we destroy the commodity; nothing remains for which to live. The monstrosity lies not in the Creature, but in the way we treat it and ourselves, in our incessant commoditization not just of necessities, but of everything. The Geats destroy the commodity that replaces their hero, thus destroying the symbol of the heroism that held them together: they will not have the treasures to give one another nor the hero-king to dole them aptly to all. Out of guilt, perhaps, the Geats remove the guilt (and gilt) on their conscience that we can't, because we are losing the capacity to recognize it: that point emerges powerfully from the film. Only the hero of *No Such Thing*, Beatrice, played by Sarah Polley, sees the monster as a *being* rather than as a passing fetish, fodder for a childish system of news reporting with an attention span shorter than the life of a mayfly or as a leftover fearsome childish imagining that incongruously exists in fact — a fact that nearly everyone wants to ignore once we have sold or bought it.[12]

Film-fandom may argue that movies return us to their antecedent classics, to read what we would otherwise have ignored. So some remnant of the old heroism revitalizes via the new medium, the one that audiences actually access in significant numbers. If we choose, we may make the process conscious and come to understand it. But I think that in this example we can see that the commodity of film has replaced the commodity of idea, and so our conscious understanding of the idea — in this case an essential idea — remains incompletely informed. We supply one another the fungible object, but fail to encourage one another to acquire and practice values central to the original, those that establish character, so original and new objects may both corrode or entirely dissolve away. We fail to search beyond whiz-bang visuals: we buy and sell a new product that has lost some of the fetishistic power of the original — to stimulate character change as well as financial change — in exchange for its own fetishistic power, the magic of the movies. We have all heard that we should value the Harry Potter novels because they turn children into readers; I have read recently that apparently they turn them only into Harry Potter readers: the children who read Harry Potter don't necessarily turn from there to Dickens or Austen or Tolkien or *Beowulf*. Consciousness changes as values change. We necessarily see the world through our values, and the cultural *quantum* of values has leaped to a new and quite different orbital, one where the value of the commodity ceases at its sale: it retains little if any fetishistic "magic" for the reader, only the fetishistic "value added" expense of a commercially successful product (which may well lead to equally empty sequels).

I don't categorically label commoditization as evil, but it does appear to me inevitably *dangerous*: the person ends up subsidiary to the material object or its associated fetishes. The epic's Beowulf even seeks to commoditize himself as hero, a process fraught with peril as much social as martial, and though the deadly peril takes a long while to materialize (in the dragon), it must inevitably do so in one form or another. Beowulf must pass challenges to his honor — the flyting with Hunferð— and to his heritage — his father's relationship with Hroðgar, plus the fear that he really seeks not heroic status but power and kingship — to gain personal and familial credibility. That credibility allows for the opportunity to do heroic deeds and so acquire fetishistic power. He must prove not only brave, but wise: he fights Grendel without weapons, but the dragon with them — he must sort out his chances to gain heroic victory, but not at the expense of dying stupidly. He must prove himself not only prudent, but humble: he must not overstep his status and accept too much from Hroðgar, he must turn over all that he wins to Hygelac, and he must not seek or accept kingship while Hygelac's sons live — and he must avenge them when they die. When Beowulf defeats Grendel, the Danish king claims he will see the young man henceforth as if he were a son: a potential danger to Wealhþeow's sons as well as to Beowulf's relationship with his own lord, Hygelac, who would prefer not to share his hero, a scarce commodity. Beowulf names himself a friend to Hroðgar's sons, and he submits all Hroðgar's gifts to his own lord. He then receives a new spectrum of gifts he may keep or share: gifts pave the way to honor, honor to more gifts, gifts to more and better friendships, better friendships to more security and access to new gifts. Thus the society holds itself together by repeated or serial personal and material commoditization.

When Hygelac goes recklessly harrying on the Continent, all the Geats but Beowulf meet their death in battle. Beowulf returns to his homeland alone carrying thirty suits of armor: he has his life and a fine haul, but in those accoutrements he has only a material fetish, a representation of strength, an insufficient replacement for a king and his warrior band. Beowulf becomes in a martial sense a better king than Hygelac, but in a *marital* sense he fails: he produces no heir, no sufficient human replacement. He cannot create the commodity to replace himself—in this case, the limitation of his heroic powers. At his death he provides his folk a useless, fetishized treasure, and at the last minute he appoints a successor he hopes can marshal the people to their own defense. The energy of the cultural quantum of heroism has dispersed, and only the idea remains, perhaps for fetishizing, at least nostalgically, as a virtue of the past that we may admire, but that we have lost.

In *No Such Thing* a mousy young woman—not a muscular male, and one whom her colleagues value mostly because she makes the coffee—works as nothing more spectacular than as a gofer for a producer of an American news show. Beatrice—the name oddly recalls Dante but also calls attention to its etymology, *blessed one*—gets the assignment to travel to Iceland to find a reputed monster partly because no one else wants it and partly because the monster killed her boyfriend. Her plane crashes into the sea, and only she survives, but with her body broken. She undergoes, awake, unbelievably torturous and painful surgery, but with time she recovers. The scene shows incredible physical courage and determination, though the character must accept her suffering passively: the heroism appears in acts of will and endurance, not of force or in violent action. Heroism, commodified, becomes quiet resistance to death or immobility, a will to persist and to discover and understand what has happened. The Icelanders who live near the monster take her in, get her drunk, and leave her as a sacrifice at the monster's lair, an abandoned American missile site. Jaded, cynical, alcoholic, seemingly immortal, older himself than the human race, the monster has no interest in their sacrifice. But Beatrice, learning his story, does come to take humane interest in his suffering. She sympathizes with his desire to die, and she takes him to New York to find a scientist who, he believes, has the technology to kill him by "proving to him he's a figment of our imagination." Once the monster arrives in that most commercial of all cities, the media exploit him and his promise to Beatrice that he will hurt no one, and everyone who encounters him, including government scientists interested in what military applications they can learn from him, tortures him mercilessly. Beatrice effects his release and takes him back to Iceland where the scientist, Dr. Artaud (in another brilliant allusion, this one to the this one to Antonin Artaud and the "theater of cruelty," which focuses on the truths of life that we prefer to ignore) apparently succeeds in taking life from him. As the doctor runs his miracle death-machine, we see finally from the Monster's viewpoint: we see Beatrice's face outlined in light.

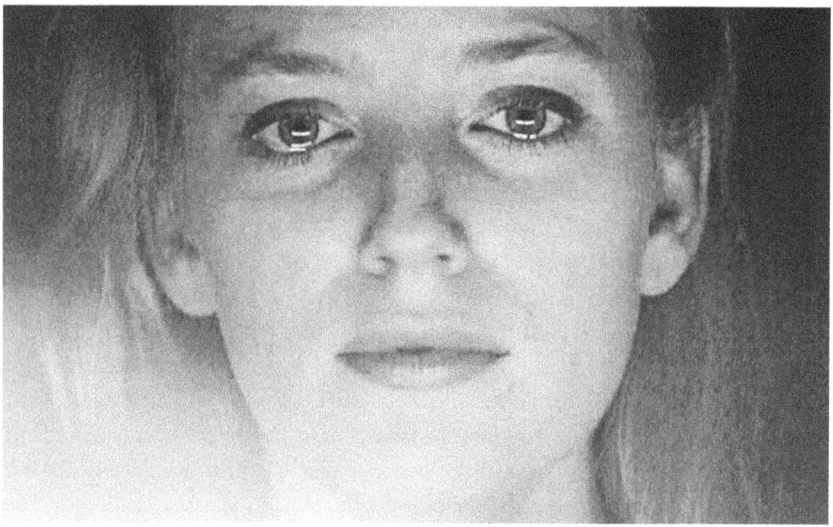

POV shot of Sarah Polley as Beatrice in Hal Hartley's *No Such Thing* (2001).

Then the screen goes blank, suggesting that at least Beatrice, for a time the viewpoint character — if not all of us — dies with him. Perhaps when we lose our monstrousness, we die, because that is what we find at the core of our being. Perhaps when we commit with compassion to another, we fear that we lose ourselves. Without the magical, co-modifying elements of suffering and cruelty, we lack what we need to survive: horrifying but perhaps true. The media exploit Beatrice as "hero," the Monster as "monster," anything they can get their hands on for as long as it can attract audience interest; they fetishize their commodities for as long as the public follow their stories, usually a day or two.

Unlike Beowulf, who has value as a commodity as long as he retains life and strength to fight, Beatrice and the monster "exist" at all only so long as the public will pay money to hear or view clips about them. The means of delivery of the commodity has moved from oral poem to visual film, but, surprisingly, the message has changed little, adapting only to a different quantum of consciousness: courage has value; compassion has value — both can help us survive; good and bad mix in us, variably; we must do some things for ourselves, but we do better when we help others as well. Some selfishness can enhance survival; too much destroys us and those around us. Without acts of heroism and compassion, bound *only* in commoditization, we, as humans, fade away into nothing.

Our reception of a story depends still on how we commoditize it. For the poet the tale of Beowulf provides a means to get lunch, a living, oral in both delivery and result, a connection to both Christian and "pagan" authority without excluding either. The poem as commodity offers a message its audience had been culturally conditioned to hear and to revere, therefore one for which they would pay. In our time Heaney did not so much translate as colonize and re-commoditize the poem, quietly claiming in a contemporary and Irish idiom the treasure-poem of the oppressor and remaking it as his own. It sold well, has colonized the *Norton Anthology*, and is quickly becoming *the Beowulf* that students will know and accept as their version, the written version they know, like, and will in turn teach, if they allow a print commodity to replace the visual one with which their students may already have familiarity. The serial commoditization isn't as a phenomenon bad, but the commodity becomes through its transformations a different product with the potential to deploy different sets of values: to commodify, as time passes and audiences change. We owe ourselves the careful attention we must employ to determine as nearly as we can what virtues those various products can provide or communicate to us; to find value beyond the price of purchase, we must re-fetishize the object and what it suggests intellectually with new power even as we try to rediscover the power it had in its own time.

While one can productively explore the other *Beowulf* films, I think Robert Zemeckis's *Beowulf* and *No Such Thing* best represent the most notable and most polar alternatives for the cinematic commoditization process. They most readily recognize textually the process of commoditization in which they participate. *No Such Thing* satirizes our commoditization, while *Beowulf* indulges it to the hilt.

Zemeckis, who reportedly hated the poem after reading it in high school, refigured the poem for another purpose, *scooping* it as "about" something totally different: using "performance capture technology" to colonize patrons' wallets and to attack uncontrollable male sexuality: a common theme in an age in which male artists may protectively and proactively adopt their own banal version of feminist criticism to try to expand the potential audience. The product finds a male audience, captivated by a nude, golden Angelina Jolie, fully though perhaps blindly culpable: the male audience may submit as readily as do Hrothgar and Beowulf—and perhaps Wiglaf after them. The story or *fabula* makes a cultural "quantum leap," not in quality, but in the issues of which audience is fully prepared to make itself conscious. Filmmakers re-value their source as a commodity manipulated to produce a visual extravagance that will sell, not freely offered to promote peace and unity among a *dryht* or even between warring factions: the goal of commodity creation in the Middle Ages. Some audience members — and not only feminists — seeing Ms. Jolie, at once deadly and desirable, as replacement commodity for the poem's Grendel's Mother may feel the tide of blood-feud rising anew. Is the sexy, naked monster a female with power to change the world or simply to arouse an audience of teenage boys? Like the hero, she too operates as fetish for both the characters and the audience. The character of Grendel's Mother in the poem attracts some sympathy: her son has been killed by an upstart people. The presence of Ms. Jolie adds to the film an unmistakable level of sexuality foreign to the original, but her presence highlights a "monster" of our time, the idea that we can't trust male sexual desire: even with the greatest of heroes it will always fetishize and fail given a sufficiently sexy object for its desire. There the filmmaker does not so much modify the poem as ignore it entirely, though for a generation who see the film first and read the poem later, the poem will have been immitigably altered.

Generally in *Beowulf*-derived movies the Beowulf/Grendel relationship has gained the most screen-time, perhaps in part from the influence of John Gardner's novel *Grendel*, which refigures the story with monster as sympathetic viewpoint character, co-modifying the poem and its sibling cinematic renderings.[13] The story re-shapes around the notion of "Other," something or someone not naturally "enemy," but turned dangerous by human (specifically white *European*) abuse or excess. Zemeckis turns Grendel into a cross between The Thing in *The Fantastic Four* and a Giacometti sculpture, the son of Hroðgar's earlier sexual liaison with the She-Monster, a sin that Beowulf will repeat. Beowulf's son, a shape-shifting dragon, has proportionately more power, though not enough to withstand his father finally. Once father and son have mutually immolated, Wiglaf remains, also facing and preparing to submit to the attractive and reproductive power of the monstrous Golden Mother: males will always be bad, yet females will always make more of us than we are, their own fetishized commodity. We come away having commoditized the Other as sexual mother, if producer of ever-more-dangerous children, still fetishized as more powerful and more worthy than ourselves — a salve to our self-indulgence.

Commodity Fetishism in Robert Zemeckis' *Beowulf* (2007; Ray Winstone as the titular hero and Angelina Jolie as Grendel's mother).

Cultural change thus hasn't uniquely economized the hero; it has changed his quantum level — though, I think, not to a higher state. *Quantum* in physics refers to energy levels, discernable units we observe with respect to sub-atomic particles. Beowulf the hero existed at one quantum level for his original audience, and he exists at another for us. For us the higher the energy of his visual presence on screen, the more elaborately enhanced his martial electricity, the greater the amount of legal tender to which filmmakers can convert him. But in raising the quantum state of his electrons for cinematic explosiveness, we have diminished the nuclear power of his tenacious sense of virtue. The original Beowulf would not fight Grendel naked, do the nasty with Grendel's Mother (even if she did have bodacious golden curves and a built-in whip tale that would make a dominatrix pass out in envy), or marry and then neglect Hroðgar's sexy widow. Medieval consciousness of the moral status of the hero has disappeared in a quantum flux that leaves the hero as typical fallible male, bounced by self-indulgence from incontinent soldier to flaccid king. The male-sexuality demon invades our consciousness, bars any passages that might lead the way from youthful courage to mature virtue, and metaphorizes our attachments for everything from beer to razor blades to ancient heroes. Macho commoditizing deflates any potential of medieval fetishizing in our contemporary tension over what it means to be male: the power that comes with success and the flaccidity that comes with failure. In the quanta-fication of entertainment we have demolished quantum layers of interest in what it means to live a good human life.

Hardly free of intention or meaning, any more than was the original, reincarnations of *Beowulf* sadly validate Samuel Johnson's cynical notion that a poet who writes for any reason other than money is a blockhead. They modify an old fetish to re-commoditize, and thereby they co-modify: with visual images fully imprinted in our commoditized imaginations, we never read the original quite the same way again, and thereby we miss its truest magic: to transform us into something braver, smarter, and more realistic than we were. If we wish to show some truth to the original, the "real" must serve more than the reel; we must allow it to provide us something for living rather than just for making a living. *Beowulf*, while it has elements of faery tale, is not fantasy: it tells us as plainly as the poet could our unflagging need for generosity, loyalty, kindness, mutuality, and steadfast courage, and that's about as real as anything gets. For me the sadness in *Beowulf*-at-the-movies, despite technical inventiveness, comes in an artistic *ubi sunt*: the *Beowulf* we read and loved has, I fear, in a flurry of cinematic images, in a series of commoditizations and commodifications, vanished.

3
Making Sacrifices
Nickolas Haydock

Mysteriously, even ostentatiously sublime, the opening of *Beowulf* has puzzled, enthused, and enervated generations of readers. Although spectacular in its own right, the narration of Scyld Scefing's funeral also contains an equally precious gem for those in search of Germanic paganism: the uncanny parallelism between the burial at sea and the miraculous survival of a cast away, a boy set adrift alone on the sea, who washed ashore in Denmark, subsequently held all Scandinavia in awe, and fathered the Shielding dynasty. There are large measures of irony, fatalism and mystery lurking within this fairy tale framework: irony, most surely, in the droll litotes comparing the treasures piled on the bark-bier of a wealthy king with the *feasceaft* origins of the waif the Danes fostered; fatalism, in the whimsical appreciation that *wyrd* should achieve so fearful a symmetry of arrivals and departures; but mystery too, in the ontological fog which besets the very end of the passage. Just as none knows whence Scyld came, neither can they determine whither he has gone. Many have remarked on the theme of a savior coming from overseas, which seems to prefigure Beowulf's arrival in another dark time. Many more have been struck by the placement of funerals at the beginning and end of the poem. But few critics indeed have bothered to ask how that child happened to be out alone on the sea in the first place or how this myth of a fortunate foundling contributes to the poem's ambivalent evocation of Germanic paganism *in illo tempore*.

This chapter reviews opening scenes in some recent film *Beowulf*s, which, although they have nothing at all to say about Scyld Scefing, suggest a sacrificial reading of the prologue and perhaps even the whole poem. Although Scyld is absent from the opening scenes of these adaptations of *Beowulf*, the specter of the prologue haunts their frank depictions of human sacrifice. My strategy here is threefold. First, by exploring the cultural pulsations and shifting horizons that Deleuze and Guatarri call "deterritorializations," I attempt to assess the impact of some recent films on the meaning of *Beowulf*. Such an exercise looks to discover in the roundabout ways of film adaptation new means of approaching the text that can productively engage with scholarly approaches. Second, by paying attention to the sacrificial undertow in the poem which film versions make egregiously apparent, we can revisit the perennial issue of Christian and pagan elements in *Beowulf*, in concert with the wealth of material on human sacrifice extant in Old English and Norse texts. To anticipate an important conclusion of this survey: what emerges throughout these materials written by Christians about their pagan forbearers is the crucial role of sacrifice in demarcating the border between Christian and pagan worlds. Third and finally, I note how heterodox concepts that emerge within movie medievalism (such as the role of human sacrifice in *Beowulf*) are quickly subsumed within the "reterritorializations" of popular cinema and film genres. As we shall see, these retrenchments follow the by-now-predictable paths of pop psychoanalysis and mass-market Marxism. However, even though such films quickly foreclose the horizons they have opened within the text — Oedipalizing the Grendel-kin or conflating *cupiditas* and the erotics of capital — one need not follow their recursions into the quotidian and clichéd. In brief, the final leg of this argument traces the poem's critique of sacrifice and its progress from the circularity of what René Girard calls "repetitive sacrifice" toward a figuration of Christ's final, transformative sacrifice.

Human Sacrifice in Beowulf Films

Two films released in 1999 (John McTiernan's *The 13th Warrior* and Graham Baker's *Beowulf*) introduce their versions of the story of Beowulf with clear, albeit dissimilar representations of human sacrifice. As seen in Chapter 1, *The 13th Warrior*'s royal funeral makes us view the sacrifice of an unnamed woman through the foreign, distant perspective of Ahmed ibn Fadlan, who watches the spectacle at a distance, through the smoky, torch-lit gloom of pre-dawn. The Arab chronicler's independent, objective point of view thus functions as a stand-in for modern perspectives, establishing the burial as something miraculous, rare — even reified — and riveting our attention on the exotic strangeness of a Viking ship burial, specifically on the ritual sacrifice of a young woman who will travel with her dead king to Valhalla. It should be emphasized that this filmic version of a Viking funeral is itself several removes from *Beowulf* and even from its ultimate source in Ibn Fadlan's detailed description of a burial among the Rus in *Journey to Russia*:

Then the people lifted her onto the boat but did not yet let her go into the tent (where the dead king had been placed). Hereupon came men with shields and staves and gave her a bowel of mead, whereupon she sang and drank it. The interpreter said to me: "With this she is bidding goodbye to her friends." Then she was given another beaker. She took it and sang for a long time, while the old woman was urging her to finish the goblet, and to go into the tent where her lord lay. I saw then how disturbed she was. She wished to go into the tent, but put her head between the tent and the side of the boat. The old woman ("the angel of death") took her by the head, made her go into the tent, and also entered with her. Whereupon the men began to beat their shields with the staves so that her shrieks would not be heard, and the other maidens become terrified. Then six men went into the tent and all had intercourse with the girl. Then they placed her beside her dead lord; two men seized her by the feet and two by the hands. Then the old woman placed a rope in which a bight had been made, and gave it to two of the men to pull at the two ends. Then the old woman came to her with a broad-bladed dagger and began to jab it into her ribs and pull it out again, and the two men strangled her until she was dead [Frye 69–70].

Perhaps most remarkable about the passage in terms of Girard's theory of scapegoating is its matter-of-factness, its reportorial objectivity. Girard details how myths routinely conceal the realities of sacrifice. He traces evidence of such erasures in myths like that of the Cretan Kouretes, who noisily clashed their weapons around the infant Zeus ostensibly to "save" him from being consumed by his cannibal father Cronos, or the "game" the Aesir played of hurling missiles at the supposedly impervious Baldr.[1] No such "mythologization" is evident in ibn Fadlan's account of the Rus: the techniques of drowning out the screams of the victim and the labored process of ritual killing are frankly described — with horrifying precision. Michael Crichton's version of the scene in his novel *Eaters of the Dead* (46–54) remains quite faithful to this account, though John McTiernan's filmic adaptation of Crichton pales by comparison, producing a heavily romanticized, even sublime version of human sacrifice. Gone are the virgin rendered nearly comatose with drink, the series of ritualized sexual violations, the raucous banging of weapons to hide her screams, the piles of animal carcasses also sacrificed to the dead king, as well as the victim's over-determined death by stabbing and strangulation. What the film offers instead is an apparently inviolate young woman in a white dress partaking in a sublime ceremony. Both cinematography and dialogue contribute to a distancing effect not present in the novel. All the sex and blood of the sacrifice is kept off stage in *The 13th Warrior*. As Herger tells Ibn Fadlan: "You will not see this again, it is the old way." The squeamishness is bewildering since the R-rated film doesn't otherwise blanch at depicting sex, violence or cannibalism. But what its adaptation of the novel's adaptation of *Beowulf* does establish is the theme of human sacrifice as a frame for all that follows.

At this exact point in the surviving epitome of ibn Fadlan's tenth-century travel narrative, *Eaters of the Dead* jumps ship, abandoning the *Journey to Russia*, which up to this juncture it had traced rather faithfully, in favor of the Old English poem, which Crichton's version substantively reconceives. With the reissue of his novel in 1992 Crichton discussed his options for the rewriting of *Beowulf* in "A Factual Note." Citing a "scholarly tradition that examined epic poetry and mythology as though it might have some underlying basis in fact" (Crichton 271), he explicitly compared his original concept to Schlieman's discovery of Troy, Arthur Evans' Palace at Knossos, and attempts to plot the legendary journeys of Odysseus or the Argonauts. Not content simply with these archeological analogies, he also tried to leverage oral formulism:

> Thus it seemed reasonable within this tradition, to imagine that *Beowulf*, too, had originally been based on an actual event. The event had been embellished over centuries of oral retelling, producing the fantastic narrative we read today. But I thought it might be possible to reverse the process, peeling away the poetic invention, and returning to a kernel of genuine human experience — something that had actually happened [271].

Something like the project here described was actually undertaken in the later film, *Beowulf and Grendel*, but, in the event, Crichton found this fictional version of scholarship too daunting; he settled instead on the related strategy of introducing a "witness to the events that led to the epic poem of *Beowulf*" (274), a witness whose cultural difference and status as an "outsider" would permit an "objective" account of the history that inspired the legend.[2] Albeit grandiose and ultimately unsuccessful, this notion of medievalism as scholarship by other means is not without merit. In one form or another, the convention of the pseudo-scholarly paratext is a founding trope of medievalism from Walter Scott to Umberto Eco. Of course, judged by the disciplinary canons of academic history or literary scholarship, few historical novels or action films are likely to pass muster. However, isn't the corollary notion that medievalism simply represents distortion and baseless fantasy equally suspect? Likewise, is Crichton's creation of an objective perspective through which we can perceive truths hidden beneath the text's supernatural encounters really all that dissimilar from scholars who enter the world of the text to find parallels between the monsters and social structures such as feud or ring givers?

The answers to both questions probably depend chiefly upon who is doing the asking, and why. If such questions are mere rhetorical gambits designed to level scholarship and popular entertainment, then we should respond by emphasizing the differences between making a film for popular audiences and writing a scholarly monograph. Yet, if asked earnestly in hopes of comprehending the extent to which each is implicated in the other, we can honestly begin exploring the inter-relationships and analogies. In each of the four films discussed in this chapter, the figure of the outsider identifies a missing link that connects monsters and men. In each, a scene of human sacrifice serves as a prologue to the main action of the film, marking the unstable borders between inside and outside, human and not human, sympathy and abjection.

To return to *The 13th Warrior*, the waning of the "old ways" of human sacrifice establishes a distinction between the Vikings and the "Wendol" Neanderthals, as well as an obscure continuity. The two civilizations in Crichton's rendering are contemporaneous but asynchronous in their development. The Viking society depicted in the film is progressing beyond human sacrifice, and in the Wendol they encounter the survival of an earlier stage in their own development as a culture. The miraculous re-appearance of the Wendol surprises many within the film because they were thought to have died out long ago. This strange double of humankind ("they are men ... they are not men") who take heads, build altars of human skulls, worship bears, and practice cannibalism seems to reincarnate an earlier stage in *human development* so that it can be destroyed once and for all. While Crichton's hypothesis about the genesis of the legend of *Beowulf* from an actual conflict between the subspecies *homo sapiens* and *homo neanderthalensis* is certainly fanciful, considerably more plausible is the notion that the poem's monsters represent the abiding specter of human sacrifice, a specter which the pagan cultures within the poem are imagined to have (for the most part) transcended.

As described in Chapter 1, the last Viking sacrifice ("you will not see it again," says Herger to ibn Fadlan), is presented in the film as exotic spectacle. These distancing strategies in both time and space do not derive from Crichton's novel; rather, the cinematic version seems designed as a kind of variation on the ship burial at the opening of the Old English poem. Herger does not share the *Beowulf*-poet's hesitancy about ship's destination: "We will burn him. In a moment he and all he owns can be in paradise." Still, shouldn't we be equally of suspicious of what René Girard would probably call the poem's *mythologization* of human sacrifice in the miraculous survival of a child exposed on the open sea? Is there not in the *Beowulf*-poet's comparison of those who launched the boy with those who launched the dead king a critique (however sublimated) of benighted rituals devoid of any real meaning or foresight? Bede's pagan priest Coifi in *Ecclesiastical History of the English People* makes a similar point when he compares pagan life to a sparrow's brief flight within a hall:

> Your Majesty, when we compare the present life of man on earth with that time of which we have no knowledge, it seems to me like the swift flight of a single sparrow through the banqueting-hall where you are sitting at dinner on a winter's day with your thanes and counsellors. In the midst there is a comforting fire to warm the hall; outside, the storms of winter rain or snow are raging. This sparrow flies swiftly in through one door of the hall, and out through another. While he is inside, he is safe from winter storms; but after a few moments of comfort, he vanishes from sight into the wintry world from which he came. Even so, man appears on this earth for a little while; but of what went before this life or of what follows, we know nothing [Bede 127].

The same metaphysical obscurity brackets the before and after of Scyld's life among the Danes, an instance that exemplifies the general rule laid down by King Edwin's priest on the brink of conversion to Christianity. The Scyld episode forecloses the spiritual horizons of those within the world of the poem, even as it evokes an awareness in the Christian audience that they are living in an age distinct from the one depicted in the poem, a new world in which the horizons of transcendental knowledge have been opened.[3] Scyld's funeral at the beginning and Beowulf's funeral at the end form another such frame, marking the limits of pagan eschatology and glory from a Christian perspective.

Released in the same year as *The 13th Warrior*, Graham Baker's *Beowulf* (1999) also opens with the specter of human sacrifice, albeit in a more gaudily neo-gothic vein, as if the title character played by Christopher Lambert were reprising the *Highlander* role that made his fortune. Think *Highlander* meets *Road Warrior* in a post-apocalyptic, iron-age vampire vs. werewolf noir.[4] In the first shot of the film at night from far above a field, bonfires and soldiers standing guard limb a boundary. The camera cranes downward to take in totem poles festooned with corpses, or rather half-corpses — everything below the torso has been amputated. In the distance on a hill rises what can only be called a post-industrial castle featuring smokestacks. Grendel is already within the hall; in fact, holed up in the dungeons beneath, he never leaves it. After a brief, enigmatic encounter with the monster — who has no visible body but does converse with Hrothgar — we follow a woman in scarlet-stockings over the wall and down into the countryside. It seems that she seeks not just a "bed in the bothies," in Seamus Heaney's justly controversial translation, but in a different zip code. Armed soldiers capture her and beat her and drag her kicking and screaming away. It is important not to slight the intentional disorientation this sequence produces for anyone even passingly familiar with the Old English poem, even more disorienting than the iron-age redux weaponry and synthesizer-laden sound track. Beowulf himself had spoken of Heorot as a hall that had to be purified, but here the border guards seem to be enforcing a modern containment strategy, familiar from a host of zombie films, in the hopes of confining the contagious agent *within* the hall.[5] This Hrothgar certainly terrifies ("egsode," 6, where it applies to Scyld, not Hrothgar) the surrounding peoples, but because of the contagion his "outpost" contains. The *ymbsittendra* have drawn very close indeed, imprisoning the Danes within a dragon-like hall that belches fire like the pressure valves on an oil-rig.

Just what's rotten in the state of Denmark becomes clearer as the shot widens to take in a primitive slab of bloodstained wood, fitted with an enormous guillotine-like retractable straight razor set atop an altar. The master of the sacrifice wears ram's horns and pronounces the sentence: "Kill the beast that is within her." Lambert's Beowulf arrives in the nick of time, heralded by the spaghetti western theme like Sergio Leoni's Clint Eastwood, shot with the broadest of winks in a surprised-to-see-me-here (?) portrait shot of Lambert on horseback (see Forni 2007, 246). Though the range of weapons is thoroughly over the top — not to mention the hackneyed ninja backflips — the kitschy pastiche seems self-consciously clever, self-mocking even. "Look who's playing Beowulf!" "Look at what we've made of Heorot!" Until the girl that the hero has rescued runs away from him and back to the sacrificers, preferring certain death over returning to the haunted hall — like the stag that chooses to die on the bank of Grendel's mere rather than enter its terrifying waters. Her death, like the stag's, does much to identify the site with an unspeakable, unfathomable fear, and in so doing inverts or reverses the locus of terror from mere to hall, from outside to inside. The poem rather obviously contrasts the two halls — Heorot and the hall at the bottom of the tarn — but this clever reference to the dying stag in what most judge a very tiresome film should perhaps give us pause. Disparate times and places are collapsed into one. Heorot, the Grendel-kin's mere, and the dragon's lair merge in the film's castle. Likewise, the three monster fights occur within the castle on three consecutive nights. A simplification of the poem's complex structure, admittedly, but in what sense *is* Heorot the site of an abiding curse, cleansed only to be defiled again the next night, then supposedly purged of the kin of Cain but abiding further kin-killings and a final holocaust?

Baker's *Beowulf* is the first of four films (the others being *Beowulf and Grendel* [2005]; *Grendel* (2006); and Robert Zemeckis' 2007 *Beowulf*) to give us not simply an aged but also a morally weak Hrothgar, burdened with a secret sin. In the 1999 and 2007 *Beowulf* films, the descent of the monsters from Cain is foregone in favor of beings that *onwocon* from the kinds of unions between humans and monsters that *The Book of Enoch* also cites as the genesis of the cursed race; though in these films Hrothgar sires the demon from hell that haunts him.[6] The 1999 Hrothgar has strangely unpleasant wet dreams, inspired by a Playboy playmate in the role of a woman he raped in the course of a reign of terror that won him his kingdom. That the monsters in both *Beowulf* films turn out to be psychosexual manifestations of imperialism (1999) and greed (2007), respectively, is not so different after all from scholarly interpretations casting the monsters as social anti-types or personifications of sin, or, indeed, the wealth of Freud, Jung, Lacan, and Kristeva-inspired readings of the Old English poem.

Georges Bataille observed that "empire is a diversion of violence to the outside" (67) and so, of course, are sacrifice and scapegoating. For Kristeva, because such abjections are constitutive of subjectivity they remain in threatening proximity to the self, pieces of the self or the social that were once expelled from within are reconstituted as fearsome objects and others.[7] The poem's insistent parallels serve an analogous function, repeatedly collapsing the fragile distinctions between inside and outside. The parallel genealogies—Scyld through Hrothgar and Cain through Grendel—function in a similar fashion: threatening, like the invasions of the hall, a collapse of difference that abjection and sacrifice attempt to enforce.[8]

This destabilization of binaries is apparent early in the poem: from the "outlawed" Grendel who nightly visits the hall, like Scyld inspiring terror and taking men from their mead benches in tribute, through the naming of this menace a "feond mancynnes" (164) to whom perhaps the Danes offer sacrifices at pagan shrines in hopes of expiating the scourge:

Hwilum hie geheton	æt hærgtrafum
wigweorþunga,	wordum bædon
þæt him gastbona	geoce gefremede
wið þeodþreaum.	Swilc wæs þeaw hyra,
hæþenra hyht;	helle gemundon
in modesfan	metod hie ne cuþon...
Sometimes they sacrificed	at the temples of idols,
Doing them honor,	prayed in words
That the soul-slayer	send help
Against the nation-scourge.	Such was their practice,
Custom of the heathens.	They remembered hell
In their heart-thoughts;	they did not know the measurer... [175–180].[9]

Ostracized early on as a particularly egregious interpolation, this remarkable passage is perhaps best understood as the Danes' failure "to live up to (the poet's) own modernized representation of them," as Klaeber suggested long ago (135). The blending of Christian and pagan shadings here is evident in the pun on *gastbana* ("demon-slayer" and "slayer of souls"), the first evoking a giant-killer like Thor, the second, precisely the kind of murderer of souls with which Danes are currently afflicted. The irony is no doubt intended: the Danes in their unenlightened paganism are sacrificing to the very demon that haunts them. These tantalizing, guarded references to pagan ritual give us very little to go on, but clearly both prayer ("wordum") and sacrifice ("geheton ... wigweorþunga") seem intended. Whatever victims they may be offering in sacrifice — Pope Gregory's letter to Abbot Mellitus records that the backsliding Anglo-Saxons sacrificed cows — are not only useless but redundant: the Danes' self-blighting, paltry imitation pales in comparison with Grendel's nightly blood-letting.

In both *The 13th Warrior* and the 1999 *Beowulf* young women are sacrificed. Among the five Anglo-Saxon poems that employ a vocabulary most similar to the description of pagan sacrifice in *Beowulf*, two virgins are threatened with rape and marked for sacrifice (*Judith* and *Juliana*), while two other poems equate pagan sacrifice with cannibalism and the torments of hell (*Andreas* and *Elene*). In Pope Gregory's discussion of Germanic sacrifices, he suggests a program of conversion that extends even to the structures where Anglo-Saxons formerly sacrificed to the pagan gods:

> The temples of the idols of that people should on no account be destroyed. The idols are to be destroyed, but the temples themselves are to be aspersed with holy water, altars set up in them, and relics deposited there. For these temples are well built, they must be purified from the worship of demons and dedicated to the service of the true God.... And since they have a custom of sacrificing many oxen to demons there, let some other solemnity be substituted in its place, such as a day of Dedication or the festival of the holy martyrs whose relics are enshrined there [Bede 86–87].

Similar rites of purification and sanctifying substitutions occur within the pagan temples of all these poems. Judith is brought to Holofernus' *træf* (lines 43, 255, 268) situated high on a hill, which is often somewhat misleadingly translated "tent" or "pavilion." The space is in fact a temple, or rather a parody of a temple. The word *træf* here refers specifically to the "gylden/ fleoh-net fæger" (46b–47a), which serves as a canopy for Holofernus' bed and functions like a one-way mirror, allowing the Assyrian leader within to see outside while no bystanders may view what happens within. The distinction is important, because what occurs in this confined space represents a conversion of pagan sacrifice — in biblical sources described as occurring behind a curtain with the utmost secrecy.[10] The dazed drunkenness of Holofernus and his followers is likewise in tune with descriptions such as those of ibn Fadlan emphasizing the inebriation of victims before the sacrifice. The beheading occurs *in camera*, behind the veil; Judith positions her victim deliberately and preserves the head *in a food basket*, which she takes with her as a powerful totemic symbol.[11]

Of particular importance for our discussion, however, is the ritualized nature of the sacrifice. The taking of the head and its display represent more than an ironic turning of the tables wherein the victimizer becomes victim, the sacrificer sacrificed; rather, the ritualized murder of Holofernus marks the end of sexual pollution, a rending of the pagan veil, which transforms pagan sacrifice into an allegory of Christian eschatology.

A second virgin threatened with sexual violation and sacrifice is Cynewulf's *Juliana*. This work deliberately conflates hell and temple sacrifices, much as *Beowulf* does, where pagan congregants "remember hell" (*helle gemundon*, 179) in their worship. In *Juliana* idolatry and sexual desire seem to be one in the same. In the wake of Maximian's leveling of Christian churches and his spilling of the blood of Christian martyrs, Eleusius worships idols as well as the virgin Juliana — all in the space of the first thirty lines. Told by her father that she must sacrifice to pagan idols and marry Eleusius or suffer terrible tortures, Juliana in reply demands that Eleusius must first abandon sacrificing to idols: "forlæte þa leasinga,/ *weohweorþunga*" (179b–180a; emphasis added). The word *weohweorþunga* (sacrificial offering), a variant of the form in *Beowulf* (*wigweorþunga*, 176), occurs nowhere else in the poetic records. Later in her prison cell, Juliana is again tempted to sacrifice or be sacrificed by a demon posing as an angel of God, quickly exposed by a genuinely divine messenger. This satanic ruse in a sense incarnates the pagan idols and establishes the *leasinga* (false, deceitful practices) of pagan sacrifice as a hell-sent simulacrum of Christian belief— perhaps not that different after all from that hell-demon ("feond on helle," 101), who drives the Danes to sacrifice to pagan idols in *Beowulf*.

In another Cynewulfian poem, *Elene*, Christ's triumph and Constantine's Christian empire continue to be opposed by another talkative demon, but the symbolic notion of a pagan shrine as an earthly hell gives way to the notion that the underworld itself is a hidden shrine from which Satan will launch counterattacks:

> ...now I am humiliated, deprived of my goods, outlawed and friendless.... But yet, out of the dwellings of the damned (*weargtræf*) I shall be able by subterfuges to find retaliation against this [trans. Bradley, 188; lines 922b–926a].

Whereas in *Andreas* (along with *Judith* the poem most often thought to contain similar scenes, clauses, and perhaps even reminiscences of *Beowulf*), what first appear from a distance out at sea the tiled shrines ("tigelfagan trafu," 844) of Mermedonia are later exposed as a *hell-træf* (hell-shrine," 1693), a prison ruled by Satan and liberated by Andrew. The inhabitants of this prison/shrine are blinded and given a monstrous potion that robs them of human thoughts and feelings. The potion makes these sacrificial victims bestial before they are consumed by the race of cannibals native to the island. The notion that human victims should be made drunkenly stupefied before their sacrifice, which we have seen repeatedly, is obviously present here as well. Without compromising the supernatural character of the passage, we should note the ritualistic character of this description of sacrificial cannibalism. Victims are given a mind-altering potion by "dryas" ("sorcerers" the word may be a borrowing from the native Gaelic word, *druidh*, druid), which robs them of their humanity. They are kept in a *træf* for a predetermined time and then consumed in a communal feast.

Perhaps Michael Crichton drew upon the similarities with *Andreas* in his adaptation of *Beowulf* as a battle between Vikings and "eaters of the dead," though he never acknowledged the source. One problem stems from the embarrassing possibility that Crichton's postulation of a reality behind the poem as we have it really derives not from archeology or ancient myth but from an avowedly Christian representation of paganism that, because of deliberate design or the serendipities of formulaic diction, happens to parallel *Beowulf* in a number of intriguing ways. Of course the Christian Anglo-Saxon poets weren't archeologists or anthropologists either. Their reconstruction of pagan religions across representations of many disparate cultures is so uniform because it too is formulaic and traditional. What the fascination of modern films with human sacrifice can accomplish is to provoke us to look again at sacrifice as depicted across the poetic corpus and encourage us to look more closely at how it functions in *Beowulf*.

One question that all these films try to answer with varying degrees of success concerns the etiology of monsters. The Oedipalizations of the two *Beowulf* films (1999 and 2007) — Grendel is Hrothgar's son — provide one kind of predictably trite answer, while the surprising (but perhaps equally trite) evolutionary hiccup in McTiernan's *The 13th Warrior* offers another. If Freudian psychology and Darwinian evolution do not hold intellectually and aesthetically satisfying etiologies for medieval beliefs in trolls and dragons, then the psychology of Kristeva's abjection and the anthropology of Girard's scapegoat may well offer more attractive perspectives from which to assess the relationships between men and monsters. John Gardner's sympathetic, existential Grendel was already a step in a much more interesting direction, and it has left its mark (along with Kristeva and Girard) on the best of the film adaptations of the medieval poem, *Beowulf and Grendel* (2005).[12]

Its prologue entitled "A Hate Is Born" could just as accurately have been called "A Monster Is Born," though this monster is made not born. An extended 180-degree pan moves from the Icelandic coastline past rolling green hills to glaciers in the distance. Toward us runs a frolicking child laughing as he skips over a hill. The opening credits had featured a faux medieval map that marked the North Sea with a sea-beast, from whose storms early myth critics once derived the monsters of *Beowulf*; here, there's no hint of that meteorological divine, only a child in a landscape sublime enough all by itself. The only hint of anything like the sacrificial preludes of the other films we have surveyed are the fat rams grazing in the foreground. Soon the father emerges over the knoll, dressed in the same furs and leathers as the boy. As the child somersaults out of frame, we focus on the physically impressive strangeness of his father: gigantic, thick-bearded, muscular, a mountain of a man among the mountain peaks, but with thick tufts of hair on his arms and legs. Could this be Beowulf, a bear of a man, who looks as if he could crush a foe in his bare arms, as the hero is reported to have done with Dæghrefn? When he moves closer, catching a scent on the air, his physical idiosyncrasies become clearer. Cut to a starkly different shot in an as yet unspecified location showing an impressive troop of mounted warriors in helmets and face guards, the foremost of which wears a simian mask. These storming riders gallop through shadow and mist. They are what the mountain man smelled, like a deer smells a wolf pack. He calls the child "Grendel," gathers the boy in his arms and limps hastily away. In that limp and those physical deformities we see the ubiquitous signs of the scapegoat whose differences mark him as a target. For the first time the boy's strangeness also becomes evident: whiskers, prominent forehead and enlarged cranium.[13] The repeated crosscuts between the armed warriors on horseback and two fugitives make us feel the point even before we realize it: the father and his son are being hunted. A subtitle identifies the beach along which the troop rides: "500 A.D.—Outskirts of Daneland." The riders come over the hill and bring the boy's father to bay at the edge of a cliff, while the child watches from his concealed perch just over the crest. The warriors encircle the giant with spears and torches. With practiced efficiency two arrows are fired into his chest, a bucket of tar splashed at his feet, a torch thrown in to set him aflame and force him over the precipice. In its overkill the killing well deserves the title of ritual sacrifice. We are all but asked: "Just who are the monsters here?" The film's prequel thus offers a very dark reflection of/on the events of the poem: it is Hrothgar's *geoguþ* that comes loping beneath the mists ("mist-hleoþum," 710). Grendel and his father become the innocent victims of an inhuman violence, no less monstrous for its faceless professionalism and efficiency.[14]

Like Scyld, Hrothgar terrorizes those at his borders, but he cannot bring himself to kill the child clinging to the edge of the cliff, who glares at king's raised sword with brave defiance. Stellan Skarsgård's role as Hrothgar is comparable to his portrayal the year before of the racist Saxon invader Cerdic in *King Arthur* (2004). Unlike the ethnic cleanser Cerdic, however, Hrothgar makes the "tragic" mistake of deciding *not* to kill the child. Grendel, also like Scyld, has become a destitute orphan whose miraculous survival will in turn terrify the Danes and demand a grisly tribute in corpses. The "feud" he will carry on against the Danes is thus motivated in ways a great deal less Manichean than a war between darkness and light, good and evil — a metaphysics that earlier *Beowulf* films made before 9/11 reproduced rather uncritically. In a sense, then, Sturla Gunnarsson's *Beowulf and Grendel* debunks the scientific approach of McTiernan's *The 13th Warrior*: the "monsters" are not a different species; they are just treated as if they were.

Beowulf and Grendel plays giddily with expectations aroused by the poem and its earlier film adaptations, exposing the received legend as the fabrication of an inveterate liar already at work within the film on the poem who invents gory stories for the neighborhood children.[15] Initially Beowulf is forced to assume the role of a detective and bounty-hunter rather than monster-slayer because Grendel, puckishly playing hide and seek, refuses to materialize when (or in) the expected manner. On consecutive nights the Geats are startled by things that go bump in the night. The first night, after Beowulf's impressive *gilpcwide* (640) to the effect that he "will see that thing's head on stick" or die trying, there is a noise at the door, which disappoints all expectations by failing to burst open as the warriors wait anxiously on the other side. Nary a green light is to be seen — and neither is Grendel in any form. The monster's abject assault includes neither dismemberment nor supernatural special effects; instead, dog-like he marks the entrance to the hall with a prolonged, satisfying, and exceptionally pungent piss. Once the warriors recover from the daunting stench, they charge out into the empty darkness. The morning after is spent cleansing with brimstone this mock-diabolical pollution of the hall. Marking his territory in this mocking way, Grendel travesties the Danes' earlier attempts to enforce and extend their borders, yet the scene also encourages the idea that, unlike the Danes, the monster does not kill indiscriminately. Beowulf and his companions follow the *laðes lastas* ("loathed one's tracks," 841) through rough country over a rocky summit to discover ... not a hellish mere but an endless, snow-covered plain. This empty expanse is the visual equivalent to Beowulf's earlier declaration that they are fighting "a thing beyond our ken," a "thing" capable of laying false trails and setting booby traps, in short a man not a troll. Although less pointed, these parodies are fully within the world of Monty Python medievalism.

Eternally a boy in a giant's body, Grendel howls as he bowls with human heads, while the mad Irish monk, Brendan, baptizes Danes in a freezing river.

Hrothgar, maddened himself by drink and despair, contemplates following Unferth into the Christian faith:

> HROTHGAR: Baptism, they call it. Unferth feels he has fallen from the grace of the gods. It's not every man's wish to sit in blood. If this Christ can stiffen Unferth's heart, what's the harm?
> BEOWULF: They swim only out of fear.
> HROTHGAR: But still, they swim.

Hardly Bede's miraculous conversion, that, rather an ecumenicalism which judges all options better than despair, even self-delusion. As Gerald Butler's downsized Beowulf continues his investigation, it becomes increasingly evident that neither paganism nor Christianity will help to solve the mystery of Hrothgar's "troll."

Beowulf next encounters an outlying witch, Selma (played by Sarah Polley), the waif-like, red-haired stepsister of Unferth, who foresees how men will die. While she does collect herbs and possesses a second sight, she seems no more a witch than the young woman in *Monty Python and the Holy Grail*, whom the villagers make up with a fake nose. Still, Selma willingly assumes this role and her place on the outskirts of Daneland — a place she much prefers to the alternative, a life of sexual slavery and abuse within the confines of civilization. Finding no answers there, Beowulf interviews Hrothgar again, probing for the secret he suspects lies behind the troll's depredations: "My wits still war with how this all began." Hrothgar offers the traditional, fuzzy explanation:

> HROTHGAR: Hate for the mead hall, I can only guess. The night we finished it, I felt it came. We hadn't seen a troll for fifteen or twenty years.
> BEOWULF: (hesitantly) So no one did anything to the troll itself?
> HROTHGAR (angrily): Oh, Beowulf, it's a f****** troll! Maybe someone looked at it the wrong way.
> BEOWULF: Some Dane?
> HROTHGAR: Who hands you this, Selma? Come on, she's been out in the wilds too long. Her head is full of spiders; her lap is full of moss.
> BEOWULF: It's said she sees things.
> HROTHGAR (yelling): Well the crazy do see things!

The lie harkens back to that time fifteen or twenty years before when Hrothgar saw the wild-eyed child Grendel at the cliff's edge. The exchange as a whole neatly outlines the film's critique of poem's supernatural. Outcasts and scapegoats are transformed into supernatural beings, their seemingly malevolent powers created by the very rituals of abjection that mark them as different — and therefore fearsome — in the first place. The mark of the beast is the also the mark of ethnogenesis; a people is created (and so are their nightmares) by what it excludes.[16]

The next night the film's parody of *Beowulf* concludes the series of anti-climaxes with another false alarm. Grendel throws rocks at the hall and elicits another outpouring of armed Danes into the darkness, all dressed up for battle with no monster in sight. But of course that is precisely the point of these Beowulfian feints: there is no monster here, and there never was one. The explanation of night terrors lies in a reading of the poem that is thoroughly Girardian. The poem's monsters are in service of what Girard calls "mythologization," a form of euhemerism that creates gods and monsters out of what were originally *real* sacrificial victims. Lest this point be missed, the same children we earlier saw listening to the poet's hyperbolic retelling of Beowulf's battles with Grendel later re-assemble as a mob and begin stoning a wretched, retarded man.

Beowulf puts a stop to this by assuring the children: "he's not of that race." The interlude leaves a bitter aftertaste: to what degree is the children's imitation of Germanic heroism true to life? In their encircling of the helpless, beleaguered scapegoat, we are treated to a nuanced reinterpretation of the film's opening scene, where Hrothgar's warriors encircle Grendel's father, firing arrows and throwing torches to set him aflame. This is textbook Girard, for whom the ground zero of the scapegoating impulse is always the circle drawn around a prospective victim. When Hrothgar is finally pressed by Beowulf to explain the murder of Grendel's father, the answer turns to dust in his mouth: "He crossed my path ... stole a fish."[17]

Beowulf's rescue of the beggar stoned by the Danish children yields at last the information he has so long sought — the whereabouts of Grendel's lair. This is perhaps the bitterest of the film's ironies, for the victim of scapegoating and recent convert to Christianity betrays Grendel's hiding place. His newfound faith in Christ means he no longer fears death or the monster. But it is the Christian convert who gives the Judas kiss, leading the Geats to Grendel's cave. Yet another anti-climax ensues; they can't make their way down the sheer rock-face to the cave, because they've neglected to bring a rope. The next morning as they set off again, they find the fearless Judas goat on the doorstep with his neck broken, face twisted back to front.

Meanwhile, Handscio has been having bad dreams. He has seen his own death. When the Geats finally make it to his lair, Grendel is predictably absent. What they discover there is a charnel house in both senses of the word: the father's gigantic head carefully preserved on an altar above a litter of human remains. The scene owes much to that in *The 13th Warrior* discussed at length in Chapter 1, but it serves a very different purpose. Handscio sees the idol of Grendel's father's head and flies into a rage: "Look, our friend Grendel doesn't come from mist and shit alone." Then, speaking very un–Hamlet like to the severed head, he rants: "I curse you and all your kin" (spitting on it). Thus in another of the film's uncanny euhemerisms Handscio, not God, marks and curses "Caines cynne" (107). Flying into a rage, Handscio continues to desecrate the idol, smashing the cured head to pieces. The outburst is shot from the perspective of his fellow Geats; when the counter-shot finally situates this perspective, the physical and emotional distance between Handscio and the other Geats has widened significantly. They are still, silent, bunched together, masked, and within a smoky haze; he is frenetic, well lit and without a helmet. As Handscio feels the shock of this collective gaze — a gaze that excludes and abjects the group's most popular member — he comes to himself in a chilling *anagnorisis*, realizing that he is *fæge* (fated, doomed). With this scene ends what we have been calling the *anti–Beowulf*: there will be no more false starts, no more "where's Waldo" bathos.

The fight against Grendel within Heorot, then, doesn't begin until 5/7 of the way into the film, after more than a 75-minute prelude. Bellowing and crashing stones together, smearing his face with his own blood, the Handscio-cursed "demon" comes loping down to the high hall to see how the Geats are resting after their desecration of his home. Beowulf's investigation has already discovered that the "troll's" attacks are motivated by revenge, not a lack of appreciation for architecture or music. Thus far he has not harmed any of the Geats, though he has mocked and stymied them, much as John Gardner's Grendel does, according to a fully comprehensible code of justice. When at last the door to Heorot finally bursts open, Grendel sends Geats sprawling in every direction, leaving them battered but not broken. But when he identifies Handscio by his smell, he finally speaks a rare comprehensible word, "Papé," and breaks the neck of the *fæge eorl*.

Henceforth, Beowulf's defeat of Grendel and his mother are staged quickly and unremarkably. At the level of diegetics, this is something that has to happen within the expectations of action cinema, but it rings hollow and pales in comparison with the screenplay's earlier parodies of the inherited tale. The screenplay doesn't just *give in* to the authorized version, it also *gives up* on its de-mythologizing critique of scapegoating. Throughout the majority of the film the supernatural is systematically demystified by exposing the scapegoating logics beneath the monsters of *Beowulf*. After the death of Grendel, the supernatural re-emerges in the figure of Grendel's mother, an albino troll. She was always there lurking within the sea; she had tried (unsuccessfully) to pull Geats out of their boat on a few occasions. She certainly poses a threat, but it is Grendel, not she, who kills Handscio in the film. As her dismembered protégé stumbles into sea..., her taloned hand emerges from the water to bear him — Arthur-like — to her version of Avalon. The film is searching here for something like the sublimity that invests Beowulf's fight with the dragon. In order to achieve this, it violates its own carefully crafted ontology, wherein monsters are the victims of congenital birth defects and scapegoating. The amphibian, albino *mere-wif* is the movie's white whale, but she doesn't belong in the world of the film; her existence violates the moral principles that underpin its euhemeristic approach. In Girard's terms this represents a re-mythologization of the sacrificial mechanism, one that suspiciously reverts to the monstrous feminine even after exposing how a number of men — the Grendel-kin and the retarded beggar — become scapegoats. This reversion to the ambiguity of the fantastic is not simply another turn of the screw; it suggests the film's makers wanted to have it both ways, perhaps because a uniform critique of scapegoating threatened to take the action-adventure film too far away from heroic action.

The hard to find and highly derivative 2007 movie *Grendel* was made for the SyFy Channel and released on DVD in 2010 by Universal Pictures. In many ways, this regrettable film encapsulates approaches to the poem emerging in all three of the earlier films discussed above. Though clearly what might well be called a *re*-adaptation of films such as *The 13th Warrior* and *Beowulf and Grendel*, it also rationalizes the relationship between human sacrifice and the monsters in a much more straightforward manner. Early in *The 13th Warrior* as the Geats enter Hrothgar's village they are shocked to find not only a lack of defensive measures but also "scarcely a man between 15–50 left alive." *Grendel* duplicates this scene, but the shocking scarcity is in children, not warriors. Just as other films *interpret* the Old English poem by searching out the anthropological truths (*The 13th Warrior* and *Beowulf and Grendel*) or the hidden sin (the 1999 and 2007 *Beowulf*) behind the poem's man-like monsters, so too do the Danes of *Grendel* keep a dark secret that lies behind the apparent infertility of Hrothgar's realm.

Like these earlier films as well, *Grendel* installs a series of unsuccessful attacks on the monster before he is finally defeated. This duration, as in *Beowulf and Grendel*, serves as the intellectual equivalent of physical battle, a battle of wits. Seemingly, before the Grendel can be dispatched, the human sin or secret that he represents must be revealed — a not uninteresting version of the *sapientia et fortitudo* topos. When the Geats' incendiary charge firing crossbow fails to kill Grendel, the monster takes revenge by savaging the outlying towns. Ben Cross as Hrothgar rebukes Beowulf from the *giftstol* set high within the Doric columned Heorot:

> HROTHGAR: And so it begins. You have failed me, Beowulf. You failed me and now the monster takes its revenge. We had reached a sort of understanding with the creature. Now more innocent lives will be lost.

> BEOWULF: It is true; I have failed in defeating the Grendel. But I ask you this, have you failed yourself and your people?
> HROTHGAR: What say you?
> BEOWULF: The beast has poisoned you with fear and hatred. Your land is dying; your people are dying. There are no children to carry on when you are gone. Because of your fear, your home has become a coffin. Your nation is perishing at the hands of Grendel. You know this is not my doing. This wickedness was put into motion long ago.

The counter-accusation casts Hrothgar as a kind of Fisher King or Tolkienian Denethor. The wasteland results from the king's spiritual not his physical debilities. In the terms of the 1981 film *Excalibur*, "the king and the land are one." Yet unlike *Excalibur* or the 1999 and 2007 *Beowulf*s, the spiritual corruption is not sexual, nor is its offspring a monstrous incarnation of Oedipal fantasies.

For René Girard the triumph of Freud's Oedipus complex as a mechanism for the explanation of violent impulses works to displace or indeed *repress* the remnants of sacrifice and scapegoating. In different albeit related ways Deleuze and Guattari argue against what they call "Oedipalization" because it functions to reproduce a triangulated family structure in service of an opposition between the family's production of desire and repression of that desire by social forces from outside the family.[18] However differently, both theories attempt to decenter Oedipal desire and to reorient the self vs. other binary. Girard seeks to recover the primitive social, Deleuze and Guattari a primitive individual desire. In making monsters of Hrothgar's sons, the 1999 and 2007 *Beowulf*s employ the Oedipal family romance to domesticate the *unheimlich* Grendel, making his attacks a war not simply against the father, but against the Name of the Father, the father as phallus, thereby exposing the illusory nature of his power. The film *Grendel*, on the other hand, leaves the monsters alone. They exist in a CGI separateness, their psyches as unknowable as their motivations. Instead, the film focuses on Hrothgar and the Danes' self-destructive attempts to control the menace. To continue with the dialogue quoted above:

> HROTHGAR: Our land was poisoned long ago. Poisoned by a dark secret.
> (At this point Marina Sirtis' rouge-caked Wealhtheow comes bursting Jocasta-like into the hall)
> WEALHTHEOW: No! No, tell him no more. (Taking Hrothgar's face in her hands.) Tell him no more, my lord, I beseech you. Tell him no more.
> HROTHGAR: Where is the sense in that, woman? Beowulf speaks the truth. To deny the truth is to continue to live in fear. It is time to stop hiding behind our secret. This may be our last chance. (She sinks to his knees in front of the throne.) Our people were first attacked long ago, when Scyld was still king.

BEOWULF: Scyld knew the Grendel?
HROTHGAR: I speak of his mother, Hag. She would come from the forest and slaughter indiscriminately. (Flashback to "Hag" fitted with dragon wings hanging like a bat from the roof of a cave.) She could not be stopped. In an effort to placate her blood thirst, the Scyld made a pact with her. A stone altar was built and each full moon ... offerings made.

Here a second, longer flashback is interposed.

Child sacrifice in Nick Lyon's *Grendel* (2007).

Child sacrifice in *Grendel*.

We see a bloody altar with adults milling around it. There is a shot of a small boy lurking *behind a shield* by torchlight. The irony undercuts what Scyld's very name would seem to promise. As the crowds watch, a child is bound to the altar, and the Hag comes flying down to devour her.

> BEOWULF: (With a condemning skepticism) Sacrifice? (At which point the film cuts to a close up of Wealhtheow's face on Hrothgar's knee. Her clown-like make-up correlative with her desire to hide the truth.)
> HROTHGAR: Yes ... terrible, but it worked. For years the Hag did not attack. And then one day she disappeared back into the forest and was never seen again. It was thought that she had died. But not before she gave birth to a son. (Cut to a shot of the infant Grendel.) The same beast who terrorizes us to this very day. When he was young, he would hunt mainly in the forest — animals, wayward travelers — but in time, like his mother before him, he began to attack the towns and the villages. So I renewed the pact. That is our dark secret, Beowulf. The reason you see no children here is because there are no more for me to sacrifice. It was then Grendel began to attack Heorot.
> BEOWULF: So there truly are no children.
> HROTHGAR: Oh, there are children here somewhere. But they are kept well hidden from Grendel and from me. Their parents fearing the day when I was forced to begin the sacrifices again. Well now that day has come. I suppose that now you think the Grendel is not the only monster in my land. And you would be right. I'm not proud of what I've done or what I have become.

At this point, Beowulf's mission becomes that of a culture hero like Theseus who must kill the monster in order to put an end to the barbaric sacrifices that ensure the "protection" of the society as a whole. The film thus makes of the backsliding of the Danes in lines 175–183 a recurring lapse into child sacrifice that characterizes the whole history of the Danes from Scyld to Hrothgar. The Freudian (perhaps even Hamlet-inspired) Oedipal conspiracy that characterizes the solutions of earlier Beowulf films is replaced by a revelation of a sacrificial mechanism that Girard believes underlies "mythologization" of sacrifice and Deleuze and Guattari the Oedipalization of an innate aggressivity between the self and others.

Arguably, these films' identification of sacrificial logics in the Old English epic deserves to be taken with more seriousness than the films themselves can sustain. The remainder of this chapter traces provisionally the course such an analysis might take.

Sacrifices in Dark Times

We do well to remember, as Roberta Frank reminds us, the paucity of Germanic legends in Anglo-Saxon literature: "a small and trampled cabbage-patch" (1991, 89). This material was never designed to transmit or reconstruct Germanic paganism; rather, it shaped a usable past worthy of continued respect. This construct formed a discourse of continuity spanning the great divide introduced by Christianity and from that distinct perspective, necessary for traditional cultures that drew strength (and legitimated political power) from a proud ancestry. In a trenchant adaptation of Foucault's "archeology of the present," John D. Niles calls for "an archeology of the past," by which he means: "a complex cultural construction — in part "ours" and in part "theirs"— rather than [...] a set of events that once occurred independent of observation. The past, in a real sense, is where we continue to dwell, to the extent that we dwell in human time, which is largely the creation of narrative" (1999, 182). Insofar as the filmic *Beowulf* may be included in our "part," note how these films' fascination with the dark side of Germanic paganism — especially human sacrifice — throws into sharp relief the poem's suppression of the pagan gods and rituals, as well as its projection of sacrificial logics and scapegoating from human beings unto monsters.

Although the mysterious arrival and departure of Scyld has always provoked intense controversies, something like a critical consensus about the function of the Scyld episode within the poem's repetitive, circular structure has reigned at least since Andrien Bonjour's study of *The Digressions in Beowulf* (1950).[19] Bonjour noted the symmetries in the pattern of a dire time relieved by saviors from overseas whose funerals bookend the poem. Marijane Osborn's important study identified the distinction in the prologue between two forms of knowledge, "that bound by the secular world of the poem and that perceived from our initiated Christian perspective" (973)—a distinction Earl (1994) has elaborated further. Theodore Andersson (1980) similarly remarked how the opening episode establishes a "larger pattern, a rising and falling of hope and fear, success and failure" that characterizes the poem as a whole. In John D. Niles' extensive remarks on the poem's use of ring structure, the funerals of Scyld and Beowulf serve to envelop the poem in "rings of eternity" that glance "deep into the past, in the story of Scyld, and far into the future [...] in the building of a burrow for a dead king" (1983, 158). More recently, John M. Hill (5–6) has seen in the Scyld story a paradigm of the "narrative pulse" of "arrivals and departures" that can also be shown to characterize the poem's large scale structure. What such formal approaches have difficulty addressing, however, is the poem's response to the trajectory of the heroic age itself, represented in the arc from Scyld to Beowulf, from the child to the aged king. If Scyld begins the heroic age, Beowulf's death ends its pre–Christian phase in a way that *self-consciously alludes to the deaths of both Scyld and Christ*. These are both in their own ways failed but honorable repetitions. Like Scyld,

Beowulf's funeral glorifies a protector of his people, but unlike Scyld this Beowulfian age of peace and prosperity will not survive his death. Unlike Christ, Beowulf's self-sacrifice accomplishes in fact very little, but the likeness of his sacrifice to that of Christ points to the means by which the poem's progeny will transcend the limits of its world.

To begin once more at the beginning, the elliptical evocation of the legendary Scyld should be understood as a deliberate contrivance designed to dovetail biblical and Danish legend: the kin-slayer Cain and the patriarch Moses, with Heremod and Scyld. The importance of Heremod to the poet's Scylding myth is often overlooked, because critics routinely assume that Sceaf, not Heremod, is Scyld's father. This is to put too much stress on the patronymic "Scefing" to the exclusion of inferences we should draw from the text itself in conjunction with the extant early genealogies in Anglo-Saxon England and Scandinavia.

There is much jostling for position in Anglo-Saxon genealogies. Overwhelmingly, however, Anglo-Saxon sources position Scyld as the son of Heremod and the father of Beaw — and, frequently, the descendent by six generations from Sceaf, whom *Widsið* designates a ruler of the *Langobards*.[20] Four separate recensions of the *Anglo-Saxon Chronicle* make Scyld the son of Heremod and Sceaf (or a character by another name holding the same place in the genealogy) a son of Noah.[21] Asser's *Life of Alfred* likewise has the genealogy Heremod-Scyld-Beaw, as do later genealogies of Alfred.[22] The nearly uniform acceptance of Sceaf as the father of Scyld derives from a single, late source, the late tenth or early eleventh-century *Chronicon Æthelweardi*, which in fact seems to be a fancifully eulogistic version of the traditional genealogy. Æthelweard's chronicle traces King Æthelwulf's generous endowment of a tenth to the Church all the way back to the fertile Sceaf ("de cuius prosapia ordinem trahit Aðulf rex/ from his family King Æthwulf derived his descent").[23] In *Beowulf*, the land that Scyld redeems — by martial force, not by fertility — is anything but a second Eden, flourishing and abundant. In fact, the poet early identifies the time before Scyld as "fyrenðearf" (dire distress, wicked lack, sinful deprivation, 14) and leaderless ("aldor(l)eas," 15), a state of affairs difficult to imagine obtaining after the abundance Sceaf represents. The Danes had a dubious leader, under whom and after whom they suffered greatly. That leader was Heremod. Many have noted the parallels between Scyld and Beowulf, who also comes to the Danes as a "fyrena frofre" (628), on one hand, and between Grendel and Heremod, on the other. Grendel is repeatedly associated with *fyren* (101, 137, 153, 164, 628, 750, 811, 1001, 1669) and so too is Heremod, into whom *fyren* enters ("hine fyren onwod," 915), perhaps in the demonic process described in Hrothgar's speech ("se þe of flanbogan fyrenum sceoteð" 1744), which also markedly contrasts Beowulf and Heremod.[24]

Whatever one makes of the second element in Scyld Scefing, it almost certainly does not mean "son of Sceaf," for the simple reason that the genealogy of the Danes traced at the beginning of the poem and later filled in by Hrothgar clearly implies that Scyld reigned over a renaissance of the Danes after the blight of Heremod — the same genealogy overwhelmingly reproduced in Anglo-Saxon regnal lists and genealogies. Scyld, I therefore suggest, is being called a *Scefing* in the same way that Hrothgar is twice called a *Scylding* (1792, 2105) and Ongentheow twice a *Scylfing* (2487, 2968). That is to say, Scyld is a descendant of Scef, not his immediate son. Entertaining for the moment the idea that Scyld's correct patronymic would be Heremoding, his miraculous survival becomes even more significant. He is descended from that fertility god–like figure Sceaf in that he comes to the Danes on a boat, when the leaderless Danes have endured a long period of dearth and suffering because they executed (or exiled) their opprobrious King Heremod.[25] Their lord-less distress results from an uprising against the cruel and murderous Heremod, infamous in the poem as well as in various other sources for a paranoia that led him to kill his retainers and members of his own family. Scyld's arrival thus serves as an intermediate stage between Sceaf, who survived the rebellion of Cain's offspring to re-establish civilization after the flood, and Beowulf, who also comes from overseas to rescue the Danes in another time of dire privation. Implicit in this genealogy is a war for the future of the *þeod* being waged throughout time between demonic killers of kin and God-sent saviors of the people. Cain's kin includes not just the monsters, but also Heremod and Unferth, as well as the dark lord Eormenric who hanged his own son on the gallows.

The major sources in Old Norse introduce euhemerizing adaptations of this Danish genealogy. Snorri Sturluson's *Prose Edda* makes Skjold and Ing founders of the Danish and Swedish peoples, respectively — rule granted them by their human father Odin. Yet five chapters later Snorri reproduces the genealogy Heremod-Scyld-Beaw.[26] Although Saxo Grammaticus traces the Danish ethnogenesis from the eponymous "Dan" and gives the names Lother for Heremod and Gram for Beaw, the pattern remains the same: an evil king who murders his own people is killed in rebellion and succeeded by a son (Skiold) different in every respect, who inaugurates a golden age, which comes to fruition in his Baldr-like offspring, a son perfect in every respect.

The spectacle of child sacrifice rears its gruesome head with some frequency in the sagas. In *The Saga of the Jómsvíkings* the lapsed Christian, Earl Hakon, puts ashore on an island when the battle at sea goes against him:

> And in his prayer he called upon his patron goddess, Thorgerd Halgabrúd. But she would not hear his prayer and was wroth. He offered to make her many a sacrifice, but she refused each one, and he thought his case desperate. In the end he offered her a human sacrifice, but she would not have it. At last he offered his seven-year-old son; and she accepted. Then the earl put the boy in the hands of his slave Skopti; and Skopti slew him [trans. Hollander 100].

Earl Hakon's sacrifice of his son helps to turn the tide in his favor when the sea battle recommences. The goddess sends a hailstorm against his enemies and is seen firing deadly darts from each fingertip. The battle concludes with the obscenely belabored ritual sacrifice of the Jomsviking prisoners of war.

Snorri's *Ynglunga Saga* presents the rather more creepy spectacle of a cowardly King Aun who artificially extends his long life to the extent of the Old Testament patriarchs:

> Then he (Aun) performed a great sacrifice, sacrificing his other son, and was told by Odin that he would continue to live if he sacrificed him a son every tenth year.... Then Aun had one son left and wanted to sacrifice him, and also to dedicate to Óthin Uppsala and all the districts adjoining it and call it Tíundaland. But the Swedes forbade him to do that, so no sacrifice was made. Then King Aun died [Snorri, *Heimskringla* 28].

For the Christian writers repeating or inventing such legends, sacrifice serves as the fundamental distinction between pagan and Christian. Child sacrifice is also telling in that it represents a reversion to the core of paganism as the sagas represent it. The more desperate things become, the more sacrifice descends from animals to human victims and ultimately to one's own children. The most powerful sacrifices, those best able to avert fate, are the most abhorrent and the closest to home.

Often the sacrifice of children in the sagas is forestalled, though within a complex of attitudes that suggests that the romance motif is still burdened with anxiety and an abiding sense of guilt. *The Saga of the Jomsvikings* begins with the exposure of the child "Knut" conceived in incest. Hunters "discover" the boy hanging from a tree and bring him before his biological father, King Gorm, who is only too happy bring up this fondling as his own. As the Scyldings derive their descent from the foundling Scyld, so too the "Knytlings" from Knut, after the cloth knotted around the baby's head containing a golden ring. In *The Saga of Gunnlaug Serpent-Tongue*, despite his skepticism about the prophetic power of dreams, Thorstein quickly resolves to expose his baby daughter when told that she will cause the death of her two suitors:

> Later in the summer, Thorstein got ready to go to the Althing. Before he left, he said to his wife, Jofrid, "As matters stand, you are soon going to have a baby. Now if you have a girl, it must be left out to die, but if it is a boy, it

will be brought up." When the country was completely heathen, it was something of a custom for poor men with many dependents in their families to have their children exposed. Even so, it was always considered a bad thing to do [trans. Attwood, in *The Sagas of the Icelanders* 563].

The explanation, while perhaps true, is quite irrelevant. Thorstein is far from poor, and his decision is not based upon a scarcity of resources, but rather constitutes an attempt to avert what has been fated through the sacrifice of a child. Like Hakon and Aun, Thorstein seems to represent that tribal father so crucial to Frazer, Freud and Girard, a father whose power threatens the future survival of the race. Frazer saw fertility rites and Freud Oedipal guilt as having a basis in the murder of this destructive father figure. Both writers have legions of detractors justified by a wealth of evidence drawn from archaic and primitive cultures. Yet what does seem clear is that the Christian writers of such Norse legends are deeply invested in an understanding of paganism not unlike that proposed by these Victorians. Pagan fathers seek divine aid through the sacrifice of their children. The miraculous survival of the children in turn establishes a limit to the father's power and the evil he has come to embody.

In the dire times of Heremod we may see references to a sacrificial crisis, driven by the mounting paranoia which Girard has called mimetic escalation. Such escalation is quite clear in figures such as Hakon, who moves from the immolation of animals to human beings to his own child, and Aun, who in trying to prolong his life sacrifices in succession each but the last of his ten sons. Unlike these sagas and somewhat more in tune with *The Saga of Gunnlaug Serpent-Tongue*, the poet of *Beowulf* keeps child sacrifice in the background, presenting the matter romantically and symbolically, perhaps even typologically.

Many have noted the obvious parallel of the Scyld prologue with biblical story of Moses, an infant cast adrift who later in adulthood averts the ethnocide of the Jews. In escaping immolation and in the exodus of the Hebrews from captivity, Moses fulfills the divine plan for God's people that began with the (non) sacrifice of Isaac. With Noah's ark, from which many genealogies trace the line of the Scyldings, through the survival of the sacrificial victims Isaac and Moses, down to the dry-shod crossing of the Red Sea, the Jews are set apart, made sacred, and distinguished in a special bond of God with human beings. In a similar way, God distinguishes himself from other gods through the covenants he makes with his chosen people, covenants that express an evolution away from divine retribution and human sacrifice.

Putting aside the question of direct influence between the two poems, the adult Moses of the opening of the Old English *Exodus* is well nigh indistinguishable from Scyld:

> Divine was the retribution of his hand and loyal his Lord: he granted him supremacy of arms against the violence of raging foes, and by this means he vanquished in battle the sovereignty of many tribes, his enemies [Bradley, 51].

As the exodus proceeds across the seabed, the narrative flashes back to compare the triumph of Moses with earlier patriarchs in his genealogical line, Noah and Abraham. As Noah saved humanity on the sea paths, so now does Moses lead the Jews to safety. The parallel with Abraham is much more elaborately drawn:

> To that place of parley Abraham led his son Isaac. First the executioner lit a fire, he was none the happier for that. He meant to yield up his heir to the flame, the best of men into the pyre's blaze, his beloved son as a sacrifice for victory, his only successor on earth, the consolation of his life, since he expected henceforth, as a legacy to his people, a long-abiding cause for hope. He gave witness, when he took the lad firmly in his hands and when he, the man of popular renown, pulled out his ancient sword — the edge rasped — that he did not esteem the days of his life dearer to him than that he should obey the heaven-King. He arose: this man meant to slay his stripling son, to bloody the boy with blade-edges, with the sword — if the ordaining Lord had let him. The radiant Father did not desire to take the child, the holy sacrifice, from him, but caught him with his hands. Then a voice from heaven came restraining him, the resonance of glory, and thereupon spoke these words: "Do not slay, Abraham, your own child, your son, by the sword [Bradley, 60–61].

The Junius manuscript, in passages such as the one quoted above, emphasizes typological connections between figures such as Noah, Isaac, and Moses. Something similar, although more complicated, appears to be at work in *Beowulf*. The poem puts this biblical genealogy in close parallel with the genealogy of the Danes, which in analogous ways appears to be in the process of transcending human sacrifice. In various Anglo-Saxon and Norse genealogies, Sceaf is associated with the biblical Seth, the son of Noah who survived the flood. The story of the child Scyld in *Beowulf*, then, can be seen not simply as a confusion of traditional elements, but as a typological repetition wherein Scyld repeats the miraculous survival of his ancestor Sceaf, homologous with Moses' repetitions of Noah and Isaac. Moses, like Isaac, survives child sacrifice, and, like Noah, he survives the flood, first in the little ark of parchment and then in the miracle of the parting of the Red Sea. The end of *Exodus* narrates the destruction of the Pharaoh's troops in a way designed to evoke the cataclysm of Noah's flood, but with a clear difference: God's chosen people are spared. In a larger sense too the Hebrews in the Junius poems (*Genesis*, *Exodus*, and *Daniel*) seem a figure for *Beowulf*'s monotheistic Danes and Geats, who always invoke a single "god" and never mention the gods of Germanic paganism, yet, like the Hebrews in *Daniel*, are prone to backsliding into idol worship and sacrifice in dark times.

Understanding Scyld as a type-figure of the favored child, who escapes sacrifice to become the representative of his line's divine favor — like Isaac and Moses — also helps to explain the poem's extensive concern with Heremod. The latter should be viewed not just as an example of a bad king, but rather as a malevolent force that the Danes outlast because of the miraculous survival of his son Scyld. The figure of Heremod in the poem partakes of the same syndrome of the blighting pagan patriarch that we have seen in both Old English poetry and the Icelandic sagas. The scop's song celebrating the victory over Grendel *opposes* Heremod to Sigemund and Beowulf, but also *apposes* the evil king to the dragon Sigemund killed and to Beowulf's killing of Grendel:

siððan Heremodes	hild sweðrode
eafoð ond ellen.	He mid Eotenum wearð
on feonda geweald	forð forlacen,
snude forsended.	Hine sorhwylmas
lemedon to lange;	he his leodum wearð,
eallum æþelingum	to aldorceare;
swylce oft bemearn	ærran mælum
swiðferhþes sið	snotor ceorl monig,
se þe him bealwa to	bote gelyfde,
þæt þæt ðeodnes bearn	geþeon scolde,
fæderæþelum onfon,	folc gehealdan,
hord ond hleoburh,	hæleþa rice,
eþel Scyldinga.	He þær eallum wearð,
mæg Higelaces	manna cynne,
freondum gefæra;	hine fyren onwod.
since Heremod's	war valor diminished,
his strength and courage.	Among a monstrous folk
he was betrayed	into the power of his enemies,
speedily sent to death.	Concerning him, sorrow-surgings
troubled too long —	he was to his people,
to all his nobles,	too great a life-grief.
So in former times	many a wise man
often grieved over	the stout-hearted one's departure,
who trusted in him	for a remedy for evils,
that the lord's son	should prosper,
receive the father's rank,	protect the people,
treasure and citadel,	kingdom of heroes,
the homeland of the Shieldings.	There he was to all,
the kinsman of Higelac,	to friends most pleasing
of the race of men.	Crime took possession of Heremod [901–915].

The maintenance of hard and fast distinctions between the Old English and Old Norse versions of Heremod has sometimes limited unnecessarily the associations he would have provoked in an audience familiar with Germanic lore.

Beowulf makes Sigemund rather than Sigurd the dragon-slayer, but this alteration strengthens the comparisons being drawn in the Old English poem between the ancient heroes and their applications to Beowulf's deeds. Sigemund and Heremod appear together in the *Hyndlulióð* as recipients of gifts from Odin. Sigemund receives a sword and Heremod a helmet and corselet — items that later play a prominent role in Hrothgar's allegorical description of pride. The two brothers were once honored by Odin as equals and are associated with famous youthful careers. Sometime later their lives took divergent paths. Sigemund survives a visit to the giants ("ealfela eotena cynnes" 883b) but Heremod — unless we ignore the obvious parallel and translate "eotenum" in line 902 as *Jutes*— dies among them. Sigemund goes on to even greater fame, while evil takes Heremod ("hine fyren onwod," 915b).

Relevant here too are the attitudes toward paganism both expressed in the condemnations of lines 175–186 (discussed above) and implied in the proto–Christian, exclusively monotheistic world of the poem as a whole. In one of the most sublime images of Snorri's *Prose Edda*, Heremod mounts Odin's horse Sleipnir and rides furiously to Hel in search of Baldr. It is easy to see how some version of this myth known to the Christian poet of *Beowulf* might have been read as an overweening, stupendous act of pride. Indeed, the passages on Heremod in *Beowulf* seem deflationary in comparison with Icelandic sources and Saxo's Danish history, shrinking this son or servant of Odin from a god to an empty shell eaten away by waves of sorrow, much as diabolical characters are shrunken down to size in Christian poems such as *Judith* or *Juliana*. Verbs expressing diminution of physical and mental powers such as "sweðrode" (subside, diminish), "forð forlacen" (trick by leading astray), "snude forsended" (quickly, easily dispatched") and "lemede" (lit. lamed) perform a triumph of euhemerism that reduces the once godly figure to a debile old man.

At line 907 the focus shifts from Heremod to the perceptions of the people he abandoned. Their laments are strangely confined to an earlier time ("ærran mælum") when Heremod left them for the giants. Given this temporal reference the verb *bemearn* is odd. Though often translated in periphrastic ways, the word typically refers specifically to sadness over a death, as in the modern English reflex *to mourn*.[27] Perhaps the verb is calculated to underline the proleptic metaphor implicit in "swiðferhþes sið" (908a), that is, Heremod's journey as a figure for his death — already recorded in the earlier lines but not yet having occurred at the time being described in lines 907–913a. Might not the wise men also and especially be mourning the child Scyld, whose journey they assumed fatal? The hypothesis seems tenuous at best, but it gains support as the passage continues. The relative clause in line 909 ("se þe him bealwa to bote gelyfde") could simply be the opening of a gnomic passage, but similar statements at the beginning of the poem are closely fitted to their context, Scyld's exemplary progeny. Of course Scyld himself ultimately arrives as consolation for the lordless Danes ("folce to frofre," 14), perhaps in fulfillment of their faith in "bealwa to bote" (as a remedy for suffering). Again, the epexegetical clause explaining of what this *bot* consists, which begins "þæt þæt ðeodnes bearn geþeon scolde," could just be a periphrastic description of a prosperous king. But of course Heremod's idea of prospering consisted of killing his subjects and amassing their wealth. Before he left, they feared for their lives ("aldorceare," 906). Given what has and will be said of Heremod in the poem, this ideal portrait of a beloved king dearly missed simply won't hold water. If we take *geþeon* as *to grow up* (as it certainly means in the description of Scyld's son Beow in line 25), then the whole clause in 910–913a is best translated: "that the lord's son must grow up, receive his father's nobles, protect the people, the hoard, the stronghold, the kingdom of warriors, the homeland of the Scyldings." If we imagine that they are bemoaning the loss of what was ultimately and miraculously restored to them, then that last phrase "eþel Scyldinga" (913a) is neither careless nor anachronistic. Scyld not only founds a dynasty, but his survival embodies its hopes and ideals.

Admittedly, the thesis that Scyld like Isaac and Moses survives child sacrifice to become a leader of his people rests on thin evidence. But given the poem's deliberately obscure presentation of pagan ritual and belief it could hardly be otherwise. The poet eulogizes the line of Scyld, but the threat of internecine violence repeatedly endangers the future of this civilization. That human sacrifice was a part of this past and continues to haunt the present is only referenced darkly, in moments such as the Danes' reversion to pagan sacrifice to palliate the demon Grendel and in an earlier dark time when Heremod murdered his table-companions and perhaps even attempted to sacrifice his son Scyld. Yet the specter of human sacrifice is kept alive at the borders of the reader's consciousness in other ways, chiefly through the anthropomorphic monsters whose portrayal imbues them with two related pagan rituals: sacrifice and feud.[28]

Both Grendel and his mother are said to be carrying out a "feud" against the Danes. It is important to recall the ritualistic as well as the legalistic implications of the term for early Germanic civilizations. Logically speaking, feud has many similarities with sacrifice; both involve a sacred obligation and ritual murder. That the Grendel-kin represent the stubborn re-emergence of such practices is repeatedly alluded to within the poem. The first mention of pagan offerings occurs quite early in the ironic comparison of the treasures which the Danes load onto Scyld's funeral ship ("lacum," 43) to those which were originally sent out with the boy upon the waves. While later sources mention weapons and some scholars have hypothesized that "Scyld Scefing" means *Scyld with a Sheaf,* the irony quite probably runs much deeper. If we are right in terming the boy Scyld a survivor of sacrifice, then the use of the word *lac* wittily evokes the destitute boy's original status as a sacrificial offering.

As the main story gets underway, the poet repeatedly calls Grendel's depredations a feud and a crime ("fæhðe ond fyrene," 137; "fyrene ond fæhðe," 153), seemingly conjoining two very different concepts. But of course Grendel's feud *is* illegal, for he neither has a killing to revenge, nor will he pay any settlement for those he has slain. When Beowulf arrives, he evokes a third legalistic concept in preparing for the battle against Grendel, the ritual of the duel. He swears to fight fairly, without weapons or armor as Grendel does, makes a grimly resolute last testament, and assures everyone that God will decide the outcome. Eventually, however, Grendel's body is dismembered in ways that provoke ritualistic and even talismanic associations. Looking up after the battle into the gabled rafters, perhaps patterned after a stag's antlers, one could see: "Þæt wæs tacen sweotol/ Syþðan hilde deor hond alegde,/ Earm ond eaxle—þær wæs eal geador/ Grendles grape under geapne hrof" (That was a clear token,/ Since the battle-brave one laid down the hand,/Arm and shoulder—there altogether was/ Grendel's claw under the vaulted roof, 833b–836). Later in the mere, Beowulf beheads Grendel's corpse, and the head too is treated ritually, lifted up on spears and paraded through the city. His two trophies—the head and the sword hilt—are mutually illuminating signs of ritual purification: God's flood, which killed the giants, and Beowulf's sacrifice of two of the monsters whose forefathers survived the flood. The poet tends to represent these things as spectacles astounding crowds of onlookers, but behind such spectacles can be glimpsed the kinds of pagan magic that he elsewhere avoids more assiduously.

Indeed, back among the Geats and recounting these events to Hygelac, Beowulf alludes to the cultic and the ritualistic significance behind the heroic spectacles. Seth Lerer's essay on "Grendel's Glove" stresses the ludic and performative nature of Beowulf's report and associates the *glof* with the comic adventures of Thor recounted in the Eddas. Beowulf's report makes

> direct allusions to the vision of Thor the comic dwarf and to the flytings preserved in the *Harbardzliod* and *Lokasenna*. Confronted with a need to tell his own tale, Beowulf presents himself as something of a comic Thor, a hero on a journey filled with transparent names, monstrous objects, and enigmatic verbal challenges (Lerer 736).

Lerer sees the signs (*tacen*) made by body parts as emblematic of sacrificial dismemberment and deftly associates these *disiecta membra* with the ritual purification of the defiled hall. The five uses of the verb *fælsian* in the poem (432, 825, 1176, 1620, 2352) all refer to Beowulf's bloody battles and the resultant cleansing of Heorot or its dark reflection beneath the mere. Pagan priests *blessed* buildings in a similar way, sprinkling blood or making sacrifices at a threshold or beneath a foundation. The notion of Beowulf playing the role of a sacrificial priest is perhaps not as far-fetched as it sounds. Grendel's arm had been called a "tacen sweotol" (a clear sign), but of what precisely this significance consists we are never informed. Certainly the claw represents pagan power, a potent synecdoche of that power and its overthrow ("hæðenes handsporu," hand-claws of the heathen, 986).[29] In context, the sign means to the Danes that their troubles are over, that the monster has been defeated. In this line, the literal significance of the claw is misleading, a synecdoche of the demonic power beneath the tarn that the Danes in their abundant relief rashly underestimate. As Thomas A. Prendergast suggests:

> The arm is supposedly, as the poem says, a "clear sign" ("tacen sweotol") that Beowulf had "remedied all the grief ("ealle gebette inwidsorge")—a mnemonics that purportedly leads to the cleansing of the past; yet, given the bloody events that follow, it seems, instead, that the arm is a *tacen* that uncleanness now lies at the heart of Heorot (ll. 825–36). Rather than point beyond itself to a conscious transcendence of violence, the arm becomes a kind of fetish object that makes manifest an idolatrous worship of violence [132].

Only later do they remember the rumors of two beings haunting the misty moors. Yet a different category of "tacen" is mentioned once the threat of the monsters has been well and truly extinguished. Grendel's head is brought within mead hall ("þær guman druncon," 1648), where Beowulf briefly expounds its significance:

> Beowulf maþelode   bearn Ecgþeowes:
> "Hwæt, we þe þas sælac,   sunu Healfdenes,
> leod Scyldinga,   lustum brohton
> tires to tacne,   þe þu on her locast.
>
> Bewoulf spoke   son of Ecgtheow:
> Hear me, son of Healfdane   we have happily brought you,
> Prince of the Scyldings,   this sea-plunder,
> the token of glory   on which you look here [1651–1654].

While this gloss pales in comparison with the elaborate interpretation of the hilt that follows, it contains its own rich allusiveness. The gift of the head is itself typical of Beowulf's macabre humor, but the joke stems from the original meaning of *lac* (offering, sacrifice). The kenning *sælac* might well be translated "offering from the sea." That the taking of the head is done as a form of ritual sacrifice is also suggested in the nomination of the giant sword a "beadulac" (battle-sport or battle-offering, 1561) that only Beowulf can wield in revenging the "laðlicu lac" (detestable offering, 1584) of corpses with which Grendel stuffs the *glof*. That Beowulf here presents himself as a pagan priest making a sacrificial offering is given further confirmation by a similar etymological pun lurking in the phrase *tires to tacne*. The token certainly represents a sign of Beowulf's glory, which he is conferring onto Hrothgar, perhaps to remain there within the hall in furtherance of both their fame. However, it is also a sign of Tiw (Germanic *Tiwaz; Old Norse *Tyr*), an offering for the Germanic god of justice in war, to whom prisoners after battle were sacrificed by beheading. Indeed the word play is perhaps all of piece with the earlier dismemberment humor personifying the door of Heorot as the mouth of the hall ("recedes muþan," 724). Yet, surely, the most blatant intimation of human sacrifice is the taking of the head itself, its display, its transition into the system of gift-giving.[30] In Seth Lerer's terms, the monster is being dismembered into signs, the "tacen sweotol" of the arm and the "tires to tacne" of the head. The reference to Tiw recalls the sky god's loss of his hand in the binding of the wolf Fenrir, a grotesque, synedochic remembrance of that famous myth by its component parts, a head and a hand. Grendel's bits become symbols of Tiw's judicial power, his ability to use battle to decide causes justly.[31]

In addition, Tiw is much more than a god of justice; he is also a victim who willingly sacrifices himself to forestall the forces that will ultimately bring Ragnarök. In his maiming we may see a mythological justification for the god's waning powers, ultimately absorbed by other gods such as Odin and Thor. Beowulf's supernaturally potent handgrip may associate him with this god, especially because the hero uses this grip to mete out justice in a war against ancestors of the giants, grabbing Grendel in an arm-lock, attempting like Tiw to "bind" the monster, and later wielding as no other human being could the gigantic sword, a weapon that also suffers a sea change, a diminution, a down-sizing from the gigantic to the symbolic and talismanic. Moreover, the association with the maimed, self-sacrificing Tiw helps to set the stage for Beowulf's own waning strength in the second half of the poem, his twilight.

Fate's Arrow, or What Balder and Beowulf Have to Do with Christ

In the second half of the poem Beowulf moves from sacrificer to the sacrificed.[32] This transition crucial to the deep structure of the poem depends on a Christian interpretation of sacrifice, which, according to René Girard, stems from Christ's deconstruction of the "sacrificial mechanism." Central to

Girard's theory of sacrifice is his view that Christianity transcends scapegoating and sacrifice. This view sets him apart from other anthropologists of sacrifice and complicates the application of his work in ways often ignored by critics who readily employ his analyses of mimetic rivalry, scapegoating and the interdependence of violence and the sacred, while ignoring the distinctive theological turn in his theorization of the sacred. Distinctive, certainly, but not unparalleled: a crucial distinguishing feature between Christianity and paganism in both Old English and Old Norse literature is sacrifice. Sacrificial rituals are also demythologized by Christian authors, who trace the precipitous, degenerative relapse into paganism at moments of crisis, from idol worship and animal sacrifice, through human sacrifice and the immolation of one's own children.

For Girard sacrifice is compulsively repetitive, viciously circular, a safety valve that functions to expel mimetic tensions through the identification of a scapegoat. The theology of Christianity, if not its history, is directly opposed to the repetitive trap of scapegoating. Christ's crucifixion is at once the inversion of sacrifice (a God who rather than demanding human victims, sacrifices himself for humanity) and a final sacrifice, one designed to end all sacrifices through the epiphany that humanity's need for scapegoats has driven them to kill the son of God. If the near escapes of Isaac and Moses demonstrate a development away from human sacrifice in the Old Testament, the basis of which appears to be the sacrifice of the first-born son, then the sacrifice of Christ inverts, obviates, and transcends the sacrificial mechanism. As we have seen, film adaptations of *Beowulf* are remarkably univocal in their use of human sacrifice as a frame for tales about monsters and the monstrousness of men. The films *Beowulf and Grendel* (2005), *Grendel* (2006), and the 1999 *Beowulf* find Hrothgar somehow guilty for the monstrous incursions that threaten to overwhelm his people. In the 2007 *Beowulf*, both Hrothgar and Beowulf fall victim to a lust for power embodied in the golden Grendel's Mother. However, such readings simplify the poem's complex response to paganism, turning its sublime meditation on the relevance of the past into a finger-waving condemnation. Perhaps the only real fault of these kings is to have grown older and weaker in a world where vigor and courage are paramount. In the sacrificial reading of the last half of the poem vetted below, Beowulf's battle with the dragon is read typologically through its implicit comparisons with Baldr and Christ, as a glorious but failed attempt to transcend the limits of the pagan world which nevertheless points beyond itself.

A Christian typological reading of the poem that neither condemns nor censures Beowulf may seem like a contradiction in terms. However, the assumptions underlying such resistances deserve further scrutiny. Pope Gregory's letter in Bede's *Ecclesiastical History* discussed earlier not only recommends converting pagan places of worship to Christianity but also a kind of translation in worship from pagan sacrifice to Christian feasts. These feasts chiefly celebrated Christian martyrs whose deaths both imitated Christ's sacrifice and made the saints and their relics worthy of veneration. The Anglo-Saxon Christ depicted in *The Dream of the Rood* is no passive victim. He ascends the cross as a warrior might a horse in order to liberate those trapped in hell's dungeons. Christian ritual remembers and reenacts this final sacrifice; unlike pagan sacrifices the power of this victim never wanes, nor need the cycle of victimization ever be repeated. Deeply implicit in Christ's sacrifice to end all sacrifices is a variety that many anthropologists have thought fundamental to the development of the practice, the ritual sacrifice of a king. In disdainfully marking him out as Jesus of Nazareth King of the Jews (INRI), the Romans deride the fact that the Jews have chosen to sacrifice their own "king." In fact, Christ's Flight to Egypt in escaping The Slaughter of the Innocents relates typologically to its earlier *figurae* in Moses and Isaac, but it also points forward to Christ's final acceptance of his role in the sacrificial drama. A remarkably homologous structure of a child escaping sacrifice and a king willingly undergoing sacrifice is reproduced in the beginning and the end of *Beowulf*.

As his own fate draws exceedingly close ("wyrd ungemete neah," 2420), Beowulf recollects an accidental death from his childhood that also seems to portend his own:

> Wæs þam yldestan   ungedefelice
> mæges dædum   morþorbed stred,
> syððan hyne Hæðcyn   of hornbogan,
> his freawine   flane geswencte,
> miste mercelses   ond his mæg ofscet,
> broðor oðerne,blodigan gare.
> Þæt wæs feohleas gefeohte,   fyrenum gesyngad,
> hreðre hyge-myðe;   sceolde hwæðre swa þeah
> æþeling unwrecen   ealdres linnan.
>
> For the eldest (Herebeald),   unfittingly,
> Was the slaughter-bed strewn   by a kinsman's deeds,
> After Hæthcyn   struck down
> his friend-lord,   with an arrow from his horn-bow,
> missed the mark   and shot his kinsman dead,
> the other brother   with a bloody point.
> That was a recompense-less fight,   an ill-done evil,
> Heart-wearying in the breast;   however, the prince
> Must be deprived   of a life unavenged [2435–2443].

The accidental death has seemed to many an oblique reference to the death of Baldr (Here-*beald*), the most beautiful of the gods and the kindest to mankind, at the hands of his blind half-brother Hod (*Hæð*-cyn). As such, the reference meditates plangently on the blind impartiality and inescapability of fate. Hamlet apologizes to Laertes in a way that also seems to remember the theme of accidental fratricide in the Baldr story: "Let my disclaiming from a purposed evil/Free me so far in your generous thoughts/ That I have shot mine arrow ov'r the house/ And hurt my brother" (5.2. 227–230). What we seem to have here is the interconnection of two important *topoi*: one on accidental death by means of projectile weapon and another on the stymying grief that comes when one can neither accept compensation nor take revenge for the death of a kinsman.

The compound theme of accidental death and unrelieved mourning, which we might call fate's arrow, echoes that earlier warning of Hrothgar about the

>   bona swiþ neah
> se þe of flanbogan   fyrenum sceateð.
> Þonne biþ on hreþre   under helm drepen
> biteran stæle   — him bebeorgan ne con —
> wom wundorbebodum   weargan gastes.
>
>   the slayer is very near,
> He who with the arrow-bow   shoots wickedly.
> Then it is in the mindstruck under the helmet by
> A bitter arrow —   he does not know how to guard himself—
> The perverse, weird promptings   of the cursed spirit [1743–47].

Yet of course the two passages are also markedly different in that the first attributes no blame to either party, killer or victim, while the second casts the archer as a demon and makes his target a victim of his own pride.[33] The ambiguous use of this compound theme sets the stage for a very ambivalent presentation of Beowulf's death, which represents the third and final iteration of the theme. Part of Beowulf's prior success had to do with his use of uncommon strategies: he fights Grendel without sword or armor but takes both with him down into the mere. Here at the last he devises another stratagem, a long shield made of iron to protect him from the dragon's fire:

> Stiðmod gestod   wið steapne rond
> winia bealdor, ða se wyrm gebeah
> snude tosomne;   he on searwum bad.
>
> The strong-hearted one stood   behind the high shield,
> leader of friends,   when the worm coiled
> together immediately. He waited in armor [2566–2568].

It is likely that "on searwum" refers to that purpose-made shield, a contrivance behind which Beowulf waits for the dragon. The repeated focus on the shield as a zone of protection for Beowulf—Wiglaf also takes refuge there alongside him—perhaps is meant to recall that eponymous Scyld of the beginning of the poem and the role of a king as the protector of his people. But the phrase "winia bealdor" should give us pause. Early editors attempted to resolve the problems inherent in "the lord of lords" by changing *winia* to *wigena* (warriors). Yet as in the phrase "tires to tacne" discussed earlier, something more may be at stake. Beowulf has gambled on a large iron shield to protect him from the dragon; this boldness may be compared with the Scandinavian god Baldr (OE *Bealdor*), who, thinking himself impervious to weapons, allows all the gods to fire arrows and spears at him. Beowulf is the "Baldr of lords," a figure of fate finding its way despite the power and glory of a justly beloved king, who is finally eulogized at the end as the most Baldr-like of rulers, "the most benevolent, most gentle and most gracious to his people of earthly kings" ("wyruldcyninga/ manna mildest ond monðwærust/ leodum liðost " 3180b–3182a). Also like Baldr, Beowulf receives his death wound despite his apparent invulnerability. The dragon's assault is figured as an arrow shot that finds its mark in Beowulf's neck despite the gigantic iron shield. The dragon itself is called a *hringboga* (ringed bow?), which certainly refers to coiling but also suggests a bow, and his fangs are "biteran banum," recalling perhaps the "flanbogan" (1744) which the fiend uses to launch "biteran stræle" (1746) through the compromised spiritual defenses of the proud in Hrothgar's psychomachic allegory. But image also recalls Hæðcyn's "hornbogan" (2437) and the "blodigan gar" (2440) with which he accidentally slays his brother Herebeald in the euhemerizing allusion to the death of Baldr.

In the first of these iterations of the fate's arrow theme in Hrothgar's oration both the demon and the proud king are at fault. In the second, neither Herebeald nor his brother Hæðcyn mean or deserve any harm, any more than Hod intends to kill Baldr. Yet what of Beowulf? Has he, as the references to his pride might suggest, become overweening like Heremod and the target of the fiend's arrow? Besides the use of such words, there is precious little in the poem to suggest that Beowulf has become evil or self-serving. In his final moments, he and Wiglaf seem to enact an emblematic celebration of the heroic ethos of the protective king and his faithful retainer, as the two shelter together behind Beowulf's shield. On the other hand, though Beowulf certainly doesn't intend the destruction of his people, Wiglaf himself predicts that it will come all the same, and as a result of Beowulf's pride. We are back to a crux that has bedeviled criticism of *Beowulf* from very early days. A common way of solving this perplex appeals to a Christian frame of reference which demonstrates the limits of worldly glory, but the frame of the poem itself offers a different kind answer based on the transcendence of sacrifice.

For Girard, the myth of Baldr is fundamentally identical to similarly euphemized myths of divine sacrifice such as the Kouretes' protection of Zeus from his father Kronos or Giants' murder of Dionysus. In all three cases a group of supernatural beings gather round a divine child. In each case the scene of collective murder is rationalized in later developments of the myth in order to obscure the reality of divine and sacred violence:

> It must be the work of a people who cannot tolerate the traditional representation of the murder because it makes all the gods, the victim aside, into criminals. The original gathering of the gods is no different from a band of assassins, and in a sense the faithful want none of it but they have no other sacred text; they cling to it; they are passionately attached to their religious representations. They want to keep these representations but they also want to get rid of them or, rather, to overthrow them in an effort to eliminate that essential stereotype of persecution, collective murder [Girard, *The Scapegoat* 68].

Similar glossing over of a myth of persecution is probably at work in the sublimation of child sacrifice in the myth of Scyld that opens the poem. Doubtless, too, Snorri's reconstruction of the Baldr story, which takes up one-tenth of the whole *Gylfaginning*, was influenced by Christianity as well as by the selective forgetting of collective murder described by Girard. In fact, a limitation of his approach becomes evident here. For Girard, paganism and primitive cultures from many times and places are set off against Christianity's deconstruction of the sacrificial mechanism. Thus Baldr's role as a gentle protector of mankind and his near ascent from Hel — ideas that certainly appealed to Christians like Snorri — are never mentioned by Girard. The senseless, perverse death of Baldr through the machinations of Loki has appealed to Christians from Snorri to Mathew Arnold and beyond, in part because of the similarities of his story to that of Christ: his innocence, his love for mankind, his senseless death, and even the prospect of his return after Ragnarök to help begin the world anew.

What, then, do Scyld and Beowulf and Baldr have to do with Christ? Nothing and everything! Scyld seems to inaugurate the heroic age as depicted in the poem and Beowulf to close it, but that age is rendered in an extensive if limited analogy with Hebrews of the Bible. Scyld, like Noah and Seth, Isaac, Moses and even the infant Christ in his escape to Egypt, represents the leader of a people especially favored by God. Like those Old Testament survivors of sacrifice, Scyld escapes sacrifice but fails to alter it. The monotheistic Danes continue to be haunted by *hæðen* monsters not coincidentally patrolling the heath ("hæð-stapa," 1368). Even after his death, Scyld's people continue to relapse into "hæðenra hyht" (179) and the specter of human immolation is everywhere present in the poem's dark reflection of it in the world of heathen monsters. But in the self-sacrificing king like Christ or (again, in a limited sense) Beowulf, there is a revelation of the sacrificial mechanism, that of a savior willing to die to protect his people. Like Christ, Beowulf is abandoned by the twelve retainers. Like Christ he dies in order to redeem a people. Here, though, all similarities end.

It is in the nature of sacrifice to demonize and deify by turns the sacred victim. Even as the poem celebrates Beowulf's glory, it is undermined by a strain of recriminations coming first from Wiglaf and then spreading throughout the people. A Girardian reading of the poem would be suspicious of attempts to blame the dead victim. At Beowulf's death, panic over future invasions is already beginning to mount. Wiglaf condemns the cowardice of the twelve retainers and suggests that they are responsible for the invasions to come; when their cowardice is known the enemies of the Geats will think them easy pickings. That is to say, with the death of Beowulf mimetic rivalry returns with a vengeance. The deep fissures within the Geatish society over the scandal of Beowulf's death are giving birth to a new sacrificial crisis, one that will demand new victims. They may already be present if only *in potentia*. The twelve horsemen who ride in ceremony around Beowulf's pyre and the Geatish woman with hair bound up ("Geatisc meolwe ... bundenheorde," 3150b–3151b) sound suspiciously like prospective victims.

4

The Hero, the Mad Male Id and a Feminist *Beowulf*: The Sexualizing of an Epic

E. L. RISDEN

Recent *Beowulf* films tend to exploit the popular notion of the dangers of sexuality. In Robert Zemeckis's film a gilded Grendel's Mother pursues men to father her children, and in Graham Baker's a shape-shifting she-lob also lures men to fatherhood at the cost of self and what little civilization remains to them. This essentially post–Freudian reading imposes new concerns on a nearly sexless epic: while the *Beowulf*-poet shows concerns with parenthood and the duties men and women have to families and associates, he or she has nothing to say about sexual desire as such. The insistent sexualization of *Beowulf* in film shows our obsessions, not the poet's; the films blend our personal and cultural obsessions and a love/hate relationship with adolescent sexuality to get a strange, hybrid medievalism, troubling over why we desire what we do. We may also contrast the titular *Beowulf* movies, which give sexuality and the exploitation of sexuality a central place in the motivation of characters' actions, with *No Such Thing* and *The 13th Warrior*: these films and some others juxtapose contemporary connections of feminism and cultural Othering with ideas of monstrosity and heroism. What if Grendel had lived into the present, removed to an isolated rock in Iceland, and become a jaded and hermetic drunk, and what if a cub reporter, working for the most cynical and pragmatic of editors, sought him because he had incinerated her explorer/ filmmaker boyfriend? We'd find a strange, postmodern love story of survival, quiet tenacity, and media-driven human monsters. What if a group of Norseman needed an additional member for their party to seek a murderous race of deadly cave-dwellers, and they found a remarkable Arab whom a sibyl identified as their mission companion, despite their vast differences in language and culture (and cleanliness)? The latter two films have sexual elements, but both films show sexuality as minimal aspects of other more pressing human concerns.

A golden, shapely, naked Grendel's Mother (with a whip ponytail!) who with her erotic power melts a would-be hero like adolescent goo: she and a sexually disappointed Wealhtheow linger near center stage in the 2007 *Beowulf*. A troll who impregnates, but then protects an abused sibyl with an American accent in the 2005 *Beowulf and Grendel*. A buff, blonde playboy bunny metamorphoses into a spidery man-crushing Monster-Mother in the 1999 *Beowulf*. A Romantic if not sexual tension between a glib, hard-drinking, fire-breathing monster and a cute, vulnerable, but brave young reporter sits quietly amidst *No Such Thing*. A tough, golden-haired Viking maiden medicates and then falls for the exotic Arab — no surprise in what seems the doomed world of *The 13th Warrior* — but a significant contrast with the stringy but murderous Monster-Mother whose poisoned scratch kills the Norse leader. In all these examples of sexualized revisions of the *Beowulf* story, filmmakers must either assume they have no audience for traditional, heroic adventure stories without the addition of sex, or they bring their own sexual tensions to the story, or they find sexuality so unavoidably embedded in all human experience that they can't image a story without it. So in the name of innovation we have brought to cinematic *Beowulf*s, along with a comic-bookish martial arts element nearly absent from the poem, a suspicion that men can never go long without dwelling on it and women can never avoid using it to acquire such power as they can and may. Sex refigures *Beowulf* entirely: we get not the epic with its ideals of heroism, loyalty, and personal accomplishment balanced with martial service and self-sacrifice, but exoticisization and titillation that reshapes the story as fable largely about the problems of male sex-drive.

In *A League of Their Own*, Manager Jimmy Dugan, played by Tom Hanks, tells a tearful player, whom he has just chewed out for missing a cut-off throw, "There's no crying in baseball!" If Dugan had thought about it — though probably not just at that moment — he might have added later, "There's no sex in *Beowulf*!" Or at least we can say there's very little sex in *Beowulf*, certainly not enough to foreground it in any version of a story one may honestly call *Beowulf*. The poem suggests the tensions between familial relationships by blood and those by marriage, for instance in the story of Hildeburh and the blood vengeance her brothers take against her husband and his family (including her children). It also clarifies, though, in Grendel's Mother, that a female attacker can be even more dangerous than a male; she may have a little less strength — as much less as a weaponed female warrior than a male, species the poet, which is clearer not much less — but she may have more cunning, courage, and determination to make up the difference. Yet in cinema sexuality creeps in where warriors were wont to tread, fogging the themes and concerns of the story, hardly on little cat feet, probably because in this age of the world, with all our obsessions and compulsions, we simply can't keep it out. It comprises not merely one small vector that that rounds a character into sympathetic realism; rather, it controls films like a dominatrix with a willing client, one who returns again and again for the same treatment, perhaps without knowing he may choose reasonable alternatives. *Beowulf* in film tends in this respect to move toward Freudian rather than Marxist fetishes.

Beowulf the poem has, on its own, remarkable cinematic qualities of landscape, fully visualizable monster battles, and personal and political tensions within and between characters, but it supplies only light sexual tension (PG 13 at most, unless we consider the potentially sexual violence of Grendel's Mother sitting on Beowulf sufficient to up the rating to R). Reading the poem for *gender* rather than *sexual* issues, one can call attention to Wealhþeow and Freawaru, the proud and petulant Modþryðo/Þryð and Higd: Beowulf may hold a little candle for them (with the exception of Þryð), though he does nothing about it. Before the Grendel battle, the poet does say that Hroðgar rises from the drinking hall to seek Wealhþeow, eager to go to bed with his queen: that's about as explicitly sexual as things get. Or as some critics have done, in a silly Freudian way, we may consider the fact that the magic sword Beowulf uses to fight Grendel's Mother melts after he cuts off her head with it. But then her head is hardly her maidenhead — she has already birthed a monster — and a real fight to the death seldom ends in what Victorians called the "little death," at least for participants (I don't know what happens among pay-per-view event audiences), not to mention that though for us any long, straight object may suggest a phallus, we have no reason to belief it did so for Anglo-Saxons. The persistent perceiver of epic peccadilloes should note, too, that Grendel's Mother may "sit on" Beowulf before he beheads her, but Fred Robinson disputes that point: he believes "set upon" better translates *ofsæt* than does "sat upon," thus relieving, perhaps, the sexual suggestion. And if Higd, following her husband Hygelac's death, is too forward in suggesting Beowulf marry her, we can forgive her for hoping to stabilize her country by establishing an even more heroic king in her husband's place and saving her young sons the inevitable challenge to the throne (made by outsiders, not by Beowulf, and, sadly, successfully).

If I were to insist on the sexually intimate rather than the martially intimate reading of *Beowulf,* I wouldn't be the first to accuse the *Beowulf*-poet of puns — see particularly Raymond Tripp's work: he finds a pun in about every third line. The perhaps too-old-for-her Hroðgar shuffles off to the marriage-bed with the perhaps too-young-for-him Wealhþeow while his retainers wait in danger of mortal attack and monstrous ingestion. The action may come across as unsuitably libidinous in light of the king's martial impotence or properly kingly for a people not so interested as we in trying to make everyone look and feel equal. Hildeburh's brothers returning home with their sister after her blameless failure as peace-weaver suggests the shortcomings of sex and marriage to knit feuding families who would much rather make war than love. Freawaru, similarly, will probably not succeed either, Beowulf suggests to Hygelac, through no fault of her own: she can be an excellent daughter, sister, and wife and still not keep husband from attacking brothers. Grendel's Mother in a sense follows the law in killing one Dane in vengeance for her son, but that doesn't free her from becoming the object of their subsequent blood vengeance: she still kills brutally, regardless of her attracting greater sympathy than her indiscriminate son. Those examples all raise interesting gender issues, but sexually they remain pretty minimal, hardly enough to move an audience to read sexuality too insistently into the story. Such tepid references hardly account for the salacious tastes of either contemporary filmmakers or the audiences they nominally seek please. Why, then, do we seem to need cinematic enhancement? Apparently in film we can't resist the lure of *sang-chaud*; the process or culture of film-making drags with it a sexual component sufficient to impose itself on any material. Violence alone doesn't raise the blood sufficiently.

Perhaps a post–Freud, or post–Hugh Hefner, or post–Erica Jong age can't avoid sexualizing texts of all sorts: one need not read sex "into" the Romantics, Jack Donne, e.e. cummings, Christina Rossetti, or Walter Benton, since attention to metaphor or proper use of the voice can do it. I don't know if William Carlos Williams felt relief after stealing his wife's plums, or if Adrienne Rich got a sense of cleansing or of revenge after rethinking and rewriting "A Valediction, Forbidding Mourning" in her own way. Perhaps Coleridge felt a bit lighter in the loins after the ecstatic explosions of "Kubla Khan." In our time the self-consciously ironic move comes to define all our interactions: every interaction oozes innuendo. But the persistent cinematic attention to sex turns *Beowulf* into a different kind of story, changing themes, layerings, and general affect (as well as effects), essentially cutting it off from its traditional epic seriousness. Instead of its original context of epic/Germanic heroism, filmmakers have replanted *Beowulf* in a field of contemporary cultural criticism and race/gender politics replete with cynicism and dis-eased sexuality thoroughly anachronistic with respect to the original.

For the remainder of this chapter I will briefly consider the sexual enhancement of the story in five movies: Robert Zemeckis' *Beowulf* (2007), Sturla

Gunnarsson's *Beowulf and Grendel* (2005), John McTiernan and Michael Crichton's *The 13th Warrior* (1999), Graham Baker's *Beowulf* (1999), and Hal Hartley's *No Such Thing* (2001). I don't know, finally, whether the sexualizing of *Beowulf* comes from filmmaker's obsessions, audiences' obsessions, latent erotic tensions in the text that only our time has dared (or felt able) to unearth, or cinema's immitigable sexual drift, but I think I can say that in the case of each film it shifts the weight of the story from a praise and critique of what J. R. R. Tolkien called the "Germanic theory of courage" to a critique of male libido and female power.

Women Are Monsters, and Men Are Worse *(Beowulf 2007)*

This most recent *Beowulf* movie focuses more than anything else on its medium, the performance capture technology; it appears to me to be "about" how to maximize the visual effects of that technology to depict adventures. But it does have a strong thematic point to make, though one that doesn't inhabit the epic. By making Grendel the son of Hrothgar and the dragon the son of Beowulf, both begotten upon a stunning, seductive, powerful, and perhaps immortal female of uncertain origins, the filmmakers turn our attention to especially current and in their way *pc* topics: men can't control their libido, especially when they gain some sort of power through indulging it, and women shouldn't do so, because men will become fully subordinate to strong females. Both powerful men in the story, Hrothgar and Beowulf, decline morally and physically and place their folk in danger after their sexual dalliance: they create more powerful, more monstrous, and less scrupulous versions of themselves (what Wiglaf will do after the end of the narrative we see we may only speculate). Beowulf's son by the She-Monster has greater beauty and power because he has better genetic material to give. The men gain through extramarital sex a talisman of their rule—a golden drinking horn that sits on a dragon-shape—but that rule belongs not fully to them. Rather, it attends a shadow of themselves. To the degree she wants it, the female monster with whom they have consorted and her offspring have acquired the best part of their strength, departed with her use of their seed and their use of the talisman. Beowulf shows a strong attraction to Wealhtheow as soon as he sees her, but even subsequent marriage to her does not allow him to retain or regain his sexual strength once he has exerted it inappropriately; Hrothgar, too, falls into physical dilapidation despite the affections of his young and beautiful wife. Monstrous human weakness follows an encounter with true monstrous strength.

After Beowulf's death, Grendel's Mother prepares to seduce Wiglaf and pass along that talisman to him. Just as in the epic and as his name implies, Wiglaf, "Battle-leavings," remains behind and has acquired some level of power. Now the "leftover" appears ready to submit, as have those before him, to the she-monster's charms. Grendel's Mother shows the men she can do as she pleases, and her chief desire seems to be to produce powerful heirs sufficient to cow and subdue her consorts: she joys less in the liaisons, one suspects, than in her ability to show her sexual productivity and superior vitality. So, men, the film warns, beware your weakness; women, beware men's weakness, but don't let it keep you from preparing to exploit your power over them. The idea to use this story to express the evils of the male libido came perhaps from the earlier *Beowulf* film, Graham Baker's of 1999, which indulges a male taste for sexy females even as it urges the problematic nature of that taste. Sexy women can have strength, wisdom, and attitude (Wealhtheow or Kyra), or they may prove monstrous (Grendel's Mother), but men will seldom if ever have the strength to show temperate respect for them and to keep a safe and proper distance.

While sexual urge doesn't entirely drive the 2007 film, it plays an important part; our next film, while it does not avoid issues of sexual and gender-related power, tunes toward a different but equally prevalent contemporary theme: the problem of racial difference and Othering.

Troll the Ancient Yuletide Sibyl (*Beowulf and Grendel*)

Sturla Gunnarsson's film focuses thematically more on racism than on sexuality, but sex enters the picture as a possible means of crossing racial boundaries and repairing racism as a social rift. The Danes have killed the father of a local boy-troll, Grendel, simply because he once crossed their path and they don't like trolls. The boy grows up strong and fast and seeks vengeance, and Beowulf comes from across the sea to defend the king and his folk against further attacks. Beowulf learns, though, that the monster isn't necessarily a bad fellow: he kills only those he believes responsible for his father's death — the hero thus falls into a moral conundrum about the Danes' right to vengeance. During one of Grendel's assaults,[1] Beowulf manages to rope him by the shoulder, and Grendel brings about his own death by cutting himself free at the shoulder-joint — the scene implies that while Beowulf has the courage, he hasn't the strength to defeat Grendel himself. The Mother, a *mere-wif*, who had nearly pulled Beowulf into the depths when he arrived at the Danish coast, attacks in return with more brutality and less restraint than her son. She, unlike her son, isn't a particularly good fellow, blithely killing the priest whom her son simply ignores. The hero must pursue her to her lair and kill her — she does sit on him, but his sword doesn't dissolve at the death-stroke.

Sexual concerns don't drive this film, but they do add to the sense of human male vulnerability to balance the traditional notion of the vulnerable female. Gender-based power issues play a greater part: Grendel's Mother is nastier than Grendel and more dangerous — more willing to act violently — and one wonders how she managed to get Grendel's father to beget her son. We also have a hint of the Christian/pagan questions that trouble the poem: the Danes are on the verge of converting to Christianity. Whether conversion will improve their habits the film doesn't clarify.

This movie includes two sex scenes, juxtaposed. The local sibyl, Selma, hardly more than a girl, explains to Beowulf that Hrothgar's father had brought her there as an unwilling concubine, and the men had horribly abused her. One night Grendel had come sniffing about and, finding her "in heat," had impregnated her. While she is unwilling, she has received that kind of treatment from men before: the Danes have treated her worse yet. She has a son by Grendel, whom she tries to conceal for his safety. Grendel, rather embarrassed than exploitative, has never taken her sexually again. Instead, he has since then protected her against further sexual violence by the Danes, so that they may never again force her, either. After telling Beowulf her story, the sibyl jumps him, straddles him in Grendel's-Mother-attack-style, and the movie's second sex scene occurs. Both scenes are brief — sibyls are strong, and men (heroes or trolls) are weak — and they provide another means of equating hero and monster and of troubling the question of who does right and who does wrong. From the Danish point of view, but not the Geatish, Grendel does wrong simply because he's a troll, not a man, though trolls have their own bit of magic and can, according to Norse tradition, strengthen the blood of human families. Sex occurs at the borders of human behavior, at the social limits that mark our animal nature, where we meet one another as like or turn ourselves into "other."

Beowulf as foreign hero and Grendel as local troll fill the roll of Other similarly: their difference, strength, and sexual experiences place them at the margins of human culture. Beowulf briefly "replaces" Grendel as Selma's lover, and he treats Grendel's son avuncularly, building a stone monument in honor of the dead troll and telling Grendel's son to "be proud" of his blood. We have moved far from the epic: though the poem ends with the declaration that Beowulf was the kindest, gentlest, and most eager for praise (or to give praise) among men, the poet would hardly have imagined a hero departing for home having gained compassion and respect for a monster and its kin. But the Grendel of *Beowulf and Grendel* is far from the monster of the poem: he seeks to harm no one but those who killed his father, and unlike the Grendel of Gardner's novel, while he may still act monstrously, he gains more sympathy than any other male in the story. "Others" want sex, too — how will they get it? Human men, we learn, are weak, exploitative, murderous, intemperate: they, more than anyone else in this text, make themselves Other.

*Dark Stranger, Buxom Blonde, and Witch-Mother: Lucky Thirteen (*The 13th Warrior*)*

This film, like *Beowulf and Grendel,* focuses more on the value of crossing racial boundaries to help solve problems: we not only should, but must work together with persons of different backgrounds and religions, *The 13th Warrior* teaches us, to defeat horrible foes. Those foes exist in fact, though they may for a time remain dormant with respect to human populations, or they may attack with no warning. They also represent the primitive part of ourselves that, having sheltered itself from the differences in the wide world, potentially becomes monstrous when it must face cultural and racial differences. Sexuality has its impact here in two ways: to confirm the success of the mutual male endeavor in battle and to propose that the ancient Mother Goddess may have cast her power more as figure of terror than of healthy fertility — again we see female power as suspect, and we must ask what we want both male and female strength to accomplish.

The Mother of the Wendol (Claire Lapinski) in *The 13th Warrior* (1999).

Ahmed Ibn Fahdlan finds his romantic interest unexpectedly: the brave and beautiful Olga tends his wounds and even chastises him for making sounds of pain when she treats him. She warns him not to resist her washing the wounds with cow's urine, which apparently has antibacterial properties. They make love not so much as the Arab's reward for joining the Norse band in their adventure as for mutual comfort in a time of war when mortality likely accompanies the next battle. Ahmed does not depart for home with the woman — apparently neither she nor he had a permanent relationship in mind — but the brief encounter means more to both than a Dark-Ages version of a one-nighter: it represents a bond in times of terror fraught with the necessity for heroism and for accepting what life offers as it passes too quickly for one to seize upon it. In no way exploitative, the brief love scene, more a hint than a scene, has in it ripples of the cinematic clichés of coming of age and the protagonist's obligatory love interest. But it deepens the sense of the characters' participation in the events of defending a people from an almost invincible enemy. The fact that he is Arab and she Nordic seems to affect no one particularly: they have become comrades in the attempt to save a people from an enemy more dangerous and more thoroughly Other.

That enemy, led until her death by a mother/guardian/shaman, meets its defeat at the hands of the brave defenders of the weak, but the primitive cave-queen administers the death wound of the Norse leader, Bullvie (the name serves as an attempt to recover from Crichton's bad anagram for Beowulf in the novel). Their patriarchal-matriarchal battle of Norsemen versus Wendol represents a struggle for power between the female-led primitives and the male-led defenders of civilization — one can hardly call it *civilization*, but at least the Norse represent humans moving toward human-ness and away from beast-liness. Bullvie kills her on the spot of their battle, but her poison kills him slowly: the infection of the female cuts short the barely post-adolescent life of the hero. Bullvie has just learned from Ahmed the first rudiments of reading, symbolizing that he has had little time to live an adult life: if the dangerous woman, who represents the fertility of the "Other," must die, she will take the best of her enemies with her, so that her reproductive loss is his as well. While the other Norsemen have courage, camaraderie, and martial skill, they lack the quiet attention and brainpower that distinguished their now-dead leader. How will they manage without him? The story doesn't say, other than that they remain generations away from monotheism. They have shown, though, a willingness to learn, to appreciate and value Others, and to persist in indomitable courage — lessons not so different than those the poem teaches. The Witch-Mother (though she is no Angelina Jolie) also has power, courage, and commitment to her people: they lose because they pursue isolation and destruction of Others rather than integration and mutual assistance.

Spiders Are Sexier Than You Think, but They Can't Beat a Princess in a Corset (Beowulf *1999*)

This film exploits comic-book sexuality more than do any of the others: it features three "babes," each of whom represents an aspect of feminine allure that compels the hero to action. As the movie begins a sexy young women, escaped from the castle that houses Grendel and his mother along with a collection of beleaguered heroes, is about to get sacrificed by the "outsiders," villagers who fear and loathe the castle's inhabitants. The hero, a Beowulf more reminiscent of Mad Max and Sting than the epic Geat, saves her, but rather than return to the castle with him she leaps off his horse and runs to her captors for quick execution — they happily oblige.

Beowulf pursues his quest for monsters into the castle and receives only a mixed welcome. He meets the second babe, Kyra, Hrothgar's daughter, and establishes with her a sexual chemistry while hinting that he is something different than the usual man, something more akin to monsters than to humans: he fights monsters partly to keep his own monstrous nature at bay.[2] After a selection of silly lines, gymnastic leaps, and flashy weapons, Beowulf kills Grendel, as in the 2007 *Beowulf* the shadowy son of the unfaithful king and the resident she-monster. Beowulf must now kill the mother as well: the third babe, she turns from hardy, muscular blonde bombshell to grotesque hard-shelled crab, a many-legged fighting machine much more vicious than her son — the transformation dissolves any remnant of the serial sexual tension that arises in her brief dialogue with the hero. Beowulf, who has proclaimed himself a thing of darkness who fights evil to avoid becoming evil himself, a man who has no place (and who therefore can have no family), then destroys the final monster, freeing the area of its natives for whoever remaining has any lingering interest in inhabiting it. He then leaves the castle with babe one, the bodacious, leather-bodiced daughter of the king: his chastity with respect to the Bunny/Monster brings an unexpected sexual reward in the form of the more beautiful, non-metamorphic princess. Essentially a laughable piece of cinematic dreck, this *Beowulf* does at least have a point: if you move to a new neighborhood, don't screw the old residents out of their homes — or in yours — or you'll pay the price in blood-feud; resist evil yourself and you may win a desirable reward that can subdue your own monstrous nature without depriving you of strength. The film's theme blends the twentieth century's love and fear of the male libido with its love and fear of colonization; it suggests pretty clearly that we can and should control the former, but we ought to avoid the latter — no real surprise there, with both the century and the millennium running their course.

How to Love the Monster Who Killed Your Boyfriend *(*No Such Thing*)*

No Such Thing flies under the critical radar as a version of *Beowulf*, but in many ways it fulfills that purpose better than do any of the other films, and it does so while usefully refiguring plot, place, and time. However, the movie maintains the idea of a kind of likeness or natural draw between hero and monster, though in this case, unlike the other movies we've explored, the draw comes more from sympathy than from sexuality: gender and kindness rather than libido and physical strength rule here. While the film raises many interesting points about gender, the lack of sexualizing may actually give interested film goers some relief from what has become the typical pattern of *Beowulf* movies.

The young female reporter takes the role of hero: she travels all the way to a remote rock in Iceland to investigate the immortal monster, born in the dawn of time, who killed her boyfriend. Having survived a plane crash and a harrowing operation to allow her to recover he mobility, she has no fear left, confronts the Monster alone (with help from the locals who get her drunk and leave her naked on his doorstep) and, after he has promised to do no more harm, brings him back to New York for media interviews and public displays. She gains fame and indulges herself, briefly, with a boy-toy sex buddy while the monster suffers media abuse and personal ignominy. There we find the only strong sexual hints in this version of the story: Beatrice allows herself a long night of meaningless shagging as a reward for her "capturing" the monster, but she realizes afterwards that not only has she found the experience meaningless and spiritually unsatisfying, but it also has shown her own innate tendency toward selfishness: a trait which she has not shown before and which she won't show again. Having exploited her success, she abandons both the exploitation and the idea that she herself has had a success. Her concern turns from herself to the Monster.

Because of her honest sympathy for the Monster, and because she quickly tires of the frivolous public life, she helps him to escape and to locate an infamous Dr. Artaud, who has a magical machine that can relieve the monster of his burdensome immortality. On the ship home, the monster laments that no one fears him anymore. Beatrice gently lays her head on his shoulder and says, "I do." "Yeah?" he responds, hopefully but uncertainly. The moment resists sexuality and sentimentality, suggesting instead compassion and even a kind of love — one feels almost silly at any sexual fears the circumstances may have provoked. When Beatrice awakes in the Monster's lair, he explains that the locals sometimes leave alcohol and a "piece of ass" for him, hoping thereby to keep him away from them. Because of his power and the condition of Beatrice when he finds her, the Monster could do anything to her that he wanted. But he feels more disgust at humanity than humans can possibly feel toward him, moving the tension from the sexual abruptly to the matter of life and death: will he kill Beatrice or not. While she doesn't fear him or death, he could kill her, and we don't want that to happen. We want what Beatrice wants: to know who he is and why he does what he does.

No Such Thing is finally the most sexually frightening but least sexual movie of the five I've discussed: what if a naturally loving character were to develop an attraction to a *real monster* (as, for example, in *Dracula*)? It hints at sexual potential, but it hinges instead on sorrow. Beatrice has sought the Monster because of the loss of her beloved; the Monster, being the only of his kind, can have no beloved: never has and never will. Gender comes into play as part of the tableau of loneliness that marks this film: it creates expectations of character and behavior, each of which it dissolves, leaving us on the bare edge of one creature interacting with another: can that interaction still the immense tide of the loneliness of sentient experience, even for a bit, or must it always turn us toward destruction of Other or of self as we descend into our obsessions and our fears? *No Such Thing* observes that gender has nothing to do with heroism or monstrosity: they hinge instead on earned courage or compassionless exploitation.

Perhaps the visual medium, the cultural and economic need for gender balance, assumptions about the puerile nature of film audiences or of early epics, increasing freedom from moral censorship, and the elliptical power of suggestion whispering from the narrative and lexical folds of the poem all contribute to the sexualizing of *Beowulf*. Perhaps it comes from our increased attention to the common and usually regrettable process of *othering*, from a remnant fascination with miscegenation. Perhaps it comes from a cultural fear of homosexuality: the possibly celibate hero of the epic must become a virile, sexuality active hero to assure us he has appropriate masculine drives. But in the films I've discussed here it seems to me to come most powerfully from a persistent embarrassment at male sexuality and a persistent fear of female power. The viewer concludes all of the films with a heightened sense of isolation rather than intimacy, of anxiety rather than relief—whatever catharsis the epic may provide, film resists it. But then if we really want a story of the dangers of self-indulgence, we can always go home and pop in a DVD of *The Godfather*, or if we prefer the absurdities of sexual frivolity, we can catch old episodes of *The Girls Next Door*.

5

O Dragon, Where Art Thou? "Othering" in *Beowulf* Films

E. L. RISDEN

No Such Thing questions the whole notion of Othering that has come to play such an important part in *Beowulf* films: what if we humans are *more* monster than the Monster? Monster, monstrosity, or the monstrous typically implies a shocking, horrible, or vicious abnormality or deviation from the norm (i.e., something frighteningly different from "us"), but the anti-hero trope has also initiated a move toward the anti-monster: instead of something to shun, the *grotesque*, the item or being in the metamorphic middleground, not one thing or another thing, but a troubling combination of non-synchronic elements, draws sympathy beyond that available to the normal. *Beowulf* films have taken to examining that move both in narrative and in character, which leads also to a shift in thematic concerns: the purpose of the monsters in the epic is to provide heroic motivation, while in recent film they serve instead to test our readiness to fall into chauvinism and stereotyping.

Monsters in the epic are thoroughly and clearly monstrous. Grendel and his mother may derive from the kin of Cain, the first murderer, therefore murderous themselves, and the dragon may have been born a dragon or may have metamorphosed into one, but by the time we meet them in the story, they have become indelibly monstrous, othered not by humans afraid of miscegenation but by their own difference in nature and in their ferocity. *Berserkrs*, "bear-shirts," men in Norse tradition who presumably shifted shape into bear form to gain greater strength, speed, and tenacity in battle, returned after battle to their own human shape, monstrous for a time, but human in origin and human at last. So beasts needn't have had "wholly Other" natures, but monsters had shed the remnant capacity for human feeling: neither Grendel nor the dragon has any compunction about munching, crunching, or annihilating humans.

Derived from Michael Crichton's *Eaters of the Dead*, *The 13th Warrior* envisions the dragon as a phalanx of fire-carrying proto-humans (or perhaps even Neanderthals), exemplifying a cinematic tendency to "realize" the idea of monstrosity even as cinema struggles with our persistent cultural tendency to problematize "outsiders." Crichton sees the "monster" as an earlier version of ourselves, one at once more solitary and more dangerous; we may also see it as something human-like, but not quite human. The Other acquires more sympathy as it becomes more like us — or at least as it displays the traits we think "human" in ourselves: love, loyalty, self-awareness, particularly in instances of what we perceive as undeserved suffering. One may also call this process "Of Trolls and Men," since such films as *Beowulf and Grendel* (2005) similarly raise the particular specter of racism: how willingly will those of one race consider those of another to be like them? The hero of *Beowulf and Grendel* takes on the problem of race more than he grapples with a specific and evil monster: Grendel, still emotionally a troll child, seeks only to avenge his father, murdered by men, and to maintain a place for himself if no longer for his race in the world. The film rewrites Gardner's novel more so than it does the epic original, and it especially exploits the anti-hero tradition to re-imagine causes for why we so persistently label and exclude rather than making peace with and integrating Others. The hero, Beowulf, may well end up just as Other as Grendel; he saves himself with respect to audience sympathy by learning to see Grendel as like himself— perhaps in some ways better than himself— rather than as Other.

The tension of the whole notion of monstrosity extends beyond concern with trolls. They look and act at least a bit like us. What about more distant and more powerful monsters? In his famous *Beowulf* essay J. R. R. Tolkien reminds us how few good dragons the European Middle Ages actually gave us, yet contemporary filmmakers have developed a fascination with medievalized dragons, evidenced recently, for instance, by the new Dreamworks children's animated movie about how to train your own. Medieval authors saw dragons as either naturally occurring phenomena or as the result of metamorphoses: men could turn into dragons if they gave in to greed and bloodletting. Cotton Vitellius A.xv, the same Anglo-Saxon manuscript that includes *Beowulf*, also includes a list of maxims, one of which explains that, just as a mast belongs on a ship or a sword lies across a soldier's lap, so a dragon lies in its barrow, jealous of its treasures. If other medieval authors lacked a definitive or convincing approach to dragons, linking them allegorically to violent possessiveness or symbolically to Satan, contemporary cinema casts a greater yet dispersion, as dragons have appeared as anything from our pets to our violent neighbors to our illegitimate children.[1] Given the powerful presence of the *Beowulf*-dragon, perhaps the most dragonish of dragons in our early literature, we might have expected films based on the epic to exploit it particularly. But *Beowulf*-derived movies — when they incorporate a dragon at all — have turned the beast from its most typical medieval representation of greed, reptilian horror, and infernal flame into a means of social commentary. Instead of taking advantage of the beast they find so prominent and dominant in the source, they have re-focused the notion of "monster" within the realm of cultural criticism, highlighting the response of an "othered," non-dominant group or race to the rising power of people emerging into dominance, or they have focused on a child "othered" by its illegitimacy. The dragon as dragon fades from view, and the "enemy" rises from the abused and repressed, foregrounding once again the question of whom we call *hero* and whom we call *monster*.

In *Beowulf* films the dragon as Other acquires a degree of audience sympathy, though neither audience nor filmmaker would send a neighborhood delegation to welcome it to the house next door. As Nick Haydock explains in *Movie Medievalism*, film has reduced the Other to the other (28), from dragon, wholly other in the infernal sense, to what humans see as sub-human, vaguely related, monstrous, but not Monster. As cinema has reduced the dragon, so has it reduced the hero, redirecting the desires of both: the dragon may simply be protecting its mother's territory, and the hero may be intruding in quarrels beyond his wisdom. Jacques Lacan links the understanding of desire to the understanding of the Other: we may, as in cinema or in some religious experience, desire the desire of the Other — such desire may prove healthy or not.[2] In his quest for *lof* and *dom*, Beowulf has acquired the idealized desire of his culture, the aims of the hero, to attain immortality through praise and glory. But the epic also presents monstrous desire, the desire of an opposite–Other rather than a like–Other, and to remain heroic Beowulf must reject that desire. The hero may desire to defeat his enemies; he may even harry for treasure; but he does not seek blood or material wealth for its own sake, nor does he eat those he defeats. So the epic World-of-the-Text provides both positive and negative examples of Other and desire. Cinematic *Beowulf*, unsettled by fear of racism and disbelief in fully moral heroes, translates the presence of *Other* into something at least potentially rationally desirable, something in its way both dignified and sympathetic, if archeologically bloodthirsty and always dangerous, especially to the imperialistic and unwary. The "Monsters" of film become the displaced, the rejected, the physically or genetically different.

The idea of Monstrosity has nearly as much importance here as does the Other, since the films play equally with both. As Robert and Karin Olsen define them,

> Monsters are ... the tangible representations of this past or persistent otherness ... imaginary, strange or marvelous creatures in combinations that seem almost limitless.... [T]eratological treatises and taxonomies of the monstrous abound.... [F]ictional monstrosities may be demons, humans, animals, or even inanimate objects [6].

Notions of other and monster join in the realm of the *fantastic*, in the *grotesque*: creatures of nature, with respect to the defining source of social power they come from and return to in regions of chaos and disorder. Monsters live in the midst of metamorphosis, between worlds, which makes them part *same* and part *other*. No wonder dragons, more *other* than *same*, have faded while Grendels, more *same* than *other*, have risen in narrative importance.

The medieval dragon, as in the case of the *Beowulf* dragon, fiercely avenges even the tiniest threat to its treasure: the dragon wakes at the theft of a single cup from its hoard, it destroys a nearby village, and it isn't likely to return to sleep until it has sated its desire for vengeance on many more lives. It resembles humans only at our worst, when we forget generosity, hoard, and keep treasures for the joy of the keeping rather than for the social value of giving. The man-dragon Fafnir of *Volsungasaga* has killed his father to acquire his treasure and so has disinherited his brother; he has thereby lost his humanity both in qualities and in shape and has become the worst of monsters, most dangerous because even the nearest of kin can't trust him. He has othered himself. Medievalismic *othering* comes often from a contemporary centralizing of racial concerns and a marginalizing of traditional notions of heroes, particularly with respect to how these issues inflect (or disenfranchise) cinematic, Beowulfian dragons.

We may note, for instance, the response to the *Lord of the Rings* films by some critics who had (perhaps) seen the films but who had not read the text: they saw (or wanted to see) racism in the depiction, for instance, of orcs. No one whom I heard or read made similar comments about ents, who can bring about even more destruction, probably because they love trees and protect the forest: they stand for environmental sensitivity and the living, breathing mobility of the natural world. From the voices of the orcs we would identify them as English, if perhaps English of lower classes rather than those who use Received Pronunciation. The orcs are debased forms of elves as ents represent the uncorrupted form of trolls. The dragons that appear in *The Hobbit* and *The Silmarillion* are as dragonish as any creatures one can find, though among them Smaug emerges as the most well-spoken (and, while not *easy*, the *easiest* to kill). Film medievalism, though, has not made such creatures integral if distorted parts of the natural world: it has partially de-monstered the monsters to use them as means to the current preferences in cultural criticism. It has mixed modes, not necessarily unproductively, from epic to fairy tale to comic book to comedy.

Hartley's *No Such Thing*, a free blending of *Beowulf* with the "Beauty and the Beast" fairy tale, fits satirically in a contemporary or even slightly future world; it omits the dragon as dragon, focusing instead on the Grendel-type monster, in this case a jaded, misanthropic, alcoholic cross between a sodden, wise-cracking musketeer and an especially knotty ironwood tree. He speaks good if mean-spirited American English, but he has also acquired at least one element of the dragon: he can breathe murderous fire. In this film one monster proves enough: the conflation of Grendel and the dragon allows for a story that instead of pursuing a traditional notion of heroism develops a friendship between a mousy human and an occasionally murderous but mostly solitary, solipsistic, glib one-of-a-species beast who hates both himself and the world.

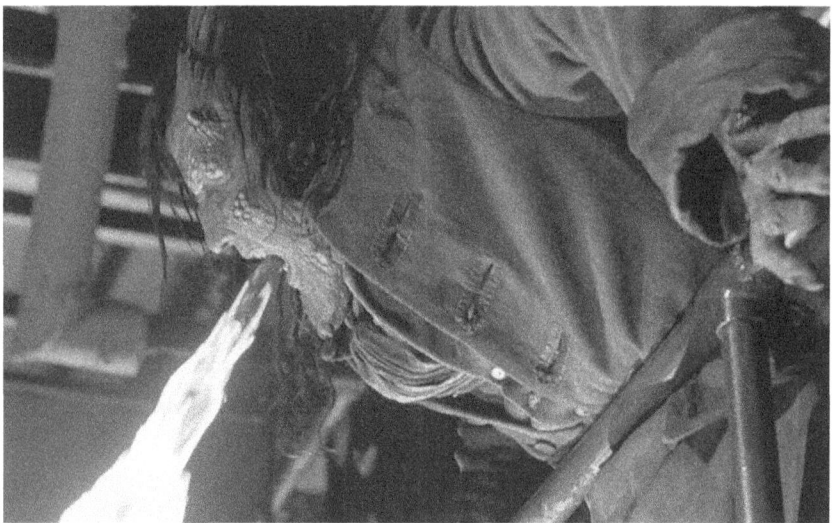

The dragon-troll (Robert John Burke) in *No Such Thing* (dir. Hal Hartley, 2001).

Something like Tolkien's Smaug in his talkativeness and the Old Norse Fafnir in his cynical destructiveness, the Monster incorporates draconic elements, but he has no possessiveness — the great sin of the medieval dragon — whatever. If humans were to keep quiet and leave him alone, he would be less troublesome than even Chrysophylax of Tolkien's tale *Farmer Giles of Ham*, though both stories play with ideas of heroic and draconic behavior. Hartley's Monster simply wants to escape a life that has lasted too long and that has got too noisy with insipid humans and their gadgetry, so that he can no longer find any rest. He kills humans not because they have burgled his treasure, but because they have robbed him of peace and quiet, and he wants nothing but freedom from his own suffering — something the Beowulf-replacement reporter sympathetically helps him accomplish, perhaps at the expense of her concurrent demise. The Monster begins as a potentially dangerous Other because of his murderousness, but he becomes a sympathetic Other because finally he produces less disgust than the even nastier, less thoughtful, less sympathetic humans who would exploit, revile, and discard him — *Beowulf*'s dragon could gain no such sympathy. The film addresses not racism, but a perspective to critique the horrors of one's own race and culture: we need no dragons because our mass culture has become more selfish and destructive than any Monster, more grotesque than any dragon. We may have Grendels lurking at the fringes of our world, but we have out-grendeled them with our own heartlessness and rapacity.

Adapted from Michael Crichton's *Eaters of the Dead*, John McTiernan's *The 13th Warrior* envisions the dragon as a phalanx of fire-carrying Neanderthal-types, exemplifying a cinematic tendency to "realize" the idea of monstrosity even as cinema struggles with the persistent cultural tendency to problematize "outsiders." The Wendol, as Crichton calls them, probably deriving the name from *Grendel*, represent either a competing species or an earlier, scarier, deadlier version of humans. While they may keep to themselves, they may also attack, kidnap, and consume people: they confront us directly with our most nightmarish worries about ourselves, our genetic heritage, our flirtations with cannibalism, and our buried cultural past. They *are* the bogies who come in the night to snatch and eat us. The film powerfully re-embodies the dragon principle — the natural/supernatural enemy — as a terrifying, ruthless, streaming humanoid attack, Other but not wholly other in its mythical, animalistic ferocity: human nature red in tooth and claw. The Norse folk, savage as well, must eliminate an even more savage version of themselves; they have reached a brink of civilization and wish to move toward it, while the Wendol have no interest in it.

With the help of the exotic Arab-Other, Ahmed Ibn Fahdlan, they destroy that unbearable and nearly unnamable past to make room for their (one hopes) cleanlier and less violent future. The Arab must use his adventures in the North to cleanse his own past as the Norsemen must cleanse their culture of rapacity and "paganism." The Wendol suggest only partly, I think, the racist destruction of another people; more exactly they represent a proto-racist cleansing of the past of one's own race. They do, however, have a matriarchal culture, and the story suggests they inhabited the land in question before the Norsemen came there: the hint of patriarchal imperialism remains, though not sufficiently to turn one's sympathies to the pre-civilization, pre-human versions of ourselves that we'd prefer to deny.

The introduction of an Arab hero-protagonist also has social (and political) purpose, much like what we see in *Kingdom of Heaven*: the Arab characters have a cleanlier, more orderly, more forgiving and inclusive civilization than their Christian attackers. The Arab brings to his Norse company a different and invaluable kind of knowledge and wisdom, athleticism, kindness, and devotion: that need not only *him*, but the skills and values he can bring to them to complete their quest. Western audiences must see him as the anti-terrorist, the brave and sensitive peacemaker — in a sense the male version of the Anglo-Saxon *freoðu-webbe*, "peace-weaver." The character asks Westerners to abandon stereotypes of Middle-eastern men and see them as friends, colleagues, equals — if not, often, rather better than our equals. Medieval Arabic culture gave the world greater advancements in mathematics, medicine, learning and perhaps culture generally than did the West. He goes from other to friend and trusted colleague; the Wendol, dressed in skins and animal teeth, remain thoroughly Other — we must embrace the human other, but extract the inhumane other from ourselves.

One may also call this process of refiguring epic notions of the monstrous "Of Trolls and Men," and other *Beowulf*-derived films, such as *Beowulf and Grendel* (2005), deal with it similarly but explicitly to raise the particular specter of racism. They tend to eliminate objective monsters such as dragons (one may compare, of course, Tolkien's *Farmer Giles of Ham*). The hero in this film takes on, without knowing it, the problem of race and racism more than he does a battle with a specific monster: Grendel, a troll child, grows up alone and seeks only to avenge his father, murdered by Hrothgar's men. He has probably come along too late to maintain a place for himself and his race in a world busied by the expansion of human outposts. The film, rewriting John Gardner's novel *Grendel* as well as the epic original, exploits the anti-hero tradition to re-imagine causes for violence and to redirect audience sympathies. Beowulf comes to Denmark to save its folk from the troll, but the troll takes no interest in him, because the would-be hero has done Grendel no harm. Grendel seeks those who have harmed him and his family: another re-direction, in this case of the traditional Germanic blood-feud motif. Grendel kills only one non-participant in his father's murder: a friend of Beowulf's who has entered Grendel's cave and destroyed the mummified head that Grendel has kept and worshipped, his only physical remembrance of his father and his father's death. The Geat has initiated a blood-feud that Beowulf has not, because he has destroyed Grendel's remnant of his father, which has become to him the sacred object of family and identity.

Grendel does not gain complete audience sympathy: he urinates on Heorot's doorstep, a fratboyish joke that elicits the disgust of hosts and guests alike, and he rapes and fathers a child upon the Danes' sibyl, herself fully othered by a people who abuse her far worse than does the Monster. Grendel afterwards protects her from further assaults by the Danes, I suspect in an effort by the filmmakers to present the monster as more humane than the humans he attacks. The odd but persistent narreme of sexual license or abuse suggests perhaps without intention that culturally we still prefer dangerous males who threaten us to scary females who know us at our worst, especially if no dragon appears to make men briefly forget the lot of them.

Beowulf and Grendel includes no dragon because it doesn't deal with the issues that warrant a dragon: the problems of greed, the need for heroes to show their courage against monsters beyond the scope of their strength and skills. This film deals purely with human problems, those related to race and gender, to why and how we identify and marginalize others. The story has turned from Beowulf and his monster fights toward Grendel, and the story remains his until he dies: Beowulf, still heroic but vastly diminished, must then respond sorrowfully, even apologetically, for Grendel's death — he would have a hard time finding a reason to apologize for killing a dragon.

We can perhaps no more expect Justice in our films than we do from our Courts. Grendel's Mother, a water witch, proves meaner and more dangerous than her son: in passing she kills a priest not because he has done any harm, but because he is available and annoying. The fear of the dangerous female, more worrisome in this film than any hint of a dragon would be, proves greater than the fear of the dangerous male: she will kill without reason, restraint, or compunction, especially frightening in a culture where males have learned from childhood to expect females to nurture, tend, and encourage them, not to outdo them in acts of violence and vengeance.

Graham Baker's 1999 version of *Beowulf* resets the epic at a timeless, post-apocalyptic outpost part post-medieval and part postmodern. The castle both within and without which the story unfolds stands on land previously inhabited by a shape-shifting monster who can take the form of a spiderish dragon or a seductive Playboy bunny. The human inhabitants as squatters or colonialists have shown no sympathy for the native inhabitants, monstrous though the audience may find them, and for their insensitivity the colonists receive a response of steady, violent revenge. The Grendel comes in this version (as in the 2007 film) from Hrothgar, begotten by him on the native female — presumably in the shape more appealing to human males. Grendel will kill any of the humans except his father. Monsters, after all, have some feelings, particularly for their parents, though the humans show little. As those inside the castle suffer violent attacks, those outside the castle kill any who escape, including a young woman the Beowulf character tries unsuccessfully to save: she would rather face execution by human hands than death-by-monster-Other. The outsiders believe anything in the castle/outpost or anything from it must be bad, tainted, or deadly, no matter how beautiful the form it takes: they show no compassion or consideration either. They act not out of anti-colonialist sentiments, but out of their own fear and disgust at what they see as Other: those who have awakened the native inhabitant(s) to violence. They kill without mercy or question: Beowulf finds the inside, as bad as it is, preferable to such judgmental and dimensionless persons.

Baker's *Beowulf* also includes no dragon, not least, perhaps, because Beowulf confesses himself akin to monsters: the monsters here have at least some human traits that dragons (except for those who speak) largely lack. This film addresses not greed, but the excesses of the male libido and our worries about the responses of the Monstrous Female to those excesses. It instead provides Beowulf with a love interest and a hope for happiness with her — apparently such a hero, having proven himself sufficiently human to love and be love, can retire from monster-battles and so need not face the ultimate, mortal test embodied in the dragon.

Robert Zemeckis's *Beowulf* reconstructs the dragon motif amidst the cinematic critical context of the earlier *Beowulf* films, particularly as they deal with issues of territorial takeover, male sex-drive, and ill-begotten children. This version also exploits the theme of the dangers of the inevitable excesses of the pampered male libido, and like its 1999 avatar, it provides instead of a she-troll a seductive Grendel's Mother, naked, curvy, purring, golden, and with a long ponytail whip perfect for s & m types. In this case Grendel, son of the golden mother and Hrothgar the now enervated king, takes the form of a tall, boney, linguistically challenged troll, and Beowulf the hero has the wherewithal to defeat him. The gymnastics have improved, partly because of the PCT, but they must also derive in part from Baker's film and the curious but pervasive influence the Shaw Brothers' trampolines. Heroism in contemporary film requires more than just gripping an arm and holding on courageously: audiences (or producers and directors) want hero-fu and beast-fu to spice the visual experience like amusement-park rides.

But the dragon here — every bit the most dangerous sort of dragon while he maintains that shape — comes from Beowulf himself: a more powerful monster begotten by a more powerful father. Beowulf, having fathered him as an exchange for power granted by the purring monster-mother, has given into the same weakness as did Hrothgar, with a similar but even more troublesome result. The she-monster's sexual attractiveness — one may even think it, in the world of the film, irresistibility — tempts the male at his greatest weakness, which combines both sexuality and power (in a time before televised sports). Should the hero take some pride in fathering so powerful and impressive a son? In this case the hero, having joined with the Other, gains a talisman of rule and longevity, but loses in a kind of cosmic payment both sexual and mental vitality, which the Mother-Other seems to have drained dry. Her sexuality — not wholly Other, since with human males she can reproduce — gains her a hope of continuity, one that gains force as heroes decline.

The best Hrothgar can do is father a bony if powerful troll, but Beowulf, greatest of heroes, begets the greatest of beasts: a flying, fire-breathing, shape-shifting dragon who turns at his death into the proverbial good-lookin' corpse that would have made the Silver Surfer jealous. To kill the dragon Beowulf must summon his remaining manhood and extract from the beast its furious heart: as he gave his heart to a monster, he must take the heart from the monster that would destroy him. He dies heroically in the process, but he need not have undergone the adventure at all, had he enough self-control and a sufficient sense of the danger of the she-monster not so much to his life as to his living vitality. While the Fafnir of Norse tales, the most famous of ancient man-dragons, changes form from greed and *miasma*, family-blood-letting, this dragon transcends the ancient notions of a dragon's powers and shifts his *raison d'être* to lack of sexual control. He lives because of weakness and lies, and he dies in the destruction that accompanies the uncovering of and the attempt to mitigate those lies.

Finally we may say that "*Beowulf* at the movies" has either "othered" the Monster or "monstered" the Other, and it has had a difficult time dealing with the dragon as a dragon. Even Yuri Kulakov's 1998 animated *Beowulf*, the closest adaptation yet to the original, hints that the dragon in some way reflects Beowulf: it isn't simply a (grotesque) product of nature, a separate being one fights simply because it will otherwise destroy all humans it meets. We still need a *Beowulf* film that allows for the separation of dragon and Grendel-kin into the different sorts of problems they represent for humans; to have a story we can reasonably call *Beowulf*, we need, as Tolkien would have suggested, to let the dragon be a dragon. The dragon fight, the hero's climactic adventure, defines him as could no other adventure: there he meets death squarely and accepts it without giving in to it. As Professor Eastwood says, we need to know our limitation, and as Professor Tolkien adds, the hero can hardly die better than in the act of defeating them, even if that requires succumbing to our ultimate human weakness even in the moment of achievement. Heroism implies the courage to win and to lose, the sense of duty that leads one to the right contests and conquests and that can face defeat with reignation tempered by generosity. *Beowulf-in-film* also has a progressively easier time relinquishing old notions of heroism, replacing them with the Freudian weaknesses of the modern male of medievalism. With Lacan we come eagerly to accept the desire of the Other, at the cost of making monsters of ourselves. To paraphrase Pogo, we have met the Monster, and he is us; the dragon-Other we have yet to meet, and until we do, it lurks dangerously around the next cultural corner.

6

Meat Puzzles: *Beowulf* and the Horror Film

NICKOLAS HAYDOCK

> What would an ocean be without a monster lurking in the dark?
> It would be like sleep without dreams.— Werner Herzog

Brought face to face at last with her monstrous antagonist, the redoubtable Ripley of *Alien 3* (1992) shivers in disgust as viscous strings of drool ooze from the xenomorph's lipless mouth. In a comparatively restrained image from *The Silence of the Lambs* (1991) Hannibal the Cannibal Lector noisily sucks saliva through his teeth, relating with relish how he once ate a census taker's liver "with fava beans and a nice chianti." These images seethe with the horror film's voracious appetite for terror and revulsion, its quivering abjectness. No surprise at all then to find Wealhtheow falling victim to goo dripping from Grendel's lopsided maw in the 2007 *Beowulf*. In *Outlander* (2008), the warrior princess Freya suffers a similar breach of bodily containment when the creature's saliva slops down onto her face as she lies upon a hill of human meat. An unacknowledged *Beowulf* analogue from the seventies bears the delicate title *Raw Meat* (1973), wherein the lone descendent of a band of cannibals lives with his pregnant paramour in a tunnel beneath the London tube. The night stalker raids the tubes above to feed his family, desperate to carry on his line. His single weak spot is a livid, swollen ear, which a potential victim strikes in order to incapacitate him, releasing a stream of gore — an idea deliberately echoed in the hero's fight with Grendel in Robert Zemeckis' *Beowulf*. In *Beowulf and Grendel* (2005), "the troll" raises an altar to his father's severed head, which he reverences by strewing human bones on the floor beneath — a *mise en scène* borrowed straight from the hut of Jason Voorhees in *Friday the 13th, Part 2* (1981). Likewise, *Beowulf and Grendel*'s *merewyf*, at first visible only as a webbed and taloned hand which tries to pull Vikings from their ship, is in homage to a signature shot from the horror classic *Crea-*

ture from the Black Lagoon (1954). At the end of *Friday 13th* (1980), Jason emerges from the lake in an attempt to pull the Final Girl, who has just beheaded his mother with a machete, from her boat down into the watery depths where he apparently resides, whereas in *Friday 13th, Part 3*, it is "the Lady in Lake" Mrs. Voorhees who rises from the bottom and the dead to drag yet another Final Girl beneath the surface. As is widely recognized, *Friday 13th* inverted the mother-son relationship in Hitchcock's *Psycho* (1960), which gave birth to the modern sub-genre of the Slasher film, but its mythic substructure — a mother's revenge for the death of her child, and the lake which holds revenant zombies waiting to waken in a slough of sequels — rather obviously updates the first half of *Beowulf*.

The venerable horror trope of an unmasking that reveals a monster beneath the mask (e.g., *The Phantom of the Opera, Friday 13th, Texas Chainsaw Massacre*) was freshened up for a scene in *The 13th Warrior* (1999), where a bear mask is pulled back to reveal the face of a Neanderthal. Generally speaking, the cinematic roots of this film stretch back to the Universal horror film *The Wolf Man* of 1941 that modeled Lon Chaney's make-up on reconstructions of Neanderthal man.[1] In the 1999 *Beowulf* a door tightly bolted in one shot is mysteriously ajar in the next, faithfully reproducing a ubiquitous horror film *topos*, one which in its failures to exclude or contain is emblematic of the genre as a whole. Roger Corman's *The House of Usher* (1960) features doors locked and unlocked in practically every scene as an objective correlative for the undead and the return of the repressed. Indeed, Graham Baker's *Beowulf* owes a debt to many adaptations of Edgar Allan Poe (e.g., *The Pit and the Pendulum*), not least at the beginning of the film where a gigantic straight razor severs victims in half. At the end of the film, the neo-gothic castle implodes in homage to the concluding scene from *The House of Usher*. The DVD box cover for *Outlander* quotes the Boston Herald critic James Verniere's characterization of the film as "*Beowulf* Meets *Predator*," though a more accurate version of the blurb would run: "*Alien* vs. *Predator* in Viking Age Denmark."

This latest installment of *Beowulf* adaptations in its derivations from hugely successful horror franchises only confirms the impression assembled piece by gory piece above: namely, that all of the films with which we are concerned in this book are chiefly amalgams of the *Beowulf*-meets-horror-films type. Many more examples of crossbreeding between *Beowulf* and horror films will be adduced in the course of this chapter. But at the outset it may be useful to state plainly that (despite admixtures from other genres like action-adventure or science fiction) *Beowulf* films are predominantly horror films. To see the Old English poem from the perspective of horror is neither perverse nor simply a concession to the Hollywood system of genres. It foregrounds a dominant characteristic of *Beowulf* which continues to linger only at the margins of much academic scholarship, despite the warnings of Tolkien and his successors, namely, that the monsters — not genealogy, archeology, history or religion — are the center of the poem. A thought experiment may help to demonstrate the extent to which these films encourage us to refocus our attention back unto the garish, nightmarish qualities of the poem. What does the evidence of films such as the 1999 and the 2007 *Beowulf*, *The 13th Warrior* (1999), *Beowulf and Grendel* (2005), *Grendel* (2006) and *Outlander* (2008) suggest about how screenwriters and filmmakers viewed the medieval poem as they went about adapting it (and related materials) for the screen? A synthesis of their approaches based on common elements from these six films might run as follows.

A once-great house has fallen into the grips of an abiding curse. It is haunted by a gigantic night-stalker, who emerges after dark to feast on human flesh and drag the corpses back to a lair somewhere within a foggy bog. The creature himself is never fully seen or comprehended, momentarily glimpsed only at distance in the mists beneath the moon or up close where its massive teeth, capable of biting through bones and joints, and its long claws, capable of rending flesh, are briefly glimpsed in its frenzied rush on the hall. Oddly, the monster haunts only this particular hall, seemingly provoked by an aching need to quell the beer-soaked parties. In one of the tale's many gothic ironies, the late-arrival poses as a guest, feasts on human victims, and drinks their blood, as the guardians drowse, asleep after the feast. Indeed, that he waits until all are asleep before attacking seems to confuse nightmare with waking reality. The survivors, victims of an unending terror, survey the hall on the mornings after the attacks. There are gory traces of violence everywhere, but the bodies have disappeared. They avoid the hall like the plague, and, thus abandoned, the once majestic edifice lapses into decay. Although the hall may be cursed by a supernatural evil, a certain frisson obtains with the human world where analogies to the curse or its causes become the topic of heated speculation. Something is rotten in Denmark; there is a dark secret, a hidden past that must be brought to light before the reign of terror will cease. Grendel's long feud with Hrothgar is the stuff of legend, making the locals suspicious of outsiders and drawing adventurers. A band of young adventurers arrives from overseas; they agree to spend the night in the haunted hall and are promised fame and fortune in return.

Night descends and mists rise on the moors. A stalker moves in shadow to the bolted door of the hall, which bursts open at his touch. Throughout, the monster is more felt than seen, we catch only glimpses of his feet on the tiled floor and his eyes glowing with an eerie green light. We survey his prey from the creature's perspective, until he grabs one of the sleeping warriors and tears him apart, bolting body parts and gulping down the blood that issues from these wounds, consuming even the boniest bits, hands and feet. Next, a claw reaches down for another victim and meets unwonted resistance, the horror trope of the victim *qua* avenger takes hold and the trap is sprung. The man-monster is capable of feeling pain and elicits a modicum of sympathy. His screams echo through the hall and terrify even the Danes awaiting the outcome from afar. Conventional weapons are of no use; they cannot penetrate the supernatural hide of the creature, but neither can he extract his arm from Beowulf's grip. More graphic carnage now, as a wound slowly widens in an arm being torn from the socket. The monster has been withstood and maimed, though there is a lingering sense of unfinished business.

Daylight comes; the people celebrate the lifting of the curse, but as in many horror films the aftermath is premature, a prelude to another blood bath. This premature release of tension, only to have it return with a vengeance, is a staple of horror plotting. Victories against evil will always be provisional or partial, sequels the rule rather than the exception in this most compulsive of genres. A new foe emerges, a copycat killer, more cautious and motivated by revenge, whose appearance only deepens the mystery — mother and son companions living together in a parallel world beneath a seething tarn. She kills only a single Dane and retrieves the totemic arm of her son. Terror vies with curious fascination as Beowulf plunges into the unknown. His battle with the female creature is sexually charged in ways the earlier one was not: his sword fails to penetrate just as her dagger does, until at the last possible moment he finds a weapon no other man could wield and strikes off her head. But the job is still unfinished: zombies are stubborn things. As everyone knows, the only way to kill a zombie is to incapacitate it, literally. Beowulf searches out the body of Grendel and beheads the (perhaps only seeming) corpse. The hero returns to shore with Grendel's head and the sword hilt, the sword blade having been melted down by the monsters' corrosive blood. The bloody waters are cleansed, but as the Geats head back to Heorot, the pool teems again with gore. There is no end to evil the mere represents; no final victory is possible.

Such an exercise foregrounds a number of salient characteristics about the relationship between the Old English poem and its many adaptations in recent years: most obviously, perhaps, no attention is paid to the second half of the poem, set fifty years hence among the Geats where an aged Beowulf dies fighting the dragon. Of the five generally released *Beowulf* films enumerated above, only one (*Beowulf* 2007) features an aged hero fighting a dragon, though he does so in Denmark defending Heorot against yet another incursion of the same undying evil. Secondly, the vast majority of academic scholarship on the poem is marginally if at all concerned with the horrific elements stressed in our synopsis or their function in producing suspense, fear, and the heady concoction of humor and disgust that the poem shares with film horror. Finally, very little of the criticism accompanying the release of the *Beowulf* films addresses in any sustained way the relationship of these cinematic texts to the film genre of horror, to which the screenplays, camera work, editing, etc. are chiefly indebted. Some of the reasons for these predilections will emerge in the subsequent discussion, but it may be useful to remember at the outset the abject status of this most abject of genres which trades on terror as pornography trades on sex. As film scholars have noted repeatedly, film horror is perhaps the most successful and durable of all the classic Hollywood genres, yet it is also the most reviled and, until fairly recently, the least likely to receive sympathetic critical analysis.

Monsters and Meaning: Horror Theory and Beowulf *Films*

> The poet was, it seems to me, attempting to evoke in his audience the sensation of terror that is experienced in nightmares ... these techniques are similar to those used by modern writers of horror fiction, and indeed by makers of horror films.— Michael Lapidge, "*Beowulf* and the Psychology of Terror"

My analysis rests first of all on the abundant, ubiquitous details scattered throughout these films taken from the generic arsenal of the horror film, such as the desultory comparisons enumerated at the beginning of this chapter. The prevalence of such details gives some weight to the contention that *Beowulf* films should be understood chiefly as horror films. More central to my approach, however, are recent theoretical explanations of the genre's structure and enduring appeal, which, when applied to *Beowulf* films, render many cinematic divagations from the text explicable. As such, this chapter contributes to the growing critical discourse on adaptation by exploring the ways in which medium-specific genres and sub-genres inflect the adaptation of canonical literary texts.

Any survey of horror theory should perhaps begin with the work of Robin Wood, who dubbed the 1970s a "Golden Age of the American horror film" (*Hollywood from Vietnam to Reagan* 63) and did as much as anyone to initiate the serious study of these films. For Wood, horror films represent "our collective nightmares" (70); specifically, these nightmares work to expose the weakness of "surplus repression," which functions to produce "monogamous heterosexual bourgeois patriarchal capitalists" (64). Collective nightmares are based on a simple formula: "normality is threated by the Monster" (71). Wood's monsters are embodiments of societal *oppression*, boogeymen who also maintain a parallel, internal existence as the subjects of psychological *repression*. Monsters quite simply represent the "other" in Wood's theory: the other people with whom one interacts throughout a system of unequal power relations — other cultures and ethnic groups, women and feminine sexuality, bisexuality and homosexuality, alternative ideologies and children. To this tension between self-identity and the other (familiar from Lacanian psychoanalysis and evocative of Sartre's famous remark that "hell is other people") Wood adds a third variable, "the relationship between normality and the Monster," which he deems "the essential subject of the horror film" (71). Cinematic horror typically mediates the tension between self and other through introduction of third variable: "the doppelgänger, alter ego, or double" (71).

Recent work on what Jeffrey Jerome Cohen calls "Monster Theory" confirms and extends Wood's triadic model to monsters in general and to *Beowulf* in particular. Here is Cohen's chilling account of Grendel's last visit to Heorot:

> The door splinters at the giant's touch, and Grendel strides into the hall. The men still sleep. He seizes Hondscio, the nearest warrior, and guts him as he dreams. The giant rips the body to pieces, "*bat ban-locan, blod edrum dranc, / synsnædum swealh*" [bit into muscles, swilled blood from veins, tore off gobbets]. The giant eats the sleeper alive, everything, "*fet ond folma*" [even hands and feet]. The fear that animates this gory evisceration is that all that is rhetorically outside, incorporated into the body of the monster, will suddenly break through the fragile architecture of the hall, which is the fragile identity of the subject, and expose its surprised inhabitants to what has been abjected from their small world to make it livable [Cohen 7–8].

Cohen's fluid elisions of objective and subjective, the hall and the head (hall = identity of the subject), are Wood's oppression and repression given material form, as these forces function in *Beowulf* and Anglo-Saxon culture more generally. The monster disrupts normality; its exclusion (in the terms of Deleuze and Guatarri) works like a machine in the re-production of social and psychological orders. Michael Lapidge's "*Beowulf* and the Psychology of Terror" (1993) was perhaps the first thoroughgoing attempt to challenge the traditional categorization of the poem as "heroic poetry." Lapidge linked the illusive description of Grendel with the qualities of nightmares and suggested that the poet's style was designed to "evoke in his audience the sensation of terror" (391). This much is certainly evident in Grendel's approach to Heorot. The monster's stealthy, gliding advance rendered through the repetition of *com* (702, 710, 720) heightens the terror "almost as in a nightmare" (Lapidge 384). Grendel is described as a *sceadugenga* (703) and his attacks as *nihtbealu* (193), terms that may be intended to associate the monster's visitations with a medical term for nightmares, *nihtgenga*. Yet Lapidge also recognizes the decidedly embodied, objective nature of Grendel's attacks — heads bitten off, bone locks broken — as well as the monster's physical, mortal nature. This slippage between nightmares and monsters, Lapidge argues, is a part of Anglo-Saxon ontology. It is also a staple of horror films, e.g., the *Nightmare on Elm Street* and *Friday 13th* franchises, as Robin Wood's focus on the freakish interchanges in horror between objective and subjective, oppression and repression, makes readily apparent. Indeed, the essay "Point of View and Design for Terror" by Alain Renoir, discussed at length in Chapter 1, suggests that the poet's modulations of perspective and suspense in the scene make it analogous to the cinematography of a horror film.

Wood's third variable — the relationship between normality and the monster — is typically embodied by doppelgängers or alter egos, whose presence encroaches upon boundaries between self and other. Recent uses of monster theory emphasize the similarities between Beowulf and Grendel, just as earlier myth and archetypal criticism did. For David D. Gilmore, "monsters and heroes arise simultaneously ... as paired twins" and their conflict amounts to a "virtually universal" "combat myth of civilization's origins" (27). "Each monster narrative," as Richard Kearney reminds us, "recalls that the self is never secure in itself" (3). Many *Beowulf* scholars remain uncomfortable with the notion that Beowulf and the monsters are doubles of one another for the very weighty reason that monsters are the enemies of God. Still, the poem encourages their partial identification through the use of similar vocabulary, humanizing the monsters and emphasizing Beowulf's superhuman size and strength. Grendel especially is described in ways that seem designed to evoke sympathy: he is a "wonsæli wer" (unhappy man, 105), a wretched exile "earmsceapen/ on weres wæstmum wræclastas træd," (the misshapen one trod the paths of exile in a man's form, 1351-2).[2] Although the reason for Grendel's "feud" with Hrothgar is never specified in the poem, the reciprocities of feud become crystal clear in the concatenations of revenge that begin with the death of Handscio. Beowulf revenges that death by dismembering Grendel and hanging his arm within the hall as a trophy of victory. Grendel's mother requites this, despoiling the trophy and placing the head of her victim Aeschere on a hill above her mere. Beowulf descends into the mere, beheads the mother and then Grendel's death-sick corpse, whose head is returned to Heorot. Though there is no doubt that Beowulf contends against the enemies of God, themselves the progeny of Cain's transgression, the hero's battles with monsters take on the character of a never-ending feud that mirrors human blood feuds, their monstrous, *undead* nature: feud is thus the most haunting of revenants. In this sense Beowulf's actions closely mirror those of the monsters, perhaps nowhere more than at the end when he has the treasure from the dragon's hoard piled up within his own tomb. Indeed, it might well be said that it is only the gigantic and inhumanely powerful hero, in his mediation between men and monsters, that allows the logic of monstrosity — its dark reflection of human societies — to emerge so sharply within the poem. Thus, reciprocity, the pattern of imitation and escalation, serves to represent not only the mimetic structure of feud in Girard's terms but also the psychic bipolarities of Lacan whereby the self originates in the other.

Still, few would argue that the hero of the poem emerges as anything but Grendel's implacable enemy, a warrior who fights on the side of God and on whose side God himself fights against a demon from hell descended from Cain. In film adaptations of *Beowulf,* the line between good and evil is deliberately blurred, and doubles and doppelgängers multiply with promiscuous abandon. *Outlander* (2008), for instance, goes so far as to christen its exilic Beowulf-figure *Kainan,* a soldier engaged in genocide whose spaceship crashes into eighth-century Denmark, laden (*Alien*-like) with a trio of secret sharers who serve as the film's version of the son, mother, and dragon. This sci-fi frame sets the stage for quite a conventional horror film in which the hero and the monster are a package deal — Kainan is initially treated as an enemy by Hrothgar's tribe and later leads the initiative to rid them of a curse he has brought down upon their heads. Kainan serves a kind of hybrid, then, of Cain, Beowulf, and the thief.

The 1999 *Beowulf,* with Christopher Lambert in the title role, represents a paradigmatic instance of the hero and monster as mirror images of one another, where the original poem's concern with genealogy is obliquely reconfigured through a series of back stories in which demons mate with human beings. As he faces off against Grendel, Beowulf lets the monster know that he has to do with something very different from simple human prey: "I've been waiting for you. One of us is the other's death. I'm like you. I'm one of the damned." Soon thereafter, in a twisted form of foreplay, he recounts for his lover, Kyra, the strangely elfish idyll behind his Manichean origins. His mother followed a strange light through a hole in the mountain that magically opened at her approach. There she encounters "Bale, the God of Darkness, Lord of Lies" and sleeps with him every night for three months. On the last night she is told that she is with child and must name the boy Beowulf — or perhaps *Bale-wolf,* as the name is typically pronounced in the film. Thus it is that he comes to be "trapped between two worlds": "The only thing that stops me from becoming evil is fighting evil." Here we see a strange conflation of comic book superheroes with the Bear's Son folktale as told of Böðvar Bjarki in *Hrolfs Saga Kraki*. Yet more integral to the film's Freudian supernatural is the notion that Grendel and Beowulf are specular images of one another, products of human/demonic miscegenation: Grendel, the son of Hrothgar and a shape-shifting succubus "older than sin"; Beowulf, the offspring of a human mother and the demon Bale.

Grendel was conceived "at the height of victorious bloodlust," when Hrothgar conquered the land and took its succubus queen as a prize of conquest. Employing the terms of Robin Wood, we encounter in the doubling of Beowulf and the monster a textbook case of the dual functioning of oppression and repression. Grendel is the offspring of imperial oppression, such that Hrothgar is haunted by the embodiment of a furious resentment he himself sired. On the other hand, Beowulf's battles are chiefly internal; he attempts to control the forces of evil that gave birth to his supernatural strength, warring like Grendel against his father, in order to repress an evil bred in his bones. The succubus appeals to this dark side in her attempts to vanquish him:

> (Grendel's mother appears when Beowulf finally kills Grendel, who has just killed his father Hrothgar.)
> GRENDEL'S MOTHER: That was a mistake.
> BEOWULF: No mistake. I only kill when I have to. You kill for pleasure.
> GM: Their blood was sweet. I sucked their veins. Chewed their bones — wet and still alive. Hot blood pumping down my throat. (sucks her bloody fingers in a shot deriving from pornographic depictions of oral sex) You should try it, it will appeal to you.
> B: You know nothing about what appeals to me.
> GM: Don't I? How will her (Kyra's) blood taste? You've wondered; you can't help it. You look at her and your blood pumps. Your mouth becomes wet. You haven't confused that hunger for something else, I hope.
> B: I'm not confused. I know exactly why I'm here.
> GM: (Moving closer to Beowulf, circling round him, touching his lips with her bloody fingers.) Tell me, whose blood mingles with yours? Who spread your mother's legs and gave you the strength to overcome my son?
> B: Someone stronger than you.
> GM: (with a scornful laugh) That's doubtful. I know you feel the pull towards me. You can't help it. I need you inside me. You're on the edge of control now. With fresh kills only inches away. And me so close — aching for you. Does it burn in you, the hunger ... for blood, for flesh? Is it sweet to you the scent of my son's kills? Tell me, hero, whose world do you really belong to, theirs or mine?

"I need you inside me": Ms. Roberts here seems to reference rather explicitly soft-core horror porn such as *The Hunger* (Tony Scott, 1983), as well as the more recent, hugely successful *Interview with the Vampire* (1994).³ When the seduction fails, she unfolds herself, metamorphosing into a gigantic scorpion that retains a human face. As such, Beowulf's final monster offers an example of "body horror," a sub-category that has received much attention lately. The horror that emerges from the body or the remnants of human form that survive its transformation will receive some discussion below, as will concerns with gender and family.

But let us return to that weirdly excessive hybrid of monsters composed of a woman, a dragon-like scorpion whose blood is flammable, and her son, whose gaseous, purple life force flows back into her body after his death. Hybrids are the stock and trade of horror. The Sphinx was a similar tri-morph made up of a woman's face, a lion's body and the wings of large raptor. The Medusa, herself part of a trio of sisters called the Gorgons, had snakes for hair and a long tongue sticking out of her mouth — both of which signified her apotropaic function in Greek myth, the terrifying power of her gaze to turn men into stone. Whatever the creature featured at the end of Baker's *Beowulf* is supposed to represent anatomically, she seems, like the Sphinx, to pose an anatomical neck riddle that the hero must solve in order to defeat her. Also, like the Medusa, she poses the mortal threat of the stultifying feminine gaze. The latter supposition finds support in the manner of her attacks on Beowulf. She makes no real effort to wound him; she simply pins him down and gazes into his eyes, tongue jutting far out of her mouth and her hair re-coiffured into snake-like braids pulled tightly back from her face. Freud's famous remarks on "Medusa's Head" saw the specter of the Medusa's gaze as a castration terror brought on by revelation of the mother's sexuality and her lack of a penis, while the hair/snakes in a sense compensate for this lack, according to a "technical rule" whereby "a multiplication of penis symbols signifies castration" (Garber and Vickers 85). In Baker's *Beowulf* the monster's transformation from a woman offering, even demanding sex to a grotesque monster threatening to incorporate the man begins as a rash of protruding, snake-like phalloi emerging from her arms, legs, abdomen and pelvis — protrusions that quickly develop dangerous elaborations into bat-like wings with tusk-like nails. Throughout she calls Beowulf "child" and even after her transformation continues to speak as if she were offering to consume him as a form of transcendent sex: "Come, child, sample the true delights of flesh with me. Feel what no human woman can offer you." At this point, Beowulf draws his sword.

Threats to masculinity bring us closer to more recent, gender-based readings of Medusa, her status as a woman raped by Poseidon within Athena's temple and that goddess's terrible punishment of the victim. Like Medusa, this apotropaic monster has reason to be angry with men. Hrothgar took her and her land, and she took her revenge by repeatedly raping him in his sleep and bearing the child that becomes his scourge. In her inside-out transformation, her breasts (much in evidence throughout the film) and vagina disappear, exfoliating into beastly talons in a horrific variation on that other Freudian nightmare, the *vagina dentate*. But what of her symbolic role as Sphinx, a tri-form being who ultimately unites in a single body all three of Beowulf's monsters? There is good reason to associate the figure in the film with Lilith and her reflexes in Jewish and related ancient and medieval traditions. Certainly her claim that she is "older than sin" would seem to put her genesis before that of Eve. Equally intriguing is the film's recurrent scenes of nocturnal emissions as Grendel's mother writhes atop Hrothgar in sexual bliss, a commonplace in traditions about Lilith and her Greco-Roman incarnation, Lamia. The related Mesopotamian demon Labartu had a scorpion between her legs, just as a scorpion's stinger emerges from the privy regions of Grendel's mother in the film. Later literary traditions such as the Pre-Rafaelites emphasized Lilith/Lamia's vampirism, a trait especially foregrounded in the film. Perhaps most important for our purposes are the medieval notions, beginning in the *Alphabet of Ben Sira*, which cast Lilith as Adam's first wife and later Jewish texts which claim she left Adam because she refused to be subservient to him.

    The point of hunting such analogues really has more to do with the kind of response the 1999 *Beowulf* solicits from audiences than with archetypal or

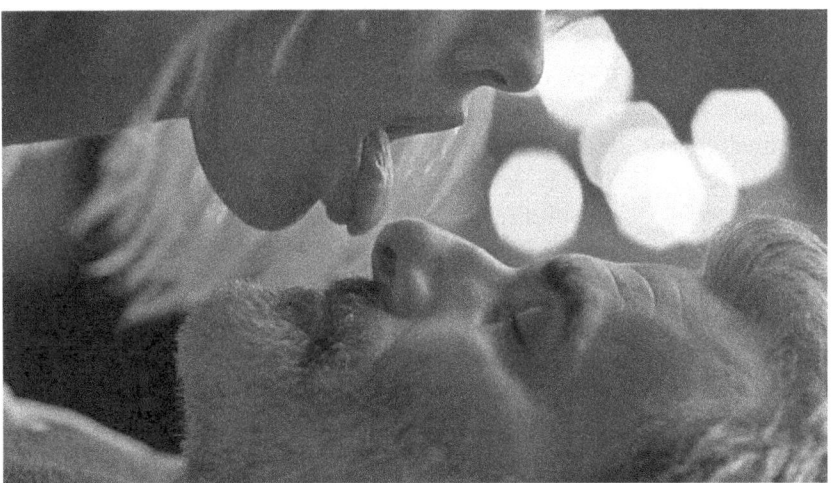

The Lilith-like succubus (Layla Roberts) in Graham Baker's *Beowulf* (1999).

The Lilith-like mother of Grendel in *Beowulf* (1999).

myth criticism *stricto sensu*. The poem poses its own share of mysteries: why can't Grendel approach the *giftstol*, and why, since she is proportionally smaller and weaker, does Grendel's mother represent the greater threat to the hero? This film, like nearly every other of its ilk, offers answers to such questions while spawning many more enigmas. Every major character has a secret — Grendel, his mother, Beowulf, Hrothgar, Kyra and Roland — and the plot is chiefly dedicated to the unraveling of these mysteries in the long interludes between monster fights. The three-in-one riddle of succubus is the chief of these riddles, but all the characters pose questions of identity and origins. Hrothgar's wife and Kyra's husband are conspicuously absent; both, as it turns out, died violent deaths because of their spouses. Grendel is the child of Hrothgar and the succubus, which explains his reply "Not you" when Hrothgar impotently pleads with the monster: "Fight me, fight me, dammit." But it is intimated that the scorpion-dragon is also Hrothgar's child, conceived not at a single moment of "victorious bloodlust" like Grendel, but over the course of many wet dreams during which she coaxes the king: "It is almost finished, my love." Finally brought to fruition, the hybrid unites all three monsters and seeks to add the force of Beowulf to its composite body, first by seduction and then by ingestion — though that is perhaps a distinction with no real difference here.

That the final incarnation of the creature retains Layla Roberts' face pays homage to famous images of body horror in films such as John Carpenter's

The Thing (1982) and George P. Cosmatos' *Leviathan* (1989), just as the bursting forth of the creature from within a human host in all of these films looks back to the *Alien* franchise. In these examples of body horror the monsters-are-us theme emerges from the fear of science under capitalism. But for Deleuze and Guatarri, of course, Oedipal complexes and the hysterical, monstrous feminine are also products of bourgeois capitalism, however insistently their genesis is traced from classical and biblical myths. According to Robin Wood, the monsters of 1970s horror films represent the family under capitalism, and this is relevant too for many film *Beowulfs*. In Baker's *Beowulf*, Grendel's mother is the *other* woman in more ways than one, a husband's fatal attraction which ultimately claims the lives of his wife and all of his people except the final girl, Kyra. According to the Internet Movie Database, Kyra's character was originally slated to take the monster Grendel as her lover. The scene was reportedly dropped because it detracted from the plot; one can speculate that the incest theme was included in the first place because it contributed to the film's central concern: the fracture of the nuclear family by uncontrolled desires, both incestuous and acquisitive. Until it is proven otherwise, Kyra assumes that the monster is a revenant of her husband, whom she stabbed to death. Kyra's unscreened monster love — as well as the scene late in the film where she reconciles with her father in his bedroom after pulling that same knife on him — suggests (in tune with Deleuze and Guatarri) how incest prohibitions are constitutive of the nuclear family under capitalism. The violation of these prohibitions assumes monstrous forms that embody forbidden desires and hybrid offspring (for instance, the Sphinx, the Medusa, the Minotaur, Lilith, monsters born of the union of giants and women, and the succubus in Baker's *Beowulf*). Heorot is a house haunted by a secret sin, the colonist's ethnocide that established Hrothgar's reign in the first place. That terror is revisited upon him and his kingdom in the form of a son who embodies the rampant bloodlust of the father. As a kind of vanishing mediator between the self and the social, the family's founding imperatives — monogamy, reproduction, ethnic and racial prohibitions — produce an embodied *jouissance* of infidelity, incest and miscegenation, which must be destroyed in order to return the reign of the family. In Robin Wood's terms, the ending of the 1999 *Beowulf* squares the circle in yielding at the end only two survivors united in a monogamous relationship, Beowulf and Kyra — like Adam and Eve with flames behind and all the world ahead of them. Although this romantic ending has nothing at all to do with the Old English poem, it does reinstitute the compulsory (and compulsive) heterosexual monogamy that Robin Wood specifies as the *telos* of the classic horror film.

Fear and Disgust: Noel Carroll's Theory of Horror

Noël Carroll's *The Philosophy of Horror: Or, Paradoxes of the Heart* (1990) represents perhaps the most theoretically astute account of the genre's trade in fear and revulsion and the paradox of its enduring appeal. Carroll asks quite simply: "why horror?" in attempting to account for our enjoyment of images designed to elicit *un*-pleasurable emotions. He begins by defining a mode called "horror," which is thought to traverse many media, including fiction, film, painting and drama. Carroll's neo–Aristotelian approach works to abstract a general theory of horror based upon the affective responses such works are designed to elicit in their audiences and the challenges monsters present to established cultural categories. Carroll distinguishes what he calls "art-horror" from real fear, suggesting that our identification is chiefly with the fearful reactions of characters within the fiction. As such, the rather thorny question of whether many horror films are really scary or for whom they are frightening is gracefully sidestepped. Horror films are those that elicit an audience's responses to that which is frightening, abject and threatening *to characters within the film*. Taking a page from Aristotle's definition of tragedy as productive of pity and fear, Carroll adapts a formula from Mary Douglas' *Purity and Danger*: monsters are interstitial beings that confound epistemological categories (e.g., human/animal; living/dead) in order to provoke fear and disgust.[4] Also analogous to Aristotle's anatomy of the structure of tragic plots (*peripatetia, anagnorisis* and *catharsis*) is Carroll's contention that most examples of art-horror are based upon a "drama of investigation" leading to knowledge and a restoration of cultural order:

> Horror stories, in a significant number of cases, are dramas of proving the existence of the monster and disclosing (most often gradually) the origin, identity, purposes and powers of the monster. Monsters, as well, are obviously a perfect vehicle for engendering this kind of curiosity and for supporting the drama of proof, because monsters are (physically, though generally not logically) impossible beings. They arouse interest and attention through being putatively inexplicable or highly unusual vis-à-vis our standing cultural categories, thereby instilling a desire to learn and to know about them. And since they are also outside of (justifiably) prevailing definitions of what is, they understandably prompt a need for proof (or the fiction of a proof) in the face of skepticism. Monsters are, then, natural subjects for curiosity, and they straightforwardly warrant the ratiocinative energies the plot lavishes upon them [Carroll 182].

In this, Carroll's approach complements that of Wood, who proposed a triad of normality, the monster and the relation between them, often figured by doppelgängers or alter egos.

Where Carroll parts company with Wood is in the latter's valorization of the monster's heroic qualities to challenge normalcy and the nuclear family. Carroll is understandably hesitant to follow Wood here, because while many monsters (Frankenstein, the Wolf Man, and the Grendel of *Beowulf and Grendel* or *No Such Thing*) encourage our sympathy, even admiration, many others elicit only fear and disgust: the monsters of *The 13th Warrior* and *Grendel*, for instance. As noted at the beginning of this chapter, the heroines Wealhtheow and Freya shuddering in terror and revulsion at digestive juices drooling from slavering maws is emblematic of the horror film's influence on film Beowulfs. Yet another, more prevalent characteristic is these films' indulgence of our curiosities about the monsters, their investigations into the origins, nature, motivations, and even the psychology of Grendel or Grendel's mother. The monsters in *The 13th Warrior* represent one extreme, the Neanderthal cannibals known within the film as "the Eaters of the Dead," who are beyond identification or sympathy. At the opposite extreme prowls the quite human troll of *Beowulf and Grendel*, a victim of scapegoating who strictly confines his attacks to those who have injured him and is easily the most sympathetic male figure in the film. Yet, however different the levels of empathy their monsters elicit, both films are equally invested in what Carroll calls dramas of proof in which the heroes along with the audience laboriously gather evidence as a prelude to, indeed as means of, killing the monster.

Just as horror often proceeds like a scientific investigation into the nature of the creature as a way to understand and combat it, *Beowulf* horror films have aped and mimicked scholarly investigations into the poem and its backgrounds. In sum, both John McTiernan's *The 13th Warrior* and Sturla Gunnarsson's *Beowulf and Grendel* construct a Rosetta stone capable of translating the supernatural terms of the poem into historical (or pre-historic) realities. Ahmed ibn Fadlan, as a stranger in a strange land, is initially skeptical that the Wendol represent anything more than an enemy tribe whose furiousness has lead to beliefs that they are impervious to weapons — not unlike in this respect the legends about berserkers with which Crichton was certainly familiar. Yet, although Crichton's novel and the film's screenplay (by William Wisher, Jr. and Warren Lewis) leverage anthropology and evolutionary biology to an extent unprecedented in movie medievalism, the science is just as fanciful as that in *Jurassic Park* or *Timeline*, a science which disrupts chronological distinctions and puts the present under the threat of a distant past. Science serves to rationalize the monsters of *The 13th Warrior* in the most fanciful of ways, just as it typically does in horror fiction and films. The myth that Crichton invents as a backdrop to the poem, the idea of "creatures of the mist," certainly reaches back through Tolkien's "Misty Mountains" and the dragon

Smaug, to H. Rider Haggard's *The People of the Mist* (1894) and its 1978 film adaptation *Slave of a Cannibal God*, but such cannibalistic clouds are also a staple of more recent horror films such as John Carpenter's *The Fog* (1980) and *The Mist* (d. Frank Darcourt 2007), based on a Steven King novel. In Crichton's later novel *Prey* (2002), a cloud of nanoparticles programmed as an irresistible predator capable of adapting to new conditions escapes from the laboratory to rain havoc on the world. Mists are such a staple of horror conceptions precisely because they represent how the unknown and unseen is embodied as a threat, becoming a monster. It is Ahmed ibn Fadlan's role in the film to penetrate these mists, to ascertain the identity of these mythic creatures, and to discover the location of their lair in the Thunder Caves.[5]

Much more realistic and requiring little suspension of disbelief is the Grendel of Sturla Gunnarsson's film. In Noël Carroll's terms, Beowulf is sidetracked into "a drama of proof" not unlike that of Sherlock Holmes in *The Hound of the Baskervilles*. Grendel emerges from this investigation a man and a victim, not the demonic troll of motiveless malignity that Hrothgar and the other Danes insisted he was. Rather, he is the victim of scapegoating whose own victims pay the price established by the code of the feud, a being that is in fact more like Grettir the Strong of the Icelandic saga than this film's Beowulf, an outcast and outlaw whose position at the extremities has made him a monster. Jeffrey Jerome Cohen's characterization of the abject Grendel, quoted earlier, is thus an even better description of Gunnarsson's film than it is of the poem, of "the fragile identity" of subjects exposed "to what has been abjected from their small world to make it livable" (Cohen 8). The film succeeds in exposing the subtle dialectic of repression and oppression in ways that are truer to the psychoanalytic and anthropological subtexts of Cohen's monster theory (Lacan, Kristeva, Girard) because the monster's hybridity is explicable in neither divine nor evolutionary terms. Films do pursue adaptations of texts that have more in common with the ways and means of professional scholarship than is often acknowledged, particularly because the same theorists who inspire a good deal of recent scholarship have also made their way into popular consciousness, just as recent theorists such as Žižek and Kristeva increasingly engage popular culture. When Jerome Cohen enlists support from the likes of Prospero and Dr. Frankenstein ("This thing of darkness I acknowledge mine"), he also invites us to take the question of the existence of monsters seriously: "Monsters are our children ... a discourse all the more sacred as it comes from the outside" (20). The Hrothgars of the 1999 and the 2007 *Beowulf* do actually father monsters, as does Beowulf in the latter film. The orphaned Grendel of *Beowulf and Grendel* becomes Hrothgar's child in the metaphorical sense of parentage that Cohen employs, thus becoming "sacred" in the fullest sense of that word. The Hrothgar of the film *Grendel*, who sacrifices children to palliate the monsters, comes to realize that in offering child victims he himself has become a monster, the child (as it were) of Grendel — the idea that terror nourishes the monster within us seems especially relevant now. The Kainan of *Outlander*— the film's Beowulf— is also forced to acknowledge a thing of darkness his when his spaceship bears the Moorwen to Viking Age Iceland. This, I hasten to add, is not to confuse Cohen's trend-setting work with that of screenwriters. These films are to theoretically informed scholarship as science fiction is to science. Yet the parallels between Beowulfian cinémedievalism and scholarship *are* intriguing, both in their manufacture of what Carroll calls "dramas of proof" and in the funhouse mirror such films hold up to *Beowulf* scholarship. *Beowulf* films conduct investigations into the histories and mechanisms of monsterization, seeking out the monsters' genesis, identity, motivations and location and thereby foregrounding the role of the abject in the production of normality. In the tabloid sense of the word, the human beings in these films are haunted by their *pasts*, to such an extent that one regrets Vincent Price was not available for the role of Hrothgar. The scandals uncovered include adultery, genocide, human sacrifice, Oedipal dramas and matriarchal cannibalism — exactly the kind of Gothic secrets revealed so ubiquitously in horror plotting and characterization. The corpus of film *Beowulf*s thus apes *Beowulf* scholarship through the conventions of the horror film.

Playing Up Female Parts: The Monstrous Feminine

A thinking woman sleeps with monsters. — Adrianne Rich

The feminine in *Beowulf* films is deliriously overdetermined, significant in ways that egregious, values-added supplements in popular culture tend to be. The tendency to dismiss such elements as simple concessions to political correctness or industrial commonplaces forecloses their role in staging, often quite self-consciously, the translations of medieval texts into media and genre-specific codes. Put more directly, the female figures whose roles are added or expanded in *Beowulf* films represent more than love interests or woman warriors; they are instead part of a larger discourse on gendered violence and the abject maternal, those especially intense and interrelated concerns of the horror film. In her attempt to rethink gender in horror films through Julia Kristeva's book *The Powers of Horror: An Essay in Abjection*, Barbara Creed remarks on the psychodynamics of identity and abjection:

> In the child's attempts to break away, the mother becomes an abject; thus, in this context, where the child struggles to become a separate subject, abjection becomes "*a precondition of narcissism.*" Once again we can see abjection at work in the horror text where the child struggles to break away from the mother, representative of the archaic maternal figure, in a context in which the father is inevitably absent (*Psycho, Carrie,* and *The Birds*). In these films the maternal is constructed as the monstrous feminine [Creed 72].

For Creed, Kristeva's insistence that abjection derives from ancient rituals of purification offers an opportunity to view modern horror as a social ritual through which the abject maternal is defeated in order to reassert the reign of the symbolic order.

John Gardner likely concluded that such a struggle was implicit in *Beowulf*. In his *Grendel*, the finest and most widely influential piece of *Beowulfiana* ever made, Gardner poses what Kristeva would call the "thetic break" as the chief stumbling block in the development of Grendel's intense interiority — for monsters the mother herself is monstrous:

> I sigh, sink into the silence, and cross it like the wind. Behind my back, at the world's end, my pale, slightly glowing mother sleeps on, old, sick at heart, in our dingy, underground room. Life-bloated, baffled, long suffering hag. Guilty, she imagines, of some unremembered, perhaps ancestral crime. (She must have some human in her.) Not that she thinks. Not that she dissects and ponders the dusty mechanical bits of her miserable life's curse. She clutches at me in sleep as if to crush me. "Why are we here?" I used to ask her. Why do we stand this putrid, stinking hole?" She trembles at my words. Her fat lips shake. "Don't ask!" her wiggling claws implore. (She never speaks.) "Don't ask!" It must be some terrible secret, I used to think. I'd give her a crafty squint. She'll tell me, in time, I thought. But she told me nothing [Gardner 11].

Though Grendel continues to vet versions of Kristeva's "symbolic" in the form of various philosophical schools, the mother's body and her womb-like cave repeatedly threaten to suspend or reverse the thetic break, reincorporating him into a world before language or a distinct sense of self:

> "The world resists me and I resist the world," I said. "That is all there is." (...) "I exist, nothing else." Her face works. She gets up on all fours, brushing dry bits of bone from her path, and, with a look of terror, rising as if by unnatural power, she hurls herself across the void and buries me in her bristly fur and fat. I sicken with fear [...] I can't breathe, and I claw to get free. She struggles. I smell my mama's blood and, alarmed, I hear from the walls and floor of the cave the booming, booming of her heart [Gardner 28–29].

The sophistical dragon, who may be the devil and fills the role of Grendel's absent father, will prove equally terrifying for the fledgling existentialist monster, but the abject maternal remains a continuing danger.

Grendel's mother threatens a chthonic recursiveness, a loss of the world of language, a threat to that narcissism which fathers identity. Yet even more distressing is Grendel's recognition near the end of the novel that he is the sign of his mother's lack, a sign of the absent phallus made apparent in a re-enactment of the thetic break:

> I saw long ago the whole universe as not-my-mother, and I glimpsed my place in it, a hole [...] For even my mama loves me not for myself, my holy specialness (he he ho ha), but for my son-ness, my possessedness, my displacement of air as visible proof of her power. I have set her aside — gently, picking her up by the armpits as I would a child — and so have proved that she has no power but the little I give her by momentary whim [Gardner 158].

Grendel's difficult passage into subjectivity occurs — as all such individuations must, according to Freud and Lacan — through identification with the father's superior strength and the law he represents but cannot control. The nihilistic, materialistic, and supremely narcissistic dragon serves this father-function for Grendel. However, the dragon himself is only another sign of the phallus, not the phallus itself, which certainly resides with that God whose existence the dragon tries desperately to forget and disprove.

As we have seen, the abject maternal is abundantly evident in Graham Baker's gothic *Beowulf*, though the threat of the *chora* to masculinity has been sexed up. There, the body of Grendel's mother serves as both her son's tomb and as the womb in which the "dragon" is slowly incubated. Both center and gaping void of this version of the poem, Layla Robert's monstrous mother calls Beowulf "child" as she invites him to enter her in a form of eroticized death familiar from vampire films. For the undead like herself and Beowulf, sexual desire is merely the *confused form* of a deeper, more elemental hunger — as she demonstrates by her lethal copulation with Beowulf's rival, Roland. The hero's insistence that he knows and can maintain the difference between these two forms of hunger thus initiates yet another thetic break, the reinstitution of the masculine symbolic as a bulwark against the looming dangers of the chora.[6]

The 2007 *Beowulf* follows the lead of the earlier film in casting Grendel's mother (Angelina Jolie) as a combination siren and succubus, but Ms. Jolie bathes in gold not blood. The association is as old perhaps as capitalism itself. Marx famously coined a vampire metaphor to highlight the undead nature of capital: "Capital is dead labour, that, vampire-like, only lives by sucking living labour, and lives the more, the more labour it sucks" (Marx 342). Barack Obama took up this idea recently, accusing the venture capitalist *cum* presidential candidate Mitt Romney of "vampire capitalism." In the 2007 *Beowulf*, the eroticization of capital is made glamorous flesh, but the monstrous, threatening nature of motherhood is no less apparent. Like Layla Robert's character, Jolie's incarnates feminine fertility as a threat to masculinity — she too is the mother not just of Grendel but of the dragon as well. There is no end to the masculine lust for power she embodies: unlike all earlier film versions of the character, this virago is seemingly immortal. Beowulf lies with her and lies when he claims to have killed her. He like Hrothgar becomes her lover and sires the offspring that becomes his bane. By such means do the figures played by Roberts and Jolie represent both the phallus and its lack, for men. Their sons endow the monstrous feminine with the power to wield the phallus — in both cases almost as if by remote control — and at the same time to render impotent the kings from whom they have taken this power in something like an abiding curse. In this version of Oedipal triangulation, the father is emasculated by his son, who becomes a powerful phallus in the hands of the mother, who in bearing a child reduces her lover to a donor and her son to an apparatus through which she wields her will in the world. The Hrothgars of both films cut very emptied, impotent, despairing figures indeed. Eventually so does the Beowulf of the 2007 film, who as in no other film version is actually allowed to grow old, albeit in Denmark rather than Gotland. The waning of these powerful men is set alongside the golden girl, a succubus who never ages and never dies and who transforms their lust for an eroticized power into a monstrous scandal.

In his thoroughly engaging history of the horror film, David J. Skal relates the body horror of Ridley Scott's landmark film *Alien* (1979) to reproductive anxieties:

> The chest-bursting scene — the single most talked about sequence in the film became the seventies' surpassing evocation of reproduction as unnatural parasitism [...] the fetus-as-bogeyman, an ever growing, shape-shifting nightmare. The culture's growing but shifting hostility toward birth is transformed into a monstrous fetal parasite hostile to the culture itself. *Alien* was a validation of something already suspected: that reproduction was a kind of death, a devastating insult to the body and personal autonomy [...] Relief only came when the beast was aborted from the mother-ship's body, sucked away by the vacuum of space [301].

The 2007 *Beowulf* casts these "reproductive anxieties" in masculine terms. In the wake of the Monica Lewinski scandal, the impeachment proceedings against President Clinton and the democratic loss of the presidency in 2000, the notion that adultery and lies about adultery could enfeeble a powerful man had an especial salience. Earlier comparisons of the Clinton presidency to Kennedy's now tended to reinforce the idea of two charismatic leaders whose credibility had been undermined by sexual secrets. Debilitating wars, first in Vietnam and then in Iraq and Afghanistan, wars that scarified beyond recognition America's moral authority and self-confidence, have seemed to many commentators the direct result of Kennedy's assassination and Clinton's fall from grace. Certainly the parallels are far from exact, but in Hrothgar's and Beowulf's adulteries, which swell to monstrous proportions and threaten to destroy their house on the hill, we may see the distant mirror of an American obsession with sex as the root of all evils.

If Grendel and the dragon represent the catastrophic return of disavowed sexual secrets, then Jolie's particular variation on the *femme fatale* represents fame and fortune in both medieval and modern senses of the words. Her femininity is monstrous precisely because it brings secrets to term rather than burying them forever. An embodiment of wealth and power, she retains the right (like the goddess Fortuna) to take away all she has given. When Beowulf descends to the underwater caves, he finds the gigantic Grendel shrunk to the shape and size of an aborted fetus, lying on a table. His mother, dripping with gold, embodies the material wealth of the hoard as well as its morbid *jouissance*. Her long golden ponytail serves as both a whip and an umbilical chord, reminiscent of the umbilical-like objects in classical *catabases*. From the beginning of the episode, masculine and feminine symbols of power are juxtaposed. Beowulf holds the radiant ornamental cup in one hand and his sword in the other — shot repeatedly from angles that make it seem a prosthetic penis. But this sword (like Hrunting in the original) makes little headway, passing without effect through her body, until she takes it into her hands in another broad reference to fellatio as emasculation ... and it melts away (like the divine sword in the poem). In this liquid dream-world nothing is stable; rather — in the Kristevan sense of "woman's time" — circular and repetitive. As she glides as if on a turntable around Beowulf's naked body, her tail presents him with Grendel's head, softly intoning:

> You took a son from me. Give me a son, brave thane. Stay with me. Love me. Love me, and I shall weave you riches beyond imagination. I shall make you the greatest king that ever lived. (Tail releases the head and weaves itself through the golden cup in a tight shot of their pelvises.) As long as you hold me in your heart and this golden horn remains in my keeping (beginning to caress the sword), you will forever be king: forever strong, mighty, and all powerful. This I promise. (As the sword dissolves and oozes through her fingers.) This I swear. (As Beowulf lets the hilt fall to his side and the golden drops puddle into a reflection of their lovemaking.)

As the source of worldly power, the womb-like lair is the place where the phallus goes to die — or rather to be coopted by the feminine. That the cave is where Beowulf gains seemingly unlimited power while at the same time

The liquefying sword in Zemeckis' *Beowulf* (2007; Ray Winstone and Angelina Jolie).

being emasculated and rendered impotent — symbolically at least — adds a certain uncanny frisson to the Faustian bargain.

Later, at the celebratory banquet at Heorot, Beowulf proffers Grendel's head and tells how the mother came back to life when he pulled Hrunting from her chest — in a broad allusion to the stake of vampire legends. He claims the only way to keep her dead was to leave the sword within her body — a phantasmagoric victory of the phallus over the feminine that the film's audience knows to be both a lie and an example of wishful thinking. As no such thetic break has in fact occurred, Beowulf has established the *imaginary* nature of the phallus in a strictly Lacanian sense. This sense Hrothgar understands all too well. He quickly surmises that Beowulf has not killed the being that the young hero calls a "hag," and thus he knows as well the foolishness inherent in Beowulf's claim that he has *escaped* her. The film substitutes a private conference between Beowulf and Hrothgar for the public sermon in the poem, all the better to reveal their complicity in a (supposed) secret about male power: it not only comes from the feminine but remains eternally subject to it. By killing Grendel, Beowulf has removed Hrothgar's curse: "She is not my curse," says the aged king, "not anymore, not anymore." No, she is Beowulf's, a curse that manifests itself some fifty years later in the coming of the dragon, Beowulf's son. In naming Beowulf his heir, Hrothgar of course ignores the poem's location of the final battle with the dragon, but he strengthens our sense of masculinity's compulsive recursivity within the larger context of "woman's time."

After Hrothgar's convenient suicide, Beowulf ages in an instant, becoming every bit as despairing as Hrothgar once was. He entreats the young invader Finn to kill him. When Finn does not accept the invitation to murder an unarmed man, Beowulf explains: "You know why you can't kill me, my friend? 'Cause I died many, many years ago when I was young." When the dragon finally comes, it bears a fragmentary message reported to Beowulf by a dying Unferth: "the sins of the fathers." Though seemingly a curtailed version of the biblical phrase, it is in fact more like a name for the race of monsters in this and indeed in almost every *Beowulf* film. The dragon and his half-brother, Grendel, are the sins of the fathers visited upon the fathers in form of illegitimate, monstrous sons. In Kristeva's sense, monstrous mothers endanger masculinity — the symbolic order of language, law, and civilization — by threatening to extend the chora across time and space. Sons, especially, become reflections and extensions of the mother's power, like the spontaneously generated "children of her rage" in Cronenberg's *The Brood*. In this film, resentments and jealousies take on the form of malformed, murderous children with no volition or identity of their own, who seek out and kill the targets of their mother's wrath. Such is also the case with the Grendels of both *Beowulf* films, to such an extent indeed that these monstrous sons become almost automata, mindless embodiments of feminine aggressiveness that have taken on flesh and terrifying power.

But monstrous offspring, as is typical of the hybridity of such creatures, take after their fathers as well. The Grendel of the 1999 *Beowulf* lays waste to a land the genocidal Hrothgar had ravaged a generation before. As such, like many doppelgängers, the monster's duplications and imitations hold a mirror up to the father, the scandal of a dark side, which figures like Jekyll's Hyde or Dorian Grey's portrait render visible. The dragon in the 2007 *Beowulf* is the hero's son and double too. Their final battle, engagingly rendered by Performance Capture Technology and CGI, shows Beowulf riding the dragon's back, Nazgul-like, as it lays waste to the hero's kingdom. In this figurative sense, then, the monster simply carries out the repressed wishes of his father riding on his back. Beowulf becomes Hrothgar's heir only after killing the king's only son, Grendel. The trajectory of his life closely apes Hrothgar's: Beowulf marries Wealtheow, sires a monster, and becomes death-obsessed and despairing in his old age. Both his crown and the cup advertise him as a dragon king, though he kills the dragon and himself in an elaborately conceived imitation of the death of Grendel. Deliberately recalling the first fight with Grendel, Beowulf's arm is tethered fast with an enormous chain from which he hangs suspended in front of the dragon's breast. He dismembers himself, slicing through the tendons in his shoulder, in order to reach through a glowing chink in the beast's scaly armor to his heart. At the end, all fury spent, father and son lie dying side-by-side on the shore. The dragon shrinks back into human form, such that Beowulf sees a golden version of his son as he might have been. In these abundant reflections between monsters and men the film demonstrates over and again the descent of both from a self-destructive, feminine *jouissance*. Hrothgar and Beowulf become creatures of the monstrous feminine every bit as much as Grendel and the dragon are. Aging rapidly under the sway of this monstrous feminine infantilizes both old men. What's more, she herself is immortal and forever young. At the end of the film, Wiglaf finds the dragon cup washed ashore while the naked avatar of Angelina Jolie swims seductively before him. The scene leaves little doubt that Wiglaf will follow in Beowulf's footsteps: there is little hope of a different result. In this last wink toward horror films and their risibly repetitious evasions of closure, we realize not so much the potential for a sequel as an assurance that the dynamics which breed monsters through the eroticization of fame and power are older and more enduringly potent than any god could ever be.

One of Slavoj Žižek's most provocative contentions about postmodernity concerns how contemporary subjects cope with what he calls the waning of symbolic efficiency and the apparent atrophy of the super-ego in permissive times. For Žižek, subjects remain passionately attached to their own subjection through a masochistic attachment to the increasingly onerous burdens of unfettered enjoyment — no longer prohibited but rather demanded by a super-ego. In the words of Tony Myers: "sensual gratification has been elevated to the status of an official ideology. We are compelled to enjoy sex. The compunction — the injunction 'Enjoy!'— marks the return of the super-ego" (Myers 53). The monstrous feminine of the 2007 *Beowulf* would seem to incarnate this newer, Lacanian understanding of *jouissance*, wherein a dogged devotion to enjoyment, an apparently irresistible impulse to enjoy to the fullest all those benefits which power and position afford, becomes a postmodern variation on Freud's death wish.

7

Our Man Beowulf: Bowra, Ker and the Contemporary Struggle with Cinematic Heroism

E. L. RISDEN

In *Star Trek Voyager*'s "Heroes and Demons" heroes of the sci-fi holodeck meet an adventure-game energy-entity with designs on taking over their starship for its own nefarious purposes: pulp TV tackles mead-hall ritual, as old notions of heroism meet new sci-fi technology. For *Beowulf: Prince of the Geats* those involved in the production donated their time so that the proceeds of the film may support cancer research; this project stresses the idea of transforming the idea of heroic battle into a new arena while stretching the boundaries of culture and art. The Sci-Fi Channel's *Grendel* arms Beowulf with a fiery crossbow, reducing his reliance on physical strength, and it stresses the idea that the real purpose of heroism is the construction of story: something by which the future may remember us and, correctly or incorrectly, our reputations may survive. Contemporary audiences (or filmmakers) seem uncomfortable with old notions of courage, strength, praise, and fame, so they find means to recast the Beowulf story to exploit different — and for the most part diminished — themes. In a sense, we have come in general culture to see heroism as either quotidian devotion to duty — what a soldier or a physician or a teacher or even a parent may do regularly — or the extreme stuff of video games. This chapter will focus on what the more successful *Beowulf* films do with heroism: why and how they do it and where it leads, particularly in the light of C. M. Bowra's epic scholarly work on literary heroism.

Beowulf has served our literary tradition as a cornerstone of heroism: as Tolkien asserts in "*Beowulf*: The Monsters and the Critics," it foregrounds heroic "men [who] with courage as their stay went forward to that battle with the hostile world and the offspring of the dark which ends for all, even the kings and the champions, in defeat" (67). As Tom Shippey suggests in *J. R. R.*

Tolkien: Author of the Century, the continuation and adaptation of the old Germanic "theory of courage" represents one of Tolkien's chief achievements in *The Lord of the Rings* and *The Silmarillion*. Along with the heroes we must die, but, as *Beowulf* shows and Tolkien specifies, even we may depart nobly and memorably with a commitment to courageous resistance against chaos.[1] The modern and postmodern worlds and their media, however, have increasingly challenged old notions of human character, and increasingly public art forms have aggressively undercut the poem for its themes and even its genre: *epic* has come to mean "big and loud" rather than humanly heroic, dignified, and spiritually significant. Even as they exploit comic-book superheroes, contemporary media have deconstructed the traditional heroism that *Beowulf* teaches so clearly and directly. Some films have redirected heroism toward nontraditional themes and concerns, while some have simply diminished it to highlight our shortcomings rather than our valor.

For example, in *Star Trek Voyager*'s "Heroes and Demons" (1995) space-going fans of classic epics meet a seeming monster that turns them into energy, too, apparently, at first, for its own nefarious purposes. The intruder takes the place of the character Grendel in Harry Kim's *Beowulf* program, but it has as its goal only to recover a couple of mini-entities that the *Voyager* crew have accidentally taken captive as they attempted to acquire a new energy source from a proto-star. The ship's doctor, himself a computer creation or energy-being, reluctantly plays hero in the holodeck program by returning the captive entities and thereby recovering the lost crewmembers. In this story the hero doesn't want to be a hero, the monster doesn't want to be a monster, and the whole heroic episode amounts to no more than a misunderstanding. Pulp TV tackles mead-hall ritual in this episode. Old notions of heroism abruptly and uncomfortably meet new sci-fi technology, *Star Trek*'s prime directive, and the contemporary sense that heroism implies reluctance rather than adventure and requires clean-up work following our own blundering colonialism. The whole event results in loss rather than gain, as the ship gets no new energy source, and the doctor learns the sad power of love-longing: a Danish warrior-maiden from the holodeck program dies saving him from a jealous, raging Unferth, who doesn't want the doctor to succeed against the monster or with the woman. At warp speed traditional heroism goes nowhere mighty fast, but an old story gets a new twist adaptive to science fiction and to audiences who want human interest even in electronic projections.

For *Beowulf: Prince of the Geats* (2007), another recent but lower-budget cinematic version of the epic, those involved in the production donated their time and talents so that the proceeds of the film may support cancer research. This project stresses the idea of transforming the traditional heroic battle into a new arena — contemporary public service — while stretching the boundaries of how art can comment on and influence culture and sticking fairly close to the original story (it includes all three monster fights). For instance, as a comment on audience expectations the director appointed a black actor to play Beowulf, and he created new back-story to make the racial *coup* plausible. Beowulf's father comes from *the south*, so he might more likely have had darker skin than lighter. Here heroism joins with the process of artmaking to serve a cause, and together they result in filmmakers' communicating social statements about audiences' expectations with respect to both characters and the purpose of film. Why shouldn't we make art for generous, tangible causes, the writer/director suggests, rather than for money and awards or even for art's sake? A nobly conceived project, *Beowulf: Prince of the Geats* (how did Beowulf become a prince?) nonetheless slants attention away from the heroic attributes that define Beowulf as an essential character in literary history. In this case the help's the thing whereby we boost the conscience of the king, and the real heroism comes less in the story than in the making of this version of the story. It represents, in a sense, heroic film-making: art for vital causes both medical and social.[2]

The Sci-Fi Channel's *Grendel* (2007) has no such claims to art or social good. The script arms Beowulf with a fiery crossbow, reducing his reliance on physical strength, composure, and a sense of fair-play, and it stresses the idea that the real purpose of heroism is the construction of story: something by which the future may remember us and our reputations may survive. That theme replaces the epic's focus on steadfast courage as our source of preservation in a dangerous and unforgiving world. Whether or not we act heroically, if we show up, the future may make of us a story that will exemplify notions of heroism that it wants to teach: thus the thematic thrust of *Grendel*. Earning *lof* and *dom* has nothing to do with this film's revisionism. Beowulf defeats the monsters, remnants of antediluvian giants embodied as a child-consuming, Schwarzeneggerian gorilla-like Grendel and a speedy, gargoylish bat-like Grendel's Mother, by means of an extraordinary weapon and with a little help from his friends. The film offers no theme beyond an assertion of the value of story, but it imbeds that theme in a silly plot, silly because the filmmakers have detached it from the heroic values that ground the epic in human dignity rather than video-game whiz-bang.

Graham Baker's 1999 post-apocalyptic *Beowulf* prepares the way for Robert Zemeckis's 2007 remake: it establishes the real problem of a human society as the lack of control of the male libido. Hrothgar has begotten Grendel upon an alternately beautiful and monstrous indigenous mother. Beowulf, fearing his own monstrous nature, of which we learn little, arrives to kill the monsters, and, aided by super-human martial-arts skills and a leather suit that seems capable of hiding an incredible array of steel-edged weapons, he does so. But he admits to Hrothgar's daughter—Kyra, rather than Freawaru here—that he fights monsters because he believes himself akin to them—abetted, unfortunately, by the poet's use of the term *aglæca* for Grendel, the dragon, and Beowulf alike. As a son of the "god of darkness," Beowulf must fight them or become one of them. Despite his success against the monsters, he does the inhabitants of the Heorot-outpost little good: they die, and their castle falls as he and Kyra ride off unharmed. At least in this case the hero and the love interest end up together, and something of what C. M. Bowra would recognize as heroic honor abides in the protagonist's commitment to action. The film concentrates on the visual experience of action, not on character, or heroic ideals.

Contemporary audiences (or filmmakers, perhaps) seem uncomfortable with old notions of courage, strength, praise, and fame, unless movies house them in sword thrusts and explosions. So many current films find means to recast the story to exploit different—and for the most part diminished—virtues. Rather than promote steadfast courage, composure in conflict, and devotion to duty—themes not only of epic poetry and *Beowulf*, but also extolled as energetically by Wulfstan in the *Sermo Lupi ad Anglos*—they turn the *Beowulf* story to address instead issues of human (particularly male) frailties, questioning the heroes' abilities, intelligence, or sexual restraint.

Bowra begins *Heroic Poetry* (London: Macmillan, 1964) thus:

> In their attempts to classify mankind in different types the early Greek philosophers gave a special place to those men who live for action and for the honor which comes from it. Such, they believed, are moved by an important element in the human soul, the self-assertive principle, which is to be distinguished equally from the appetites and from the reason and realizes itself in brave doings. They held that the life of action is superior to the pursuit of profit or the gratification of the senses, that the man who seeks honour is himself an honourable figure... [1].

Contemporary cinematic productions of *Beowulf* exhibit a declining interest in Bowra's notion (or any nostalgia) of heroism as a blend of action and honor, replacing it often with either empowered or sympathetic monsters (after the fashion of John Gardner's *Grendel*) or heroes troubled with Freudian anxieties or realistic human weaknesses — or occasionally with that sense of their own monstrous nature.

A particular value of *epic* poetry, too, a specialized kind of heroic poetry, comes, as W. P. Ker explained, in its "immediate association with all that a people know about themselves, with all their customs, all that part of their experience which no one can account for or refer to any particular source."³ The hero comes from the values, desires, and lives of the people (in the singular sense) that produces him. Ker separates epic from Romance, the former more concentrated and solemn, embedded in an old Heroic Age, and the latter more expansive, attentive to the varieties and vagaries of chivalric encounters. The sense of worldly breadth in errantry overtakes the resolved defense of the home, the ambushed pass, or the mead hall as Romance replaces epic historically. Film, too, takes a different course, one of its own age: it specializes in the visual analysis of character, the close-up on facial expression juxtaposed to the panoramic expansion of action. It hasn't the concentration of epic or the expansiveness of epic, though the nature of its medium allows brief moments of either or both. The visual, auditory, and motive qualities allow, though, for more thorough audience identification with characters, a more complete sensual experience of story — and we have far more filmmakers take up the art than we ever had writers of epic or Romance, so, despite the prohibitive costs or the limitations of the studio system, an element of democritization adds to its inclusiveness. Film can adapt stories repeatedly, as could oral performance, but it can record and archive performance for generations to come.

We would expect film to embody a Beowulf-inflected story according to the cultural patterns of the time and place that produces it — but we may still reasonably expect anything called *Beowulf* to follow the epic as closely as it can, especially in the heroic ideal absolutely central to what the poem is and does. Anything we call by the name should, I think, remain true or at least respectful to the original; *auteurs* who simply use or allude to the original and then take their own course reasonably have fair license, and filmmakers generally can of course make interesting heroic films with no connection to *Beowulf* whatever. Thereby we see some of the interesting and problematic tensions in the reception of the various *Beowulf*-derived films. All tend, though, at least to deal in some way with questions of heroism, though they may well downplay or even undercut it rather than centralizing it as the poem does.

Three other *Beowulf* films also diverge greatly in purpose from the epic, though they do so to raise interesting and thematically valid alternatives with respect to heroism. They aim to address different problems that we may associate with the need for courage in daily living, issues evolving from contemporary concerns rather than from medieval Germanic culture. They come in part, I think, from popular culture's notions of the indeterminacy of meaning and value, but also from real attempts to struggle with the social and personal problems of our time. Infected by the Deconstructive aspect of Cultural

Criticism, cinematic *Beowulf*s have undercut heroism to redirect our thinking about essential social values. *No Such Thing, Beowulf and Grendel,* and *The 13th Warrior* all explicitly transform hero and heroism so that Bowra or Ker would hardly recognize them: they do, however, establish notions of heroism that, while counter-cultural, reinforce such positive qualities as courage in the face of suffering, composure amidst confusion, compassion and tolerance toward Others, and mutual commitment to a task — values useful and salable even in a postmodern environment. Beowulf becomes less *agonistes* and more concerned reporter, frustrated hired gun, and displaced ambassador. But each new Beowulf has or learns admirable qualities, and each at least exhibits (or aims to) honor, as their stories point toward culturally centralized questions.

In *No Such Thing* (2002), where Beowulf is replaced by Beatrice, a cute cub-reporter, heroism comes in the questing character's ability to learn to consider the Monster on his own terms, even though he has killed her boyfriend — not a good start in traditional Germanic-heroic contexts. Beatrice's courage, sang-froid, and compassion redefine Beowulfian heroism for our time. Her flight to Iceland plunges into the sea — compare Beowulf's swimming match with Breca — and the special extensive surgery that returns her to active life requires that she endure the worst part of it awake, without pain-killers. Having experienced incredible physical suffering, she then meets the Monster, as does the epic Beowulf, with absolute composure, and through patience and sympathy she learns to understand and appreciate his unending loneliness and his disgust with ever-encroaching humans. She helps the otherwise immortal Monster bring about his own death, and she meets it standing with him, bravely, face to face. Whether she dies with the Monster — and whether we, the audience, do as well — the film doesn't specify. The point is that she faces it with him, with an open mind, clear vision, and a willing heart.

Beowulf and Grendel (2005) reshapes the story so that the hero serves more as an observer than a monster-slayer. He uncovers the reason for Grendel's attacks: the Danes killed Grendel's father for no better reason than "He crossed our path; he stole a fish." Beowulf kills Grendel's mother, the more violent and less human of the two, but Grendel causes his own death during his escape from Heorot, as he cuts his arm free from a chain that binds him. Grendel kills only those who destroyed his father: he doesn't act out of malice as the Danes in the film did and do. When the bemused Beowulf meets Grendel's own son, rather than harm the child he says "Be proud": he attempts through slowly gained understanding, through compassion, to end the family feud by honoring the dead troll, himself a protective father. The film addresses issues of race and pointless violence rather than heroic defense against monsters. It addresses one of the central concerns of cultural critique of our time: we must avoid the easy move of "othering" and accept not only other races, but also other creatures as equally part of our world. Standing up to our cultural attempts at othering requires courage. When we enter conflicts with other countries or peoples, the propaganda machine immediately seizes on the idea that, since they are our enemies, they must be monsters, and we must be those appointed by God to deliver the world from such monsters. *Beowulf and Grendel*, like *No Such Thing*, urges us to resist such simple-minded thinking and overzealous leaps into martial conflict.

The 13th Warrior (1999), I have argued elsewhere,[4] down deep is a "buddy film": a sibyl predicts that a group of Norsemen will need a thirteenth warrior to help them defeat the Wendol, a primitive and violent folk who attack northern settlements. Ahmed Ibn Fahdlan, nominally an Arab ambassador to the realms of northern Europe, but actually an exile enduring punishment for sexual indiscretions with the wife of a powerful lord, must pass linguistic and cultural barriers to work with his brave and good-natured but less cleanly and civilized companions. Though he is physically smaller than the Norsemen, swings a smaller sword, and rides a smaller horse, his courage and the mutual commitment he makes to their task helps them succeed in driving off the flesh-eating attackers and destroying their bloodthirsty queen. He has every bit of their courage, sense of honor, and commitment to action. Ahmed, the main character, doesn't fall in the Beowulf role — we already have a Beowulf-type, the leader of the Norsemen, who dies in their defense — but he provides a perspective on their heroism and their religion and represents cross-cultural understanding and cooperation, one of the great if not the greatest of the urgencies of our age. The film foregrounds those values rather than heroic battle, though it employs both. *The 13th Warrior* stresses, though, that a tolerant and adaptable hero makes a much more successful hero, and any group must prove willing to accept an "outsider" as one of its own — perhaps in some ways better than its own.

If we find in these films small elements of parody, they haven't yet become parodies of parodies. In *Our Man Flint*, a 1966 poor-man's James Bond and unrecognized parent of the Austin Powers films, our hero faces three mad scientists set on taking over large governments by threat of serial natural disasters. With the help of an adaptive cigarette lighter, self-induced suspended animation, and some exploding cold cream, Derek Flint rescues his sexy playmates and an even sexier opposing agent along with the bad governments he represents but that probably deserved taking over. While the parodic themes and motifs of *Our Man Flint* and its ilk have perhaps distantly infected *Beowulf*-at-the-movies, they have not yet turned it into outright parody. The

Olga (Maria Bonnevie) mocks the hero for making "a woman's sound" in *The 13th Warrior* (1999).

best *Beowulf* films retain a desire to get their audiences and cultures to the liminal boundaries they need to visit so they can understand something important about contemporary heroism: to succeed one must show compassion, tolerance, and teamwork — virtues that must precede and undergird heroism if we wish, as individuals and cultures, to survive. To parody heroism itself, the essence of the story, would not only destroy the film and perhaps damage public reception of the poem (or willingness to receive it), but would also undermine our ability to make films free of self-destructive sarcasm. Much of contemporary political discourse nominally deals with values such as courage, dedication to duty, compassion, and service to others only to undermine any hope of our learning them (or from them) through the use of language gaudy with hatred, lies, and stereotypes. When film plots a similar course, it replaces the potential beauty of art with the ugliness of self-absorption and the desire for personal influence that now renders communication in the political sphere all but impossible. Whether filmmakers always recognize it or not, they have a duty to their audiences, a duty well beyond making money for themselves and investors, a duty to truth in art that reflects truth to human experience both in our limitations and in our more glorious aspirations. The truth in *Beowulf* lies not in war or possessiveness or failed libido, but in finding our strengths and sharing them to the preservation and betterment of the human lot; *Beowulf*-at-the-movies may yet more heroically plot that course.

The question of honor, too, troubles our time, when artists feel willing to raise it. Beowulf films tend, whether intentionally or not, to raise questions of honor, something that the poem, in its hero, takes for granted. The humans in *No Such Thing*, with the exception of Beatrice, have none; though she never casts the question as such, honor leads her to find the Monster, understand him, and appreciate his problems. The Beowulf of *Beowulf and Grendel* learns about honor, but occasionally fails in it: he participates in the death of Grendel before he learns the reason for his attacks and indulges sexually where he may have done better to act temperately. His sexual experience recapitulates that of the "monster," and he thereby learns more about him and about himself; the sexual response shows his humanness, even his weakness, but not necessarily his honor — again a motif that pervades *Beowulf* films. The *13th Warrior*'s Ahmed ends up in the adventure he does perhaps because of a failure in honor; he learns by that adventure not so much about the wrong he has done as about a different kind of honor, cross-cultural appreciation and mutual help for the sake of persons one doesn't even know, for the sake of something one can call good: easing human suffering. *Beowulf* (1999) succeeds where *Beowulf* (2007) fails: he keeps his sense of honor and establishes what may at the end of the film suggest a committed loving relationship — the epic, of course, never goes in that direction, as we learn only that Beowulf has not left an heir of his own body (a failing in that culture where a good king must provide a son of his own caliber to lead his folk in the next generation).

Beowulf films go so far as to ask, though tacitly, in what they omit, whether in our time we even believe in honor. We appear to believe in adventure, in what expedites our success (however we choose to define it), in working together — if that cooperation also gets us what we want. Our war films often deal with issues of honor, whether soldiers show it or not, how they feel about it, and whether or not it necessarily represents a part of soldiering. Horror films may show the terrifying results of a person's failing to act honorably or decisively: monster may just appear, terrifying in their drive to evil, or they may appear to persons who have acted badly to take their own acts of vengeance. Wall Street films typically suggest honor doesn't have much to do with business — they don't always comment on whether it should, though they may show the ill results of excesses in the pursuit of money and property. Sports films — if not sports news or broadcasts of sporting events — often bring it into relief. Professional sport may imply getting away with whatever abuses of the rules one can, but we still preach the value of sport to teach teamwork and effort. Adventure films often show the "bad guy" failing to show honor and the "good guy," wanting to or not, coming to act honorably at last: we want to *like* the hero. *Beowulf films* include elements of war, horror, business, and sport as well as adventure. The hero first chooses and later must go to battle bravely and with commitment to win. Monsters sometimes walk from the marches of our civilization right into our dining halls. Beowulf commoditizes himself to contribute to the success of his king and his people: he acts for praise and glory, but also for treasure, the peaceful exchange of which solidifies a peaceful society within and good relations with one's neighbors. The Beowulf of epic has swimming contests, wrestling matches, a hand-grip match, weapon-wielding and hand-to-hand combat: he shows unbelievable athleticism, but not the gymnastic hurtling about of Beowulf-in-film. Beowulf of the Geats, though, remains within and explicitly true to his culture's sense of honor, and that means even more than courage in conflict. It implies, as the last lines of the poem express, that the hero succeeds most and best as the "mildest, most gentle, kindest to his people, and most eager for praise (or even with praise to others)" of the kings of this world. Whether or not in our time we really believe in honor, the best lesson we can learn from *Beowulf-*at-the-movies may come in what it lacks that the epic foregrounds — all the more reason for yet more attempt, and a better one, at cinematic *Beowulf.* That attempt must now rehabilitate the honor of the woman warrior as well as that of the man, as we shall see in the next chapter.

Conclusion — The Postmodern *Beowulf*
NICKOLAS HAYDOCK

"You got business with me, Beowulf?" —*Xena the Warrior Princess*

Timeline[1]

1977: *The Hobbit* (animated feature)
1978: *Lord of the Rings* (animated feature)
1980: *The Return of the King* (animated feature)
1981: **Grendel Grendel Grendel* (animated feature)
1995: **Star Trek: Voyager* (television series, episode 11, "Heroes and Demons")
1998: **Animated Epics: Beowulf* (animated television short)
1999: *Beowulf* (estimated budget $20M)
1999: *The 13th Warrior* (estimated budget 85M, worldwide gross 62M)
2000: **Xena: The Warrior Princess* (television series, episodes 7–9)
2001: *No Such Thing* (not available)
2001–2003: *Lord of the Rings* trilogy (estimated budget 93M, 94M, 94M= 281M; estimated worldwide gross 861M, 922M, 1.12B= 2.92B)
2005: *Beowulf and Grendel* (budget not available)
2007: **Grendel* (*SyFy* Channel made-for-television movie)
2007: *Beowulf* (estimated budget $150M, estimated worldwide gross 191M)
2007: *Beowulf, Prince of the Geats* (limited release)
2008: *Outlander* (estimated budget 50M, estimated gross $160,000)

Kevin Harty's filmography *The Reel Middle Ages* was first published in 1999. It lists no film adaptation of *Beowulf* and only one related film: the animated musical *Grendel Grendel Grendel* (1981) based on John Gardner's novel. Why did the most read work in English literature go begging for cinematic treatment for so long? And why did five major film adaptations of the poem appear in the ten-year period between 1999 and 2008, especially given that only one of the five made a profit? Adding to this remarkable total an embarrassment of riches in *Beowulf*-dedicated episodes in television programs, made-for-television movies and independent, limited release films yields quite a large sampling of popular adaptations of the Old English poem. By way of a conclusion this final chapter surveys some things such remediations have in common in the hopes of tracing the contours of this intensive vetting of *Beowulf* by popular culture. The temptation to explain the rash of *Beowulf* films by reference to socio-political factors is palpable, but technical and industrial trends seem to have been the determining factor.

Unlike the story of Arthur and his knights, Joan of Arc or Robin Hood, *Beowulf* has no cinematic tradition — why? One hypothesis is the centrality of the monsters to the plot, upon which Tolkien himself insisted. He also thought *The Lord of the Rings* un-filmable for not dissimilar reasons. The technical challenges posed by both works represented a substantial barrier to their adaptation as motion pictures. It is instructive that a number of animated versions rather than live-action films were produced in the period from 1977 to 1998 (see Timeline above). The first Beowulfian vehicle, Alexander Stith's animated musical *Grendel Grendel Grendel*, which actually *adapts* John Gardner's 1971 novel, begins with a long documentary-style prologue:

> Monsters. From the Minotaur to the Boogeyman, from the dragons of legend to the Creature from the Black Lagoon, monsters have haunted the human imagination, going *bump* in our night. It's almost as though we needed monsters — those metaphors for death — as aphrodisiacs for life to unite us in our common struggle against the implacable fates.... Our version of Grendel is seen through twentieth century eyes when perhaps we're a little suspicious of the military hero and more inclined to see humanity in a monster. For Grendel, ancient Grendel, who has watched human society developing, growing more complex as it invented things like politics, religion and art, is deserving of our sympathy and our thanks, for without our monsters, our misunderstood monsters, who are after all only doing their job, which is to stimulate our imaginations and encourage social cohesion, we wouldn't be in the civilized mess we are today. Ladies and gentlemen, it is with pride that we introduce the lonely, loveable monster, who has been living and dying for fifteen centuries with our very best interests at heart.

In nucleus, or perhaps *in ovo*, we encounter a number of concepts here that are more stable in Beowulfian films than anything in the poem itself. In fact, the attempt to square Gardner's novel with popular mythology is itself a bit of a reach, but one that also embraces all the films with which we have been concerned in this book. As we saw in Chapter 5, the 1999 *Beowulf* deliberately troubles the distinction between men and monsters and reimagines Grendel's mother as a combination of the Gorgon and Lilith. Ahmed ibn Fadlan in *The 13th Warrior* is proto-modern in his willingness "to see humanity in a monster," though his vacillation on this question is in keeping with that film's uncanny evolutionary biology. The made-for-television movie *Grendel* makes the monster a figure like the Minotaur, which the Danes propitiate by offering children as sacrificial victims, which in turn brings Hrothgar to admit that he (like Minos himself) is the real monster. In the 2007 *Beowulf* both Grendel and the dragon are the offspring of the Danish kings Hrothgar and Beowulf, respectively.

As Chapter 3 attests in some detail, the majority of *Beowulf* films include depictions of scapegoating and human sacrifice. In the two films released in 1999 (*Beowulf* and *The 13th Warrior*), these themes remain peripheral to the main action. The later films, *Beowulf and Grendel* and *Grendel*, make scapegoating and human sacrifice central to their versions of the poem. It is as if an interpretive concept, tentatively vetted in these early films, continues to develop across later treatments, emerging as a central element in the latter two films' adaptations of the poem. Certainly much of the impetus for the development of a theme across separate films is owing to the semi-conscious iterations of popular culture. Such similarities seldom reach the ironic distance required for parody, and the quality and popularity of the 1999 films was hardly of the sort to inspire homage. A possible exception exists in Sturla Gunnarsson's *Beowulf and Grendel*, which cannily exposes the scapegoating mechanism behind the demonization of para-human monsters in the earlier films.

Still, a progressive accumulation of devices, details and solutions to the problems of representability seems to be the rule in this decade-long fashion for *Beowulf* adaptations. Michael Crichton's cannibals dress up as bears in *The 13th Warrior*, while the cannibals in *Xena: Warrior Princess* sport the hides and heads of boars. Indeed, *Xena*'s pastiche reaches something like a degree zero of adaptability: as such, the series' *Beowulf* trilogy (2000, episodes 7–9) lays bare many of the components common to this fashion for Beowulf adaptations. The trilogy is a delirious pastiche of three mythic elements: Wagner's *Ring* cycle, *Beowulf*, and Tolkien's *Lord of the Rings*. Teaming up with Beowulf, Xena ventures forth to right an evil she herself created 35 years before when she seduced and betrayed Odin, stole the Rhine gold, and corrupted both Vikings and Valkyries with her lust for power.

Like the Hrothgars and Beowulfs of many films Xena is also the victim of a checked past; she battles, however noisomely, against monsters of her own creation. In an erotic interlude in a subaqueous cave, the warrior princess seduces a Rhine maiden, steals the gold, and fashions a ring of power that can only be safely wielded by someone who has "forsaken love." (Here, the warrior princess assumes the role of Wagner's dwarf, Alberich, in *Das Rheingold*.)

The scene certainly influenced the more elaborate one in the Zemeckis' *Beowulf* where the hero is seduced in a watery cave by a nymphet who is literally dripping with gold.

The sixth year of the series was filmed entirely in New Zealand during the time the *Lord of the Rings* was being shot there. Principle photography for Peter Jackson's hugely ambitious project was shot at more than 150 locations around New Zealand, spanning the period from October 11, 1999, through December 22, 2000. The *Xena* Beowulf trilogy obviously sought to capitalize on the rampant buzz created by the production of Jackson's film. Yet it also cannibalizes two of Tolkien's major sources — *Beowulf* and the Norse mythology of Wagner's *Ring* cycle — in the production of what might well be termed *queer pastiche*, a queering of *LOTR* and its sources where lesbian love (like Tolkienian male friendship) is the only bond stronger than the pull of the Ring. The cinematography of the trilogy also incorporates a wide range of literary and cinematic influences: the Valkyries ride real horses across the sky in homage to Ralph Bakshi's rotoscoped sequences from *Wizards* and *The Lord of the Rings* (1977); the design of the arboreal Beowulfian monsters Grindl and Grinhilda seems based on Tolkien's Ents; Xena slices off the finger/branch of the latter to recover the golden ring that destroys anyone who has not "forsaken love."

Xena thus appropriates a number of recognizable roles. Beowulf himself (demoted to one of her followers) is cast in a supporting role and for the most part just looks on as she defeats the two Grendel-kin. Before meeting the love of her life, Gabrielle, Xena was a dark queen who cast a shadow over the north world, much as Galadriel fears to become should she accept the ring. Putting on the ring, Xena is suffused with light, anticipating a more elaborate shot from Peter Jackson's *The Fellowship of the Ring*. Like Isildur, she wins the ring only to lose it soon thereafter. When she recovers it and attempts to use its powers, the ring diminishes her just as it does Gollum, and she wanders lost, forgetting who and what she was. During her wanderings in Denmark her amnesia makes her to fall prey to an opportunistic Hrothgar, who marries her under the name Wealthea. In the final episode, "Return of the Valkyrie," Xena returns to rescue the sleeping beauty Gabrielle — her soul mate — from a ring of fire, like that guarding Brünnhilde from potential suitors in Wagner's *Die Walküre*. The *mise en scène* of this final "battle" deliberately evokes both Beowulf's fight with the dragon — by now "Wiglaf" has joined the fellowship of those who love Gabrielle — as well as Sauron's fiery eye. Leaping through the flames, Xena wakes her one true love with a kiss and subsequently returns the cursed gold to the lissome Rhine maidens.

The *Xena* trilogy's playful pastiche of *Beowulf*, Wagner, and Tolkien is nevertheless paradigmatic of the cinematic *Beowulf* in a number of ways. First, it employs Tolkien's *Lord of the Rings* to mediate between the poem and its adaptation, just as films such as *The 13th Warrior* and *Beowulf and Grendel* employ the novels of Crichton and Gardner, respectively. Indeed, even the comparatively direct adaptation of the 2007 *Beowulf* conflates Tolkien's ring with the poem's cup, a symbolic representation of how power debilitates and enslaves its possessor. Second, it allows us to sympathize with its monsters and supplies motivations for their ravages. Grinhilda, the mother of Grindl, was once a virtuous leader of the Valkyries, whom the "bad" Xena displaced, just as Hrothgar and even Beowulf create the monsters that haunt them in films such as *Beowulf* (1999), *Beowulf and Grendel*, and *Beowulf* (2007).

The tree-bearded trolls of *Xena*'s low-budget special effects bring us back to the question of technology. Of the five major films, three use CGI and other techniques to render the poem's supernatural. *The 13th Warrior* and *Beowulf and Grendel* employ considerably less technology. These films are also the most influenced by modern novels and the most determined to euhemerize the supernatural. On the other hand, the relative success of films that invest deeply in technology to render the poem's supernatural — such as the 1999 and 2007 *Beowulf*, *Outlander* and even the made-for-television *Grendel*— was largely determined by their budgets. The cheep CGI of the 1999 *Beowulf* and the 2007 *Grendel* seem precious and even ridiculous in comparison with Zemeckis' *Beowulf*, where monsters and men actually do seem to inhabit the same cinematic space. In Zemeckis' film, the fish-faced avatars *do* lack expression, and certainly actors in sensor-studded wetsuits interacting with a blue screen is about as far from actor's studio immersion in a role as one can so far get, but human and supernatural beings all appear to exist on the same plane and their bodies to interact in much more natural ways. In a sense, then, Zemeckis' *Beowulf* solves the problem of visualizing men and monsters by animating human beings, where earlier films had sought to humanize the monsters.

This performance capture *Beowulf* has relevance too for the thesis vetted in our first chapter, namely that film has the capacity to actualize styles of visualization which are essential elements of the Old English poem itself. As demonstrated in that chapter, both the 1999 *Beowulf* and *The 13th Warrior* evince — however spottily — a respect for the visual nature of the poem and attempt to reproduce effects such as form cuts and deep focus. But Zemeckis' film is for the most part an attempt to showcase the plasticity of the technology. An early "tracking shot" through an impossible camera angle follows a hawk snatching a rat from a roof beam and takes us up beyond the hall high into the sky to view the landscape from the eye of the eagle. Impressive, certainly, but to what purpose, exactly? Is it perhaps meant as a foreshadowing of Grendel's later attacks on the hall? And what are we to make of Grendel's exposed eardrum, which vibrates painfully with the racket from the hall many leagues away? Again, we might hypothesize that the visibly aching ear explains Grendel's hatred of merrymaking, but a full-scale motivation for his bloodlust is given later, lifted directly from Graham Baker's *Beowulf.* Seeing through the eyes of a bird of prey soaring high through the air and the visualization of sound are examples of Zemeckis putting the technology through its paces. These shots don't make actual anything virtual or latent within the poem, as Peter Jackson's *LOTR* trilogy does for Tolkien's novel. As such, while its technology is cutting edge, the film itself is among the most derivative of *Beowulf* films. Grendel knocks open the door of Heorot, and the wind sends warriors sprawling across the floor — an effect invented by the 1998 *Animated Epics: Beowulf.* Angelina Jolie's succubus troll is very obviously taken from Graham Baker's MILF. The notion that the dragon is also her child is likewise borrowed from Baker's film. Zemeckis' hero falls for her charms and promises, but subsequently gains a modicum of redemption like Tolkien's Thorin, while the Hrothgars of both the 1999 and 2007 *Beowulf* fall victim to a Denethor-like spiritual palsy. The fight with the dragon also seems chiefly concerned to outdo the CGI acrobatics of earlier dragon films such as *Reign of Fire* and *Eragon.* Thus, while Zemeckis' film is in many ways the most visually striking of the *Beowulf* films, it is also the most derivative and most regrettable. The success of Jackson's *LOTR* trilogy (with a combined theatrical gross of nearly three billion dollars) certainly helped pave the way for his friend and collaborator's big-budget *Beowulf.* Backed to the tune of some $150 million dollars, it is the only *Beowulf* film to make a profit, but Jackson's personal investment in Tolkien's work is light years beyond Zemeckis' uninspired approach to *Beowulf.*

Zemeckis' film was shot in a studio in Burbank, California, and, finally, it is not simply a product of that world but in many ways a mirror of it — the lure of fame and power, artificially retouched bodies and faces, the promiscuous reproduction of details and motifs from earlier films, the Faustian bargain of blockbusterism. Much more interesting to look at and think about are two films shot chiefly on location in Iceland: Hal Hartley's *No Such Thing* (2001) and Sturla Gunnarsson's *Beowulf and Grendel* (2004). Hartley's chagrin-inspiring combination of *Beowulf* and *The Beauty and the Beast* imagines that Gardner's introspective, world-weary Grendel has survived into the twenty-first century and taken up residence on an abandoned U.S. military base. His Beowulf is Beatrice (Sarah Polley), his Grendel a cross between Milton's Satan and Lord Byron, his female monster a soul-less scandal sheet editor (the delightfully wicked Helen Mirren, sporting red fingernails and an American accent), and his dragon takes the form of the near-sighted, anti-matter genius, Artaud. What identifies the monsters as such is that they are all chain-smokers. Finally, all band together to conspire against the Military Industrial Complex in a quest to euthanize the world's last living troll, whose Beatrice ushers him lovingly from the hell of an eternity in this world. Generations of critics have wondered whether Beowulf might have made it to heaven. *No Such Thing* leaves us wondering whether the troll might just join him there. As he is being transformed into nothing, a beatific vision of Beatrice remains before his eyes, beloved killer and redeemer. Whether as a memory, afterimage, or a glimpse of transcendence, we shall never know.

Sturla Gunnarsson's *Beowulf and Grendel* (2004) presents an equally sympathetic, if less philosophical monster also coupled with the divine Sarah Polley. Polley doesn't so much reprise her role in *No Such Thing* as she confirms the centrality of a particular type of feminine character in *Beowulf* films: a woman trapped in a subservient role who transcends the limits of her position. The 1999 *Beowulf*'s Kyra (Rhona Mitra) kills an abusive husband and is the sole survivor of her civilization, riding off with Beowulf at the end. Sophia Myles' Freya in *Outlander* is the beloved daughter of the good king Hrothgar. She is betrothed to a man she does not love, survives her father and suitor, and marries the film's astronaut Beowulf at the end. Both Kyra and Freya are battlers who play out a rebellion against the gender expectations of their fathers, not unlike Eówyn in the film version of *The Return of the King*. Yet Polley in both her Beowulfian roles conquers through impassive resolve. The sole survivor of a jet crash into the ocean in *No Such Thing* (reprising Beowulf's miraculous survival at sea), she finally arrives in Iceland only to be slipped a Mickey Finn by the haunted locals at a banquet thrown in her honor. They strip her naked and offer up the unconscious hero as a sacrifice to the troll, along with bottles of whiskey. As the troll himself explains: "Every, uh, once in awhile those maniacs down in the village toss some unsuspecting piece of ass up on the rocks down there. A gift, I guess, for me." As noted in Chapter 3, many films have explored the sacrificial underpinnings of *Beowulf*, but none so incisively as here. René Girard might well hear the story of a stranger royally feasted and then lying down to sleep naked and without weapons to await a flesh-eating monster as a mythologizing of the sacrificial mechanism, but this is not a connection I made before viewing Hartley's subtle adventure in iconoclasm. Indeed, alongside this delightful interrogation of gender and sacrifice, the locker room jokes in Zemeckis' *Beowulf* about the hero's gigantic penis and the pintel-less Grendel show how easily fantasy slides into puerility.

In *Beowulf and Grendel*, Polley's Selma also emerges as a scapegoat and the moral center of the film. A red-haired stepchild and an outcast, she leverages her marginal status into a position of power and safety as a kind of *sacra femina*. Unlike the demonic temptresses of the 1999 and 2007 *Beowulf*s or even the tiny but lethal mother of the Wendol in *The 13th Warrior*, Selma's power is a function of the fears embodied in the scapegoat. In this, her position doubles that of Grendel, who likewise suffers victimization and subsequent monsterization. But neither portrayal is ever allowed to slide away into the phantasmagoric. The role of Grendel's amphibian, albino mother is reduced to little more than a cameo. The real monstrous couple is Grendel and Selma, both human and both victims with few illusions about what Danish civilization means for those they exclude. As in the last shot of *No Such Thing*, our last glimpse in Gunnarsson's film is of the face of Sarah Polley. She is pregnant, apparently with Beowulf's child, the cycle of monster-making almost certainly poised to begin anew. Polly's "monster" works like a parody of the Lamia-like monstrous feminine of the 1999 *Beowulf*, her fertile womb more of challenge to the future than any dragon could ever mount.

This trend toward irresolute endings continues in Zemeckis' *Beowulf*. We are left with Wiglaf holding the golden cup and pondering his options, as Grendel's resilient mother treads water just off shore, her abundant charms undiminished. These later film *Beowulf*s reach something like a consensus about the recursive nature of the poem's monsters, even if they come to different conclusions about how this recursivity applies to the contemporary world. The lackluster *Outlander* reprises this new ambivalence about heroism and the process of creating monsters but turns it inside out. Beowulf, alias Kainan, is a man who falls from space, burdened with a genocidal past, which he carries with him as monstrous baggage into eighth-century Norway. He ends up as the savior and king of a people, having annihilated the scourge he himself brought down on their heads. Thus, the critique of scapegoating or the lust for power vetted in prior films is sublated by a narrative in which the hero proves himself a savior by killing in this new world what few monsters he had failed to destroy in the old one.

Outlander brings to an apparent (and inglorious) end this remarkable, decade-long fashion for *Beowulf* films. By 2008 the film's director, Howard McCain, was under significant pressure to distinguish his version from earlier ones. The film was originally to be shot in New Zealand, and its special effects were to have been produced by Weta, but financing fell through and the film was ultimately lensed in Canada on a relatively meager budget. Perhaps the most salient feature of the worst major *Beowulf* film yet produced is that it responds chiefly not to the poem but to earlier film *Beowulf*s. Its superficial deviations from these films do not derive from a reconsideration of the poem's proto-cinematic style, but rather from unrelated popular blockbusters such as *Alien*, *Predator* and *Jurassic Park*. David W. Marshall's insightful reading of *Outlander* identifies two major themes in the film, feud and colonial expansion, noting how the traditional opposition between Vikings as brutal raiders and daring explorers structures as well as compromises the film. Marshall rightly states that "This *Beowulf* (i.e., *Outlander*) suggests that colonial conquest breeds resistance" (Marshall 144). Yet this is hardly director McCain's original contribution to filmic *Beowulfiana*! Indeed every other major *Beowulf* film draws similar connections between feud and colonialism; perhaps the most successful iteration of the compound theme is Sturla Gunnarsson's *Beowulf and Grendel*, not least because the "monster" is actually a man/troll, not a dinosaur-like predator, unlikely to arouse much sympathy in audiences. But Hrothgar is also an imperial oppressor suffering the vengeance of the Grendel-kin in the 1999 *Beowulf*. Marshall cites with justified approval Seth "Lerer's sense that Grendel's attacks amount to a reassertion of territorial rights" (146).[2] Fair enough, but Graham Baker (in *Beowulf*, 1999) and Gunnarsson (in *Beowulf and Grendel*, 2004) drew this connection and explored its consequences in some detail before Lerer asserted it in 2005. A chief concern of Lerer's essay "On fagne flore: The Postcolonial *Beowulf*, from Heorot to Heaney" is to associate the description of the floor in the poem with remnants of the Roman occupation in Anglo-Saxon England, those Romans who built in stone and walked upon tessellated mosaics. While this is quite a lot to hang on one of the most frequent words in the poem, *fag*, Lerer's general point about the architectural remains of Roman Britain influencing the English poet's representation of an *in geardagum* past is persuasive. Yet the made-for-television *Grendel* (2007) hypothesizes exactly the same thing. This film depicts Hrothgar ruling from a throne within a stone-columned Roman building, complete with flagstone, mortared floors — no mosaics, unfortunately. Throughout this book we have touched on similar coincidences between scholarship and popular films, where there is little likelihood of direct influence in either direction. Similarly, it is important to recognize the extent to which the "postcolonial *Beowulf*" is inescapably a *postmodern* construct, diffused across a leveling field of cultural production where distinctions between high and low, scholarly and popular, the philological and the phantasmagoric are increasingly unstable.

A related point might well be made about a congeries of trends in contemporary scholarship that Eileen A. Joy and Mary K. Ramsey assemble under the rubric *The Postmodern Beowulf*. By this they seem to mean something like the state of the question of *Beowulf* scholarship, increasingly inflected by approaches that fall under the broad umbrella of "postmodernism." Surely, though, the term "postmodern *Beowulf*" applies at least equally well to the film adaptations treated in this book, in both the theoretical as well as the enduringly pejorative sense of the term *postmodern*. On the positive side, what these films share with many of the essays collected by Joy and Ramsey is a general and abiding incredulity with master narratives, such as the march of civilization or the false totalizations that inhere within un-deconstructed binaries. On the negative side, postmodernism is often associated with blank parody or ludic pastiche and a lack of historical consciousness, which leads directly to political quietism and despair. In both senses of the term Howard McCain's *Outlander* thoroughly fits the bill of a postmodern *Beowulf*. The futuristic space traveler, Kainon, crash lands into "an abandoned seed colony" in early eighth-century Norway, thereby tracing the ancestry of human development and its subsequent history to an interstellar master race of genocidal settlers. The film thus sets out to critique imperialism but ends up reinstalling it as a transcendent, otherworldly constant. Likewise, its formerly genocidal hero traverses a humanistic arc which ends in his establishment as a just and peaceful king at the end of the film — a couple of generations before the onset of the Viking Age, when an Anglo-Saxon chronicler would compare the raid on Lindisfarne to a dragon sweeping across the sky.

As the (for now) final entry in a veritable torrent of *Beowulf* films sweeping across our multi-media world, we should perhaps ignore the temptation to read the film as a free adaptation of the Anglo-Saxon poem. It is less that than an accumulation of themes inherited from earlier film *Beowulf*s, a re-stirring of sedimented ideas from all that preceded it. But it is perhaps in this concoction of inherited themes, repeated with variation and thoroughly in keeping with the formulaic character of the cinematic *Beowulf*, that McCain's film most closely approaches the traditional, repetitive, conventional poetics of the Old English poem. It performs a recombination of inherited themes that have as much to do with the original poem as the original poem does with Dark Age history. As the poem is a product of oral formulism, *Outlander* is a production of cinematic conventionality, where an incredulity toward metanarratives, no less than a love-interest for Beowulf, becomes the cinematic equivalent of the hero on the beach.

* * *

E. L. Risden began this book by justly remarking that "a full-length *Beowulf* film that actually sticks pretty closely to the poem" remains a desideratum. The rather large sample of film *Beowulf*s suggests that this is unlikely, if not impossible, within mainstream cinema. In fact, what these films rather suggest is the production of a level playing field where novelizations and earlier filmic treatments mediate or filter adaptations of the original poem. Indeed, many of these films are posed as the true version of events (e.g., *The 13th Warrior* and *Beowulf and Grendel*) behind distortions introduced in the long process of the story's oral transmission — yet another example of the myriad ways in which these films mirror the scholarly history of the poem. This decade-long fashion for *Beowulfian* adaptations and appropriations serves as a variegated palette, such that any new iteration will be a recombination of previous treatments, a remediation of prior mediations, at times rising to the level of parody but more commonly remaining a pastiched bricolage of earlier solutions to the problematics of representation and the need to address the concerns of a contemporary audience. It is as if these films are adapting not the text itself, but rather a popular understanding of the text, appealing to an inherited series of readings, gestures, tropes and techniques. What is most remarkable, finally, about this corpus of films is their similarity, such that it is justifiable to speak of the cinematic *Beowulf* as though it were a single, generally coherent approach to the poem.

Yet it is fascinating to speculate, if only idly, how a more satisfying and nuanced film adaptation of the poem might come about *within the Hollywood system of production*. The monster fights weigh large in the story. To provide context and meaning for these monsters and their ravages, films have turned to combinations of psychoanalysis (family romance) or science (evolution) or anthropology (scapegoating and sacrifice) or postcolonial discourse (imperialism) to serve as a ground for these figures. The sense of historical depth that Tolkien found in the poem is thereby completely obscured. Is there an alternative? The commonly heard solution — Just follow the text! — is not only unhelpful but woefully naïve, not just about popular cinema but also about that very text itself, with its long speeches and off-hand references to obscure heroes like Ongentheow. Still, the insistence that more really is more has a great deal to recommend it. To include more would be to alter the very kinds of problems the film is forced to solve. The film *Beowulf* of my dreams would therefore have to be a *trilogy*, with a budget to fund the kind of effects such a project demands.

Such a trilogy might well begin at the beginning with the creation of the world, the severing of light from darkness, and the establishment of the heavens as a roof. It would fade gradually to an internal, domestic scene of two brothers before their father's table. They each bear foodstuffs: one from the fields, the other bloody meat from the pasture. As the father surveys these gifts, we cut to the farmer with his throat slit at the edge of the fields. Next comes a furious time-lapse montage of images spanning generations: fields of barley and rocky mountain slopes, cities and caves, giants scaling a mountain, and a rushing flood rising at their heels. An ark rides these waves past mountain peaks jutting from the water. As the camera pulls back away from the enormous ship, the seas calm and boat bearing every kind of animal diminishes into a tiny bark, bearing a tiny, blue-eyed baby boy. His eyes gaze peacefully up towards clear blue skies. Another jump cut yields a similar shot, only now the face is aged and bearded and the eyes are shut. He is dressed in polished war gear; the camera zooms out to a full shot of the body, gradually taking in the whole boat — loaded with treasure — and then mourners who shove the ship down a makeshift track to the sea. The cinematic analogy for such an extended montage sequence is the opening of Lars von Trier's *Melancholia*.

My treatment must become more suggestive, less detailed here. But I see the first part of the first part of the trilogy working through a parallel narrative that juxtaposes the ravages of Grendel and the "inglorious youth" of Beowulf. This latter subplot would borrow its tone from early chapters of *Grettis Saga*. The point of this juxtaposition has less to do with creating a monstrous Beowulf than with yielding a fully human one. Cross cutting between the parallel plots in Gotland and Denmark would be designed to reinforce the idea that fate (or something greater) is quietly nurturing — in the person of a reckless boy — someone who will come to be more than a match for Grendel. The best strategy to achieve this parallelism would be to fashion a chiastic structure, whereby, as the Scyldings wane, Beowulf waxes ever larger and stronger. Juxtapositions should be emphasized between the two worlds, first as a direct contrast between tragedy and comedy, later in a more uniformly serious way as Grendel's depredations meet no more resistance in the abandoned hall and Beowulf can find no youth willing to compete against him in games such as wrestling or bone-throwing. Perhaps too a scene should be filmed in which the young hero breaks off a sword at the hilt. I would have him fighting an older Breca (in sport and as practice) and break the sword upon his opponent's shield boss. This *Bildungsroman* sub-plot would come to an end in the swimming match with Breca. Here it is necessary to emphasize the young hero's willingness to stay beside the more seasoned warrior as well as his frustration when he comes ashore, having killed nine sea beasts, but having lost again to Breca. Because Beowulf is not Grettir, he will not seek to harm the older man, but he will find it difficult to withstand the embarrassment of being worsted in two tests of strength with an older but smaller, less powerful warrior. Though certainly no outlaw, Beowulf has not escaped adolescence wholly unscathed. His journey to the Danes now occurs just when it must.

As the first chapter in this book demonstrates in some detail, the poet's visualization of the fights with monsters needs little or no elaboration by filmmakers. It is already quite an elaborated, variegated shot schedule. In these moments without spoken dialogue and a great deal of information about spatial relationships, point of view, and alternations between subjective and objective camera, it would be possible, even salutary, to follow the poet's directions almost word for word.

There is not much to be gained by belaboring this very sketchy treatment, but I want to bring this exercise to a close by drawing lines under what such an approach does and does not attempt to accomplish. First, it does not try to fit everything into the film, but it does hold close much that all other treatments simply abandon. Second, it takes note of the poem's appositions and juxtapositions, its proto-cinematic style and attempts to employ such structural patterns, both at the level of the shot and of the plot. Third, it borrows freely from other texts, such as *Grettis Saga*, but to elucidate character and complicate motivation in ways that are suggested by the text itself.

There will be no monstrous, monotonous MILFs in my version, no Oedipal dramas or misunderstood trolls, either — not out of any naïve wish for an absolute fidelity to the source, but because such solutions resolve in puerile ways things much better left in the darkness where they live and breed. I *would* include a love interest for Beowulf, and it would be Freawaru, both in willingness to satisfy action cinema's demand for a love interest and as feature that would help build tension within Heorot. Here Wealhtheow has a real part to play, protecting the rights of her sons against a foreign adventurer, whom Hrothgar is only too willing to offer both giftstol and daughter. The notion that Hrothgar must in the end give his daughter to an enemy rather than a friend is one of the story's grandest ironies, though left largely implicit in the poem. Such a tactic makes the inclusion of the Finnsburg material a great deal more feasible. Freawaru will see her own future shadowed forth in the tragedy of Hildeburh, and Wealhtheow's protection of her son's rights will seem blinkered if not downright destructive when another mother comes to claim the rights of another son later that evening. This first installment of my trilogy would close with a shot of Grendel's mere, its waves churning blood — the same shot would end the second film as well.

Satis est. I hope I can be excused for previewing a screenplay I will almost certainly never write. Still, one can hope for something in the future more like what I have outlined and less like what we have had. As I write this in early December 2012, the release of the first of Jackson's three *The Hobbit* films is being touted across every imaginable media outlet. I find myself wishing Jackson had confined himself to a single film that gets there and back again in two hours. That would have left him ample time to make the *Beowulf* trilogy about which I shall continue to dream.

Chapter Notes

Introduction

1. A strange and interesting recent film, *Albert Nobbs* (2011, dir. Rodrigo García), while set in the nineteenth century, questions the degree to which we really have freed ourselves of imposed sexual identities in our own time.
2. I have found reference to a 1981 animated Australian film, *Grendel Grendel Grendel*, directed by Alexander Stitt, that purportedly responds even more directly to Gardner's novel, but have not seen it.
3. A *Star Trek Voyager* episode, "Heroes and Demons," makes interesting use of the Othering motif: when life forms more like an energy field are accidentally beamed onto Voyager, the alien invades Harry Kim's holodeck Beowulf program and takes the role of Grendel, devouring crew members who enter the holodeck until the Doctor figures out what has happened and frees the trapped aliens.
4. Thanks to Sarah Titus for transcribing the original lecture from which this introduction comes.

Chapter 1

1. Even a representative bibliography of the extent of such work would fill dozens of pages, not only by dint of increasing and intensifying activity in this area but also because, as Haydock puts it: "The point is to avoid the temptation to define medievalism as error and to recognize that in the long view medieval studies is a sub-set of medievalism [...] The differences between popular medievalism and academic medieval studies are those of degree — not of kind — and these differences of degree erode quite precipitously with the passage of time ("Medievalism and Excluded Middles" 19). The line between philology and medievalism within the corpus of writers such as J. R. R. Tolkien or Umberto Eco is also very blurry. In the case of Tolkien, explored below in this chapter, the essay "Beowulf: The Monsters and the Critics" serves not only as a touchstone for most subsequent scholarship on the poem, but also has a great deal in common with Tolkien's fantasy medievalism and his artwork. Let us content ourselves, then, with citing only three influential books to serve as emblematic of a rising trend: Carolyn Dinshaw, *Getting Medieval: Sexualities and Communities, Pre- and Postmodern* (1999); John Ganim, *Medievalism and Orientalism* (2005); and the anthology of essays edited by Eileen A. Joy, et al. *Cultural Studies and the Modern Middle Ages* (2007).
2. Any study of movie medievalism should begin with Kevin Harty, *The Reel Middle Ages: American, Western and Eastern European, Middle Eastern and Asian Films About Medieval Europe* (Jefferson, NC: McFarland, 1999). Some of the problems with the fidelity approach to this mode were outlined in my *Movie Medievalism: The Imaginary Middle Ages* (Jefferson, NC: McFarland, 2008), where I offer psychoanalytic and philosophical alternatives (chiefly those offered by Lacan, Zizek and Deleuze) to the Real/Reel Middle Ages distinction. My introduction to the edited collection of essays *Hollywood in the Holy Land: Essays on Film Depictions of the Crusades and Christian/Muslim Conflicts*, eds. Nickolas Haydock and E. L. Risden (Jefferson: NC: McFarland, 2009) demonstrates at some length the inter-implication of scholarly, filmic, and mass media discourses in framing public policy debates on the relevance of the Crusades to modern interventions in the Middle East. Also recommended are Laurie Finke and Martin B. Shichtman,

Cinematic Illuminations: The Middle Ages on Film (Baltimore: The Johns Hopkins University Press, 2010), inspired in part by an attempt to read the juxtaposition of medieval book and modern cinema "illuminations." A similar approach, undertaken with rigor and pizzazz, is Richard Burt, *Medieval and Early Modern Film and Media* (New York: Palgrave Macmillan, 2008). Also see Burt's fascinating introduction to a special issue of *Exemplaria*, "Getting Schmedieval: Of Manuscript and Film Prologues, Paratexts, and Parodies," *Exemplaria* 19.2 (2007): 217–242. Stephanie Trigg's essay, "Transparent Walls: Stained Glass and Cinematic Medievalism," *Screening the Past* 26 (2009): http://www.latrobe.edu.au/sc reeningthepast/current/issue-26.html, accessed 8/29/2012, represents perhaps the most thoroughgoing attempt to read medieval and modern images in productive relation. Books on medievalism in film which employ the more widespread strategy of comparing movies with medieval history are: John Aberth, *A Knight at the Movies: Medieval History on Film* (Jefferson: NC: McFarland, 2003) and Andrew B. R. Eliot's *Remaking the Middle Ages: The Methods of Cinema in Portraying the Medieval World* (Jefferson: NC: McFarland, 2010).

3. W. J. T. Mitchell, *Picture Theory* (Chicago: University of Chicago Press, 1994).

4. The influence of Renoir's visual stylistics was greater in subsequent scholarship on Middle English alliterative poetry. See, for instance, Sarah Stanbury's *Seeing the Gawain Poet*.

5. Ted Nasmith in tracing the development of his own style in paintings illustrating Middle-Earth makes a similar point: "I came to recognize that since a work like *The Lord of the Rings* was basically anachronistic thematically (that is, set in a mythical past age), as well as stylistically related to nineteenth-century adventure novels and fairy tales, paintings that could capture its feeling and complement its grandeur ought to look back to what I saw as the corresponding golden era of detailed landscape painting" (193). This represents both an insightful use of inter-arts comparisons as well as a window into Nasmith's creative process, but it elides the influence of Tolkien's own indebtedness to nineteenth-century landscapes and the rather more direct influence of his artistic style on Nasmith's illustrations—abundantly clear, for instance, in the latter's version of *Rivendell* (1984).

6. Tolkien's fondness for perspectival metaphors and inter-arts comparisons is also readily on display in the essay on *Sir Gawain and the Green Knight*: "Antiquity like a many-figured back-cloth hangs ever behind the scene. Behind our poem stalk the figures of elder myth, and through the lines are heard the echoes of ancient cults, beliefs and symbols remote from the consciousness of an educated moralist (but also a poet) of the late fourteenth century. His story is not *about* these old things, but it receives part of its life, its vividness, its tension from them" (73). In fact, the *Gawain* essay seems to offer a less elaborate version of the "allegory" familiar from *Beowulf: The Monsters and The Critics* in order to make a related point: "Out of whatever more ancient stones may have been built the gleaming but solid magnificence of this castle (Hautdesert), whatever turn the story may take, whatever details may be discovered that the author inherited and overlooked or failed to accommodate to his new purpose, this much is clear: our poet is bringing Gawain to no haunt of demons, enemies of human kind, but to a courteous and Christian hall" (*Essays* 78).

7. Tolkien's call for a recognition of the "impression of depth" in *Beowulf* scholarship also finds an echo in his comments in the essay "On Translating Beowulf": "your language must be literary and traditional: not because it is now a long while since the poem was made, or because it speaks of things that have since become ancient; but because the diction of *Beowulf* was poetical, archaic, artificial (if you will), in the day the poem was made" (54). The survival of usages like *beorn* (bear) and *freca* (wolf) for "warrior" in traditional poetic diction are the philological equivalent of receding pictorial compositions, words (if you will) that contain their own dark history and provide remnants, "when much else of the ancient diction had perished" (54), of the tantalizing links between language, myth and tale.

8. Tolkien's artwork has been widely reproduced and marketed in art books and calendars, etc. Hereafter, references within this chapter are keyed to the numbered illustrations in the edition of Christopher Tolkien. Also see, Hammond and Scull, *J. R. R. Tolkien: Artist and Illustrator*.

9. As has been often remarked, computer graphics imaging brings film production into a much more intimate relationship with painting.

10. See, James Elkins, *The Object Stares*

Back: On the Nature of Seeing, (New York: Simon and Schuster, 1996).

11. For a discussion of themes and structures common across Tolkien's *oeuvre*, see Jane Chance, *Tolkien's Art: A Mythology for England*, 142–146.

12. See, Erich Auerbach, *Mimesis: The Representation of Reality in Western Literature*, chapter one: "Odysseus' Scar."

13. Indeed, though such a speculations could never rise beyond pure conjecture, one might well connect Alain Renoir's expressed preference for his father over his grandfather with his obvious preference for moving over static pictures.

14. My discussion of film style here is necessarily brief and confined to Renoir. The history of staging in depth and manipulations of depth of field is a rich and intriguing one. See David Bordwell's *On The History of Film Style*, 158–271.

15. See Niles, *Beowulf: The Poem and Its Tradition*, 152–162.

16. Thus the methodology is similar that used by Edward B. Irving, Jr. to analyze the poem's presentation of heroism in chapter one of *A Reading of Beowulf*, 1–42. Irving finds "rhetorical heightening" in negative clauses followed by adversative conjunctions.

17. Old English text is taken from *Klaeber's Beowulf*, edited by Fulk, Bjork and Niles; the translation is from Risden (2006).

18. Indeed, one is reminded of an analogous leave-taking in *Sir Gawain and the Green Knight*, where the court watches Gawain set off for his appointment at the Green Chapel: "he wende for euermore," (line 669).

19. "Rack focus," typically manipulated by a camera man designated the Rack Puller, alters the focus within a single shot. As Bordwell (212) explains: "By racking focus, the director could draw attention from point to point at dramatic moments. Though sometimes used in the silent period, rack focus became a principle tool in the director's kit during the sound era, and it would later help solve some problems posed by color and widescreen."

20. Said repeatedly of Grendel and the dragon; Grendel's mother is once called *aglæcwif* (1259). In line 2592, both Beowulf and the dragon are characterized together as *aglæcean*. Klaeber's glossary offers two possibilities for *aglæcan* in line 1512: as a genitive singular with verb *ehton*—as the quoted translation by Edward Risden takes it—or, as a nominative plural. The latter option is attractive because it makes neater sense. Beowulf has pursued the *mere-wif* and by extension all the monsters, who are now pursuing him as well. This collective plural encompassing and collapsing Beowulf with other monsters would be in rather close parallel with the only other plural usage of the word in the poem, which unites Beowulf and the dragon under a single rubric. There, like here, each opponent rushes at his rival. In both cases the reason why Beowulf becomes indistinguishable from the other monsters may be explicable by visual elements within the scene which work to obscure distinctions: in the former the dark sea, and in the latter, a cave-mouth billowing with flames.

21. The fire, described from Beowulf's perspective, encourages the inference: firelight is only this intense ("blacne leoman breohte scinan") at close quarters.

22. Most scholars would now insist upon translating this half-line something like the following: "Then she set upon her hall-guest." This distinction, however, has sometimes tended to obscure the lack of any real difference in the physical situation being described here. Beowulf is on the ground; she is on top of him. God will set things to rights, but only *after* Beowulf extricates from beneath her. The striking hypotaxis in the last clause, "*syþðan he eft astod*" (1556b), albeit delayed, makes Beowulf's position beneath her and *sub specie aeternitatis* quite explicit.

23. E. L. Risden concludes that: "finding the magic sword even represents a kind of epiphany: it shines in the dark, a talisman first and a weapon second, a crossover artifact between the realm of the practical smith and that of the god-inspired smith" (*Heroes, Gods, and the Role of Epiphany* 70)

24. Note too that the kenning *rodores candel* looks forward to the melting of the sword later on in the episode.

25. Quoted from edition by Fairclogh and Goold.

26. For the wealth of Celtic analogues to the sword's light see Puhvel (25–38). The sword in *Beowulf* may indeed be drawn from the realm of fairy tale, but it's worth noting here that in the Old English poem the sword functions as a light source, not simply a sign of the miraculous.

27. Note Jean Renoir's juxtapositions of mayhem committed within an interior with external crowd scenes in films such as *La Chienne* (1931; a prostitute is murdered while revelers sing songs beneath her window), *La Bete*

Humaine (1938; the murder of a woman is cross-cut with a dance). See Katherine Golsan, "Murder and Merrymaking."

28. Compare an analogous moment in *Dream of the Rood* where the gory stains of Christ's wounds and precious jewels alternate back and forth at the four corners of the cross: "Geseah ic þæt fuse beacen/wendan wædum ond bleom; hwilum hit wæsmid wætan bestemed,/beswyled mid swates gange, hwilum mid since gegyrwed" (21b–23).

29. In his retelling of the moment to Hrothgar, Beowulf would seem to confirm the notion of light as a function of God: "ac me geuthe ylda Wealdand/tha ic on wage geseah wlitig hangian/eald-sweord eacen" (1661–1663a).

30. Peter Jackson's *The Lord of the Rings: The Return of the King* presents a revealingly apropos analogy to this scene, in which Frodo in Shelob's lair, sword in one hand and the glowing Star of Eärendil in the other, searches the cobwebbed cave for the feminine spider. A publicity still, available on the Internet Movie Database and used in the cover art for the critical anthology *Picturing Tolkien* (2011), demonstrates very obviously what we're describing here.

31. See: John Garnder, *Grendel*, and Michael Crichton, *Eaters of the Dead*.

32. See Risden's more detailed discussion of this film in chapter four.

33. See Hoffecker: "One of the reasons why the Neanderthals are so difficult to understand is that they are not ancestral to modern humans, but rather the product of a parallel and separate line of evolutionary development. In some respects, they may be considered an alternative form of modern human. Just as they evolved certain unique anatomical features, the Neanderthals probably developed some peculiar patterns of behavior that never appeared in modern humans and are unknown among earlier hominids. Their burial of the dead — without convincing evidence of ritual — could be an example of this" (49).

34. "To the modern humans who eventually met up with them, the physical appearance of the Neanderthals must have seemed odd and perhaps grotesque. They possessed a long and low cranial vault with a low receding frontal bone and large brow ridge (*supraorbital torus*). Their brain volume nevertheless was large — comparable to that of modern humans — averaging slightly more than 1,500 cc. The back of the cranium projected outward to form an *occipital bun*. The face projected forward with inflated cheeks and a large nasal cavity. The front teeth were exceptionally large relative to the cheek teeth, and the jaw lacked a chin" (Hoffecker 51–52).

35. "In many ways the evolutionary origins of modern humans parallel those of the Neanderthals. Modern humans also evolved gradually from *Homo heidelbergensis* during the same broad interval of time (roughly 600,000 to 200,000 years ago)" (Hoffecker 71). The *Beowulf*-poet derives the evil progeny ("untydras") of orcs, giants and elves from Cain (lines 111–113).

36. Behind this language lies another largely unsupported conjecture, namely, that Neanderthals were matriarchal.

37. On the storm scene as a paradigm for the struggle against chaotic outbursts of fury that threaten the establishment of Roman order, see Viktor Poschl, chapter one.

38. I.e., the matriarchal society represented by the archaic mother who permits no cut, the abject horror of a world without abjection: Kristeva, *New Maladies of the Soul*, 218.

39. "The reason such accounts are ekphrasis, and hence the bedrock of art history, is that all these descriptions conspire to translate the visual and sensual nature of a work of art into a linguistic formulation capable of being voiced in a discursive argument. The act of translation is central" (Elsner 12).

Chapter 2

1. In "*Beowulf*: The Monsters and the Critics," J. R. R. Tolkien discusses the "theory of courage, which is perhaps the greatest contribution of early Northern literature" (*An Anthology of Beowulf Criticism*, ed. Lewis E. Nicholson, Notre Dame: University of Notre Dame Press, 1963, page 70, reprinted from the British Academy *Proceedings* of 1936)). Tom Shippey elaborates on this point (pages 148ff.) in *J. R. R. Tolkien: Author of the Century*, Boston: Houghton Mifflin, 2000.

2. In the epic Beowulf must convince his king, Hygelac, to permit him to undertake the Danish adventure: Hygelac doesn't want him to do it. But Beowulf's success actually increases his value as hero commodity.

3. See for instance Charles Donahue, "Potlatch and Charity: Notes on the Heroic in *Beowulf*." *Anglo-Saxon Poetry: Essays in Appreciation for John C. McGalliard*. Ed. Lewis E. Nicholson and Dolores W. Frese. Notre

Dame: University of Notre Dame Press, 1975, pages 23–40.

4. Note for instance Robert Zemeckis' 2007 CGI *Beowulf* film (screenplay by Neil Gaiman and Roger Avary) and the accompanying XBOX360 video game.

5. See Karl Marx, *Capital*, Volume 1, Chapter One, Part 4. German edition 1867, first English edition 1887, trans. Samuel Moore and Edward Aveling. The text is readily available online in the Marx/Engels Internet Archive at www.marxists.org, 1995, 1999. The (ironic) act of fetishizing places the nominal value of the object in its material nature or in its existence as product without regard to the amount or quality or difficulty of labor that went into its production, thus it represents, for Marx, a misunderstanding of both material and labor.

6. The Geats' disposing of rather than keeping the treasure may have practical as well as honorific value: ancient treasures restored may revive ancient feuds, or they may fear the arrival of a new dragon. Tradition held, as in the example of Fafnir in *Volsungasaga*, that greedy men can become dragons, or dragons may come from the guardians of old treasures. As William A. Chaney puts it in *The Cult of Kingship in Anglo-Saxon England: The Transition from Paganism to Christianity* (Manchester; Manchester University Press, 1970), "The princely dead guards his hoard against any who breaks into the cairn, and to do so he take the monstrous form of the dragon. Its treasure was the princely treasure of the howe, its residence was the howe of the great departed, and its presence was associated with death" (page 130).

7. "[Þ]ær hit nū gēn lifað/eldum swā unnyt, swā hi(t æro)r wæs" (*Beowulf and the Fight at Finnsburg*, 3rd edition, edited Fr. Klaeber, Boston: D. C. Heath, 1950). The translation is mine.

8. In *The Narrative Pulse of Beowulf: Arrivals and Departures* (Toronto: University of Toronto Press, 2008) John M. Hill makes a case that Wiglaf does reasonably successfully replace Beowulf. He "takes charge and marshals the Geats' resources and strength, he shows courage, direction, and eloquence since, "although hand-maimed by the dragon fire, he is a powerful warrior wise in words and deeds" (page 88). Having helped Beowulf kill the dragon, Wiglaf has re-commoditized himself, co-modified his position and that of his folk in their post–Beowulf age.

9. Note, for instance, the scop in *Beowulf* and the two scops in the Old English *Deor*.

10. See "On Fairy Stories" in *The Tolkien Reader* (where it is part of "Tree and Leaf"), New York: Ballantine, 1966, page 41.

11. Notably the poet uses the word *āglæca* for Grendel, the dragon, and Beowulf. Editors and translators have normally rendered "monster" in the first two cases and "warrior" in the third, but neither captures the point, and the uses co-modify each other.

12. In *No Such Thing* the hero(ine) serves her cold-hearted editor as a commodity — she herself becomes a story as she brings the monster to New York for interviews — and the monster, too, becomes a commodity to exploit for as long as he remains news. Through their growing understanding both co-modify, each coming to understand and appreciate the other, albeit that understanding leads neither to any greater happiness or fulfillment: the movie explodes notions of a happy ending.

13. The 2005 *Beowulf and Grendel* (Movision, directed by Sturla Gunnarson) takes another interesting if also original thematic direction: it addresses racism through the unwarranted hatred that the humans bear toward the trollish Grendelkin.

Chapter 3

1. See Girard, *The Scapegoat*, 66–75.

2. Cf., Magennis (2001, 35): "The introduction of the mediating figure Ibn Fadlan, who functions as our educated guide and representative in a world beyond the pale, is a key feature of Crichton's adaptation. We, as readers, can identify with him and sympathize with his responses as an un-heroic outsider on a heroic expedition."

3. James Earl employs the passage in Bede to make a similar comparison in *Thinking About Beowulf*, pp. 71–72: "*Beowulf* opens with a poetic variation on Bede's parable of the sparrow in the story of the Danish patriarch, Scyld Scefing. He arrives from nowhere with no possessions, creates peace with heroic deeds, is honored as a good king, bears a noble son to succeed him, and dies — all the course of 25 lines." What Earl calls "the ultimate meaning of this exemplary life" (72) is contained in the mysterious disembarkation of the funeral ship: "the brevity of his life and the certainty of death do not rob him of his glorious existence — he did in fact achieve

much. More than this we cannot say, however, because he sails back into the unknown ocean whence he came, shockingly diminished in the last line to no more than a 'load' committed to an unknown destination" (72–73). As Earl powerfully concludes, "But here the world of the parable is the world of the poem — a hall in a storm, promised to ruin, distinctly material, strongly determined, wholly immanent. Here the transcendent is simply unknown, everywhere bordering the world of the known as the ocean surrounds the earth" (73).

4. Kathleen Forni describes the generic pastiche: "One surprising artistic decision, however, was to place the story in the future. The setting for *Beowulf* is in the tradition of post-apocalyptic science-fiction tales such as George Miller's *Mad Max* trilogy (1979, 1981, 1985), Kevin Costner's *Waterworld* (Reynolds, 1995), or *The Omega Man* (Sagal, 1971), in which the future is marked by anarchy, economic ruin, primitive technology, roving gangs, and environmental collapse. Intentionally or not, this dark pessimism about the future replicates the mood of the poem" (2007, 245). Forni also adduces further generic elements such as Gothic horror and comic book superheroes. The film also bears comparison with the financially successful *Blade* trilogy (1998, 2002, and 2004), starring Wesley Snipes, who likewise plays a leather-wearing, kick-boxing, vampire-killing vampire.

5. The reversal takes its clue from a series of disaster films, which turned cities or even whole regions into prisons. In *The Peacemaker* (1997), for instance, Clooney and Kidman race to find an atomic bomb within New York City, which has been forcibly cordoned off by the United States Army. Similar strategies are pursued in *Outbreak* (1995) and the more recent British film *Doomsday* (2008) where plagues are contained by violent force. In Graham Baker's earlier film, *Alien Nation* (1988), the "Newcomers" from outer space are first quarantined and then uneasily integrated with the human population.

6. As Hodapp (2010, 101) trenchantly remarks, such films "use the identity of the father to explain at least in part Grendel's invasion of Heorot. Their answers to this question reveal more about each film's twenty-first century audience than about the poem or its cultural context."

7. See, for example, her chapter "Something to Be Scared of" in Julia Kristeva, *Powers of Horror: An Essay in Abjection*, 32–55.

8. In his wide-ranging work on alienation in nation-building narratives, Richard Kearney relates the killing of Grendel to myths of the "sacrificial origins" of nations: "In particular, the scaled monster, Grendel, haunts the unstable borders of the struggling nation divided as it is between Geats, Norse, Swedes, Saxons and Celts" (37). Later in the same very general discussion he concludes, "In time, the genealogical descendents of Grendel become the colonial enemies of the conquering British empire, both overseas (Africa, Asia and the Americas) and closer to home in Ireland, where the 'natives' were caricatured as simian-like, mindless savages: the *degens* serving as dialectical foil to the *gens*" (38). These provisional assertions deserve further exploration as to how the scapegoating of the kin of Cain function in Anglo-Saxon state formation and in nineteenth-century connections between medievalism and colonialism.

9. Quotations from *Beowulf* are taken from: *Klaeber's Beowulf and The Fight at Finnsburg*, fourth edition, ed. R. D. Fulk, Robert E. Bjork, and John D. Niles. Translations from: *Beowulf: A Student's Edition*, trans. E. L. Risden. Text and translation are hereafter referenced by parenthetical line numbers.

10. The Holy of Holies was a place of yearly sacrifice in the Tabernacle, the curtain of which was rent at Christ's sacrifice as described in Hebrews 6.

11. The relevant lines in *Judith* designate the container as a pouch ("fætelse," 127) brought along by Judith's servant girl to hold food ("nest," 128). Later, back among the Hebrews, Judith commands the girl to "uncover (*onwriðan*) the head of the war-wager and show (*ætywan*) it all bloody to the citizens as proof (*to behðe*) of how she succeeded in the contest (lines 171–175; trans. Fulk 2010, 310–311). Also note the similarities of this celebratory, ritualized use of the head as a sign to the scene discussed below where Beowulf presents the head of Grendel to Hrothgar in Heorot.

12. Earlier attempts to reconcile the poem's monsters with human sacrifice pale in comparison with Andrew Rai Berzins' provocative (if politically correct) screenplay. Berzins also wrote *Chasing Cain* (2001) and a TV-movie sequel, *Chasing Cain: Face* (2002).

13. Since the gigantism is later demonstrated to be genetic, Grendel and his father are probably being portrayed as sufferers from an inherited disorder such as multiple en-

docrine neoplasia, in which small, non-cancerous tumors grow on the endocrine glands, making them overactive. In the pituitary glands these tumors produce an excess of male growth hormone, which leads to abnormal growth in childhood before the bone growth plates close. Such a condition would explain their unusual size and strength, the pattern of male baldness coupled with excessive body hair, the father's apparent joint problems, their unusually prominent foreheads and jaws, as well as Grendel's headaches and hormone-induced rages. For a fuller description see The University of Maryland Medical Center website at: http://www.umm.edu/ency/article/001174all.htm.

14. For another discussion of the opening scene, see: Hodapp (2010, 103–104).

15. As Hodapp (2010, 103) notes, the film also offers itself as the "real" story behind the hyperbolic accretions in the making of the legend.

16. Although there is probably no question of influence, the film's implicit reading of the poem will bear comparison with similar approaches in the scholarly literature. See Kearney (2003), Wilson (1996) and the discussion later in this chapter.

17. "The configuration of the scene is always the same — the murderers are in a circle around the victim — but the obvious or intentional significance of the scenes can vary widely. It may share only a single characteristic: the awareness that they do not signify collective murder" (Girard, *The Scapegoat*, 66).

18. See Deleuze and Guattari, *Anti-Oedipus: Capitalism and Schizophrenia* (51–137).

19. For critical overviews see, Robert E. Bjork, "Digressions and Episodes" in *A Beowulf Handbook*, Bjork and Niles, eds. (201–205), and Orchard, *A Critical Companion to Beowulf* (100–105)

20. Cf. *Widsið* (32b): "Sceafa Longbeardum."

21. For instance, the A-Text of the *Anglo-Saxon Chronicle* has Beaw Scyldwaing, Scyldwea Hermoding, Hermod Itermoning, Itermon Hraþraing, se wæs geboren in þære earce" (Beaw, the son of Scyldwea, the son of Heremod, the son of Itermon, the son of Hrathra, who was born in the arc). The B, C and D recensions maintain the same order of Beaw, Scyld and Heremod, though they cast Sceaf as the son of Noah born on the arc. For the texts see: Bruce (96–99).

22. See Bruce (101–103; 109–110).

23. Bruce (91–92).

24. The word seems to be associated with dark times that are then relieved by a savior or a miraculous turn of events. Such a time obtains before the coming of Scyld, during the ravages of Grendel, before the change which comes to the destructive Modþryð ("fyren' ondrysne," 1932), and during the attacks of the sons of Ongenðeow upon the Geats (2480). On the use of the term in association with an arrow, see below.

25. In an intriguing, detailed article by R. D. Fulk it is argued that even the derivation of the myth of the child refugee from Sceaf is a later transferal from the original myth extant in both the prose and poetics *Eddas* where Bergelmir (related to OE *Beow*, barley) makes the fateful, fertile journey. Fulk's conclusion is almost certainly correct: "the weight of probability is in favor of the influence of heroic verse on the Anglo-Saxon genealogies, rather than the reverse" (322). This being so, there is good reason to infer that the oldest and most widespread order in the genealogies of Heremod-Scyld-Beow descends from an older tradition in agreement with the poem, if not directly gleaned from it.

26. Bruce (144–145): "Heremoð; hans son Skjalldun, er vér köllum Skjöld; hans son Bjaf, er vér köllum Bjar" (Heremód, his son Skjaldun (whom we call Skjöld), his son Bjaf (whom we call Bjarr).

27. The verbs *bemurnan* and *murnan* are arguably used in this way throughout the poem. At line 50 Scyld's people are described as "murnende" at his funeral. Grendel returns for more slaughter on a second night "ond no mearn fore" the murders in line 136. Hildeburh *bemearn* (1077) the deaths of her kinsmen, Beowulf counsels revenge rather than mourning for a dead friend in line 1385 and doesn't mourn the possibility of his own death at the hands of Grendel's mother in 1442 or her death at his hands in 1537. Finally, the followers of Beowulf don't mourn the dead dragon and open hoard at the end of the poem (3128).

28. Orchard (1995, 48) notes that the "shadow" of Heremod appears after each of Beowulf's victories (lines 901–915 and 1709–1724).

29. The term *hæðen* is twice applied to parts of Grendel, his soul and his claw ("hæðene sawle," 852; "hæðenes handsporu," 986); twice to the dragon's hoard ("hæðenum horde," 2216; "hæðen gold," 2276); and once to the belief of the backsliding Danes ("hæðenra hyht," 179).

30. Cohen sees the sign made by the head in somewhat different but related terms: "The ritualized display of the severed head is public theater within narrative theater. The highly charged exhibit validates the conservative, nostalgic ethos of the poem's imagined culture and unambiguously announces Beowulf's full status as hero, as the proper leader who realizes that identity exists only within the corporate hierarchy of community. Having accepted his symbolic mandate by conquering the giant, Beowulf can sail homeward to embrace his destiny as king" (Cohen 65). Certainly Cohen is justified in emphasizing the specular and theatrical elements in the ceremonial presentation of the head, but within his Lacanian analysis of the scene one glimpses the totemic and rites of passage. Adding to this the Girardian approach, we gain an explanation for the chronically repetitious nature of such rituals, their never-complete nature.

31. For a superb discussion of Tiw in *Beowulf* and other Old English poetry, see John M. Hill (65–70): "As a mythological sovereign presiding over lawful war, as a pledge-giver who sacrifices his hand, Tiu essentially oversees war as the biding of that which is terrible or else the unbinding of reigns of terror. This language of bonds and unbinding is at the heart of Tiu's actions" (66). There may be a similar etymological play in the description of the track of blood left by the wound to Grendel's arm as "tirleases trode" (footprints of the inglorious [armless] one, 843).

32. See Wilson for a similar Girardian reading of Beowulf as both sacrificer and sacrificial victim.

33. For the allegory and its roots in the homiletic tradition descending from Ephesians 6. 11–16, see: Hermann (39–42) and Orchard (51–52).

Chapter 4

1. Grendel's attacks mix brutal violence and boyish pranks; for instance, in one scene he urinates on the Danes' doorstep partly as an animal might mark territory and partly just a joke, to leave behind the odor of his contempt as well as the fear and blood that his attacks generate.

2. The poet does refer to Grendel, the dragon, and Beowulf all as *aglæca*; translators usually render the term as "monster," but that would make Beowulf a monster, too — the notion Baker's film partly exploits.

Chapter 5

1. Film dragons range from horrifying and destructive (as in *Dragonslayer*, 1981, and *Reign of Fire*, 2002, to somewhere between dangerous-but-redeemable and naturally good (as in the Shrek films, *The Flight of Dragons*, 1982, *Dragonheart*, 1996, and *George and the Dragon*, 2004). Ancient Germanic sources express no doubt about the evil nature of dragons, but in film the problem of Othering has led to the creation of positive and appealing dragons.

2. See especially *The Four Fundamental Concepts of Psycho-Analysis*, trans. Alan Sheridan, New York: Norton, 1981, particularly pages 215 and 251, but *passim*.

Chapter 6

1. Another classic film from 1960, Ingmar Bergman's *Virgin Spring*, inspired its own uncanny doubles in Wes Craven's hyper-violent, influential *The Last House on the Left* (1972) and the related revenge film, *I Spit on Your Grave* (1978). Similarly, the expressionless white face of Death in *Seventh Seal* (1957) looks forward to the equally cold, white mask of Michael Myers in the *Halloween* franchise, Jason's hockey mask in the *Friday the 13th* franchise and the white, ghost mask used by a number of serial killers in the *Scream* franchise.

2. See Orchard (1995, 29–34).

3. Vastly superior to both of these is Chanwook Park's *Thirst* (original title *Bakjwi* 2009).

4. "If what is of primary importance about horrific creatures is that their very impossibility vis a vis our conceptual categories is what makes them function so compellingly in dramas of discovery and confirmation, then their disclosure, insofar as they are categorical violations, will be attached to some sense of disturbance, distress, and disgust. Consequently, the role of the horrific creature in such narratives — where their disclosure captures our interest and delivers pleasure — will simultaneously mandate some probable revulsion. That is, in order to reward our interest by the disclosure of the putatively impossible beings of the plot, said beings ought

to be disturbing, distressing, and repulsive in the way that theorists like Douglas predict phenomena that ill fit cultural classifications will be" (Carroll 184).

5. A *Beowulf* inspired episode in *Star Trek: Voyager* titled "Monsters and Heroes" substitutes a luminescent cloud for the Grendelkin.

6. Indeed, Beowulf's melodramatic counterpart in this masculine, sexual control is the *Twilight* films' vampire Edward Cullen (Robert Pattinson). In *Twilight: Breaking Dawn, Part 1* (2011), the honeymoon suite is torn to pieces as a testament to the terrible strain of suppressing Edward's bloodlust, barely held in check by his love for Bella Swan (Kristen Stewart).

Chapter 7

1. In *An Anthology of Beowulf Criticism*, ed. Lewis E. Nicholson, Notre Dame: University of Notre Dame Press, 1965, 51–103.

2. "What are the most courageous films in cinema history?" may make an interesting question for discussion and research. Barry Levinson's *Wag the Dog* (1998), John Carpenter's *They Live* (1988), Stanley Kubrick's *Paths of Glory*, and Warren Beatty's *Bulworth* appear on lists of films that created political stir. Michael Moore's documentaries, beginning with *Roger and Me* (1989) and *Bowling for Columbine* (2002), required similar courage as they take on hefty opponents. Spike Lee's *Do the Right Thing* (1989) powerfully raises difficult questions abour race, and other films such as *Coming Home* (Hal Ashby, 1978), *The Deer Hunter* (Michael Cimino, 1978), The Thin Blue Line (Errol Morris, 1988), and *The Best Years of Our Lives* (William Wyler, 1946) raise similarly painful societal issues. *The Elephant Man*, *My Left Foot*, and *Philadelphia* candidly treat frightening illnesses or disability. We may call Peter Jackson's *Lord of the Rings* trilogy courageous for the magnitude of its undertaking, the success of its visual accomplishment, and the enormous expectations of the fans who waited for its installments.

3. *Epic and Romance: Essays on Medieval Literature*, 1896, reprinted 1957, New York: Dover, page 28. Please see also my discussions of the cultural centrality of the issues and approaches of epic poems in *Heroes, Gods, and the Role of Epiphany in English Epic Poetry*, Jefferson, NC: McFarland, 2008.

4. "Nobody but the Other Buddy: Hollywood, The Crusades, and Buddy Pictures." *Hollywood in the Holy Land*, ed. Nickolas Haydock and E. L. Risden, Jefferson, NC: McFarland, 2009, pages 186–99.

Conclusion

1. Boldface denotes a feature length, generally released film that adapts the Old English poem, either directly or through intermediaries such as the novels of John Gardner or Michael Crichton. An asterisk marks other treatments (animations, made-for-television films or episodes in a television series) that to a greater or lesser extent derive from *Beowulf*.

2. The referenced essay is Seth Lerer, "'On fagne flore': The Postcolonial *Beowulf*, from Heorot to Heaney," in *Postcolonial Approaches to the European Middle Ages*, 77–104.

Works Cited

Bibliography

Aberth, John. *A Knight at the Movies: Medieval History on Film*. Jefferson, NC: McFarland, 2003.

Andersson, Theodore M. "Tradition and Design in *Beowulf*." *Interpretations of Beowulf: A Critical Anthology*. R. D. Fulk, ed. Bloomington: Indiana University Press, 1991. (Reprint from *Old English Literature in Context*. John D. Niles, ed. Cambridge: D. S. Brewer, 1980. 90–106, 171–172.

Auerbach, Erich. *Mimesis: The Representation of Reality in Western Literature*. 1957. Trans. Willard R. Trask. New Haven: Princeton University Press, 1968.

Barthes, Roland. *The Pleasure of the Text*. 1973. Trans. Richard Miller. New York: Hill and Wang, 1975.

Bataille, Georges. *Theory of Religion*. Trans. Robert Hurley. New York: Zone Books, 2000.

Bede. *A History of the English Church and People*. Leo Sherley-Price, trans. New York: Penguin Books, 1968.

Bjork, Robert E. and John D. Niles. *A Beowulf Handbook*. Lincoln: University of Nebraska Press, 1997.

Bonjour, Adrien. *The Digressions in Beowulf*. Medium Aevum Monographs 5. Oxford: Oxford University Press, 1950.

Bordwell, David. *On the History of Film Style*. Cambridge: Harvard University Press, 1997.

Bowra, C. M. *Heroic Poetry*. London: Macmillan, 1964.

Bradley, S. A. J. *Anglo-Saxon Poetry*. New York: Everyman Paperbacks, 1995.

Bruce, Alexander M. *Scyld and Scef: Expanding the Analogues*. New York: Routledge, 2002.

Burt, Richard. *Medieval and Early Modern Film and Media*. New York: Palgrave Macmillan, 2008.

Carroll, Noël. *The Philosophy of Horror: Or, Paradoxes of the Heart*. New York: Routledge, 1990.

Chance, Jane. *Tolkien's Art: A Mythology for England*. Lexington: The University Press of Kentucky, 2001.

Chaney, William R. *The Cult of Kingship in Anglo-Saxon England; The Transition from Paganism to Christianity*. Manchester: Manchester University Press, 1970.

Cohen, Jeffrey Jerome, ed. *Monster Theory: Reading Culture*. Minneapolis: University of Minnesota Press, 1996.

Creed, Barbara. "Horror and the Monstrous-Feminine." In *Horror: The Film Reader*. Ed. Mark Jancovich. London: Routledge, 2002. 67–76.

Crichton, Michael. *Eaters of the Dead*. New York: Knopf, 1976.

———. Crichton, Michael. *The Eaters of the Dead*. New York: Ballantine, 1992.

Deleuze, Gilles and Felix Guattari. *Anti-Oedipus: Capitalism and Schizophrenia*. Robert Hurley, Marks Seem, and Helen R. Lane, trans. Minneapolis: University of Minnesota Press, 1983.

Dinshaw, Carolyn. *Getting Medieval: Sexualities and Communities, Pre- and Postmodern*. Durham, NC: Duke University Press, 1999.

Donahue, Charles. "Potlatch and Charity: Notes on the Heroic in *Beowulf*." *Anglo-Saxon Poetry; Essay in Appreciation for John McGalliard*. Ed. Lewis E. Nicholson and Dolores W. Frese. Notre Dame: University of Notre Dame Press, 1975. 23–40.

Earl, James W. *Thinking About Beowulf*. Stanford: Stanford University Press, 1994.

Eliot, Andrew B. R. *Remaking the Middle Ages: The Methods of Cinema in Portraying the Medieval World*. Jefferson, NC: McFarland, 2010.

Elkins, James. *The Object Stares Back: On the Nature of Seeing*. New York: Simon and Schuster, 1996.

Elsner, Jas. "Art History as Ekphrasis." *Art History* 33.1 (2010), 10–27.

Finke, Laurie and Martin B. Shichtman. *Cinematic Illuminations: The Middle Ages on Film*. Baltimore: The Johns Hopkins University Press, 2010.

Forni, Kathleen. "Graham Baker's *Beowulf*: Intersections between High and Low Culture." *Literature/Film Quarterly* 35.3 (2007), 244–249.

———. "Popularizing High Culture: Zemeckis' *Beowulf*." *Studies in Popular Culture* 31.2 (2009), 45–59.

Frank, Roberta. "Germanic Legend in Old English Literature." *The Cambridge Companion to Old English Literature*. Cambridge: Cambridge University Press, 1991. 88–106.

Frye, Richard N., trans. *Ibn Fadlan's Journey to Russia: A Tenth-Century Traveler from Bagdad to the Volga River*. Princeton: Markus Wiener Publishers, 2005.

Fulk, R. D. *The* Beowulf *Manuscript*. Cambridge: Harvard University Press, 2010.

———. "An Eddic Analogue to the Scyld Scefing Story." *Review of English Studies* n.s. 40. 159 (1989), 313–322.

Fulk, R. D., Robert Bjork, and John D. Niles, eds. *Klaeber's Beowulf and The Fight at Finnsburg*, 4th edition. Toronto: University of Toronto Press, 2008.

Ganim, John M. *Medievalism and Orientalism*. New York: Palgrave McMillan, 2005.

Garber, Marjorie and Nancy J. Vickers. *The Medusa Reader*. New York: Routledge, 2003.

Gardner, John. *Grendel*. New York: Vintage, 1971.

Gilmore, David D. *Evil Beings: Mythical Beasts, and All Manner of Imaginary Terrors*. Philadelphia: University of Pennsylvania Press, 2003.

Girard, René. *The Scapegoat*. Yvonne Freccero, trans. Baltimore: The Johns Hopkins University Press, 1986.

Golsan, Katherine, "Murder and Merrymaking: The 'Seen' of the Crime in Renoir's 1930s Cinema." *Film Criticism* 32.2 (2007), 28–47.

Hammond, Wayne G. and Christina Scull. *J. R. R. Tolkien; Artist and Illustrator*. Boston: Houghton Mifflin, 1995.

Harty, Kevin. *The Reel Middle Ages: American, Western and Eastern European, Middle Eastern and Asian Films About Medieval Europe*. Jefferson, NC: McFarland, 1999.

Haydock, Nickolas. "Medievalism and Excluded Middles." *Studies in Medievalism* 17 (2009), 17–30.

———. *Movie Medievalism: The Imaginary Middle Ages*. Jefferson, NC: McFarland, 2008.

Haydock, Nickolas, and E. L. Risden, eds. *Hollywood in the Holy Land: Essays on Film Depictions of the Crusades and Christian/Muslim Clashes*. Jefferson, NC: McFarland, 2009.

Hermann, John P. *Allegories of War — Language and Violence in Old English Poetry*. Ann Arbor: University of Michigan Press, 1989.

Hill, John M. *The Narrative Pulse of Beowulf: Arrivals and Departures*. Toronto: University of Toronto Press, 2003.

Hodapp, William F. "'no hie fæder cunnon': But Twenty-First Century Film Makers Do." *Essays in Medieval Studies* 26 (2010), 101–8.

Hoffecker, John F. *A Prehistory of the North: Human Settlement in the Higher Latitudes*. New Brunswick: Rutgers University Press, 2005.

Hollander, Lee M. *The Saga of the Jómsvíkings*. Austin: University of Texas Press, 1955.

Joy, Eileen A., and Mary K. Ramsey, eds. *The Postmodern Beowulf: A Critical Casebook*. Morgantown: West Virginia University Press, 2006.

Joy, Eileen A., Myra J. Seaman, Kimberly K. Bell and Mary K. Ramsey, eds. *Cultural Studies of the Modern Middle Ages*. New York: Palgrave McMillan, 2007.

Kearney, Richard. *Strangers, Gods, and Monsters: Interpreting Otherness*. London: Routledge, 2003.

Ker, W. P. *Epic and Romance: Essays on Medieval Literature*. 1896. New York: Dover, 1957.

Klaeber, Fr., ed. *Beowulf and the Fight at Finnsburg*. 3rd edition. Boston: D.C. Heath, 1950.

Kristeva, Julia. *New Maladies of the Soul*. Trans. Ross Guberman. New York: Columbia University Press, 1995.

Powers of Horror: An Essay in Abjection. Trans. Leon S. Roudiez. New York: Columbia University Press, 1982.

Lacan, Jacques. *The Four Fundamental Concepts of Psycho-Analysis*. Trans. Alan Sheridan. New York: Norton, 1981.

Lapidge, Michael. "*Beowulf* and the Psychology of Terror." *Heroic Poetry in the Anglo-Saxon Period: Studies in Honor of Jess B. Bessinger, Jr.* Eds. Helen Damico and John Leyerle. Kalamazoo, Michigan: Medieval Institute Publications, 1993. 373–402.

Lerer, Seth. "Grendel's Glove." *ELH* 61.4 (1994), 721–751.

———. "On fagne flore: the Postcolonial *Beowulf*, from Heorot to Heaney. *Postcolonial Approaches in the European Middle Ages: Translating Cultures*. Ed. Ananya Jahanara Kabir and Deanne Williams. Cambridge Studies in Medieval Literature, vol. 54. Cambridge: Cambridge University Press, 2005. 77–104.

Leyerle, John. "The Interlace Structure of *Beowulf*." *Beowulf: A Verse Translation, Authoritative Text, Contexts, Criticism*. Trans. Seamus Heaney, Ed. Daniel Donoghue. New York: Norton, 2002. 130–151. Originally published in *University of Toronto Quarterly* 37 (1967), 1–17.

Magennis, Hugh. "Michael Crichton, Ibn Fadlan, Fantasy Cinema: *Beowulf* at the Movies." *Old English Newsletter* 35.1 (2001), 34–38.

Marshall, David W. "Harrying and Infinite Horrizon: The Ethics of Expansionism in *Outlander*." *The Vikings on Film: Essays on Depictions of the Nordic Middle Ages*. Ed. Kevin J. Harty. Jefferson, NC: McFarland, 2011. 135–149.

Marx, Karl. *Capital: Volume 1: A Critique of Political Economy*. Trans. Ben Fowkes. New York: Penguin Classics, 1992.

Mitchell, W. J. T. *Picture Theory*. Chicago: University of Chicago Press, 1994.

Myers, Tony. *Slavoj Žižek*. New York: Routledge, 2003.

Nasmith, Ted. "Similar but Not Similar: Appropriate Anachronism in My Paintings of Middle-Earth." *Tolkien's Modern Middle Ages*. Eds. Jane Chance and Alfred K. Siewers. New York: Palgrave Macmillan, 2005. 189–204.

Niles, John D. *Beowulf: The Poem and Its Tradition*. Cambridge: Harvard University Press, 1983.

———. "Widsith and the Archeology of the Past." *Philological Quarterly* 78.1–2 (1999), 171–213.

Olsen, Robert and Karin Olsen. "Introduction: On the Embodiment of Monstrosity in Northwest Medieval Europe." *Monsters and the Monstrous in Medieval Northwest Europe*. Ed. K. E. Olsen and L. A. J. R. Houwen. Leuven, Belgium: Peeters, 2001. 1–22.

Orchard, Andy. *A Critical Companion to Beowulf*. Suffolk, UK: Boydell and Brewer, 2003.

———. *Pride and Prodigies: Studies in the Monsters of the* Beowulf*-Manuscript*. Toronto: University of Toronto Press, 1995.

Osborn, Marijane. "The Great Feud: Scriptural History and Strife in *Beowulf*. *PMLA* 93 (1978), 973–81.

Overing, Gillian R. *Language, Sign, and Gender in* Beowulf. Carbondale: Southern Illinois University Press, 1990. 33–67.

Poschl, Viktor. *The Art of Virgil: Image and Symbolism in the* Aeneid. Ann Arbor: University of Michigan Press, 1962.

Prendergast, Thomas A. "'Wanton Recollection': The Idolatrous Pleasures of *Beowulf*." *New Literary History* 30.1 (1999), 129–141.

Puhvel, Martin. *Beowulf and the Celtic Tradition*. Waterloo, ON: Wilfred Laurier University Press, 1979.

Renoir, Alain. "Point of View and Design for Terror in *Beowulf*." *The Beowulf Poet: A Collection of Critical Essays*. Ed. Donald K. Fry. Englewood Cliffs, NJ: Prentice Hall, 1968. 154–166. (Originally published in *Neuphilologische Mitteilungen* 63 [1962], 154–167.)

———. "The Terror of the Dark Waters: A Note on Virgilian and Beowulfian Techniques." *The Learned and the Lewd: Studies in Chaucer and Medieval Literature*. Ed. Larry D. Benson. Cambridge: Harvard University Press, 1974. 147–160.

Risden, E. L. *Heroes, Gods, and the Role of Epiphany in English Epic Poetry*. Jefferson, NC: McFarland, 2008.

———, trans. *Beowulf in Faithful Verse*. Albany, NY: Whitston, 2006.

Robinson, Fred C. Beowulf *and the Appositive Style*. Knoxville: University of Tennessee Press, 1987.

———. "Did Grendel's Mother Sit on Beowulf?" *Anglo-Saxon to Early Middle English: Studies Presented to E.G. Stanley*. Oxford: Clarendon, 1994. 1–7.

Sagas of the Icelanders, The: A Selection. New York: Penguin Books, 2000.

Skal, David J. *The Monster Show: A Cultural History of Horror*. Revised edition. New York: Faber and Faber, 2001.

Sklar, Elizabeth S. "Call of the Wild: Culture Shock and Viking Masculinities in *The 13th Warrior* (1999)." In *The Vikings on Film: Essays on Depictions of the Nordic Middle Ages*, ed. Kevin J. Harty. Jefferson, NC: McFarland, 2011, 121–134.

Shippey, Tom. *J. R. R. Tolkien: Author of the Century*. Boston: Houghton Mifflin, 2000.

Sturluson, Snorri. *Heimskringla: History of the Kings of Norway*. Lee M. Hollander, trans. Austin: University of Texas Press, 1964.

Stam. Robert. *Film Theory: An Introduction.* Boston: Blackwell, 2000.
Tolkien, Christopher, ed. *Pictures by J. R. R. Tolkien.* Boston: Houghton Mifflin, 1992.
Tolkien, J. R. R. *The Essays of J. R. R. Tolkien: The Monsters and the Critics and Other Essays.* Ed. Christopher Tolkien. New York: Harper Collins, 2006.
———. "Beowulf: The Monsters and the Critics." *An Anthology of Beowulf Criticism.* Ed. Lewis Nicholson. Notre Dame: Notre Dame University Press, 1963. 51–103.
———. *The Tolkien Reader.* New York: Ballantine, 1966.
Trigg, Stephanie. "Transparent Walls: Stained Glass and Cinematic Medievalism." *Screening the Past* 26 (2009): http://tlweb.latrobe.edu.au/humanities/screeningthepast/current/issue-26.html, accessed 8/29/2012.
Tripp, Raymond. *Literary Essays on Language and Meaning in the Poem Called Beowulf: Beowulfiana Literaria.* Lewiston, NJ: Mellen, 1992.
Virgil. *Aeneid 7–12, Appendix Vergiliana.* Ed. H. R. Fairclough, rev. ed. G. P. Goold. Loeb Classical Library, vol. 64. Cambridge, MA: Harvard University Press, 2000.
Wilson, Eric. "The Blood Wrought Peace: A Girardian Reading of Beowulf." *English Language Notes* 34.1 (1996), 7–30.
Wood, Robin. *Hollywood from Vietnam to Reagan ... and Beyond.* New York: Columbia University Press, 2003. (Revised and expanded edition of the 1986 book.)

Filmography

Alien. Dir. Ridley Scott, 1979.
Alien Nation. Dir. Graham Baker, 1988.
Alien 3. Dir. David Fincher, 1992.
Beowulf. Dir. Yuri Kulakov, 1998.
Beowulf. Dir, Graham Baker, 1999.
Beowulf. Dir. Robert Zemeckis, 2007.
Beowulf and Grendel. Dir. Sturla Gunnarsson, 2005.
Beowulf: Prince of the Geats. Dir. Scott Wegener. 2007.
The Brood. Dir. David Cronenberg, 1979.
Chasing Cain. Dir. Andrew Rai Berzins, 2001.
Chasing Cain: Face. Dir. Jerry Ciccoritti, 2002.
La Chienne. Dir. Jean Renoir, 1931.
Creature from the Black Lagoon. Dir. Jack Arnold, 1954.
Doomsday. Dir. Neil Marshall, 2008.
Excalibur. Dir. John Boorman, 1981.
The Fellowship of the Ring. Dir. Peter Jackson, 2001.
Friday the 13th. Dir. Sean S. Cunningham, 1980.
Friday the 13th, Part 2. Dir. Steve Miner, 1981.
Friday 13th, Part 3. Dir. Steve Miner, 1982.
Grendel. Dir. Nick Lyon, 2007.
Grendel Grendel Grendel. Dir. Alexander Stitt, 1981.
Highlander. Dir. Russell Mulcahy, 1986.
The House of Usher. Dir. Roger Corman, 1960.
Human Beast, The. Dir. Jean Renoir, 1938.
The Hunger. Dir. Tony Scott, 1983.
I Spit on Your Grave. Dir. Meir Zarchi, 1978.
Interview with the Vampire. Dir. Neil Jordan, 1994.
The Last House on the Left. Dir. Wes Craven, 1972.
A League of Their Own. Dir. Penny Marshall, 1992.
Leviathan. Dir. George P. Cosmatos, 1989.
The Lord of the Rings (trilogy). Dir. Peter Jackson, 2001–2003.
Melancholia. Dir. Lars von Trier, 2011.
Monty Python and the Holy Grail. Dir. Terry Gilliam and Terry Jones, 1975.
No Such Thing. Dir. Hal Hartley, 2002.
Our Man Flint. Dir. Daniel Mann, 1966.
Outlander. Dir. Howard McCain, 2008.
The Peacemaker. Dir. Mimi Leder, 1997.
The Phantom of the Opera. Dir. Rupert Julian, 1925.
The Pit and the Pendulum. Dir. Roger Corman, 1961.
Predator. Dir. John McTiernan, 1987.
Psycho. Dir. Alfred Hitchcock, 1960.
Raiders of the Lost Ark. Dir. Steven Spielberg, 1981.
Raw Meat. Dir. Gary Sherman, 1973.
The Return of the King. Dir. Peter Jackson, 2003.
The Rules of the Game. Dir. Jean Renoir, 1939.
Seventh Seal. Dir. Ingmar Bergman, 1957.
The Silence of the Lambs. Dir. Jonathan Demme, 1991.
Star Trek: Voyager (episode 11: "Heroes and Demons"), 1995.
Texas Chainsaw Massacre. Dir. Toby Hooper, 1974.
The Thing. Dir. John Carpenter, 1982.
Thirst. Dir. Chan-wook Park, 2009.
The 13th Warrior. Dir. John McTiernan, 1999.
Twilight: Breaking Dawn, Part 1. Dir. Bill Condon, 2011.
Vertigo. Dir. Alfred Hitchcock, 1958.
Virgin Spring. Dir. Ingmar Bergman, 1960.
The Wolf Man. Dir. George Waggner, 1941.
Xena: Warrior Princess (episodes 7–9: "The Rheingold," "The Ring," and "Return of the Valkyrie"), 2000.

Index

abjection, abject maternal 85, 88–91, 94, 159–61, 194*n*38, 196*n*7
Abraham 106
Achilles 4
action-adventure (film genre) 57, 63, 97
Adam 61, 153, 155
adaptation 4, 27, 57–8, 60, 62, 65–6, 81–3, 91, 93, 97, 101, 103, 113, 141, 144, 146–7, 150, 158, 168, 177–81, 186–7, 195*n*2
Aeneid 32–3, 46, 62
Aeschere 16, 149
Afghanistan 163
Aglaeca(n) 40, 193*n*20
Ahmed ibn Fadlan 21, 59–61, 63, 82–5, 89, 127, 137, 157–8, 173, 175, 178, 195*n*2
Alberich (in Wagner's opera, *Das Rheingold*) 179
Albert Nobbs (film) 191*n*1
Alfred the Great, King 102
Alien 3 (film) 185, 204
Alphabet of Ben Sira 153
anachronism 14, 29, 36, 109, 122, 192*n*5
Anagnorisis 96, 156
Andersson, Theodore 101
Andreas (Old English poem) 89–91
Anglo-Saxon Chronicle 102, 186, 197*n*21
anthropomorphic monsters 109
anti-hero 5–7, 132–3, 138
apocalypse 50–1, 86, 139, 169, 196*n*4
apotropaic function, apotropaic monsters 152–3
appositive style, apposition 29, 37, 58, 189
Arabs 21, 59, 82, 119–20, 127, 137–8, 173
Aragorn 31
Argonauts 84
Aristotle 27, 156
Arnold, Mathew 117
art-horror 156; *see also* Carroll, Nöel
Artaud, Antonin 24, 76
Artaud, Dr. (character in *No Such Thing*) 24, 76, 129, 183
Arthur, King 6–7, 61, 96, 178

Athena 152
Auerbach, Erich 33, 193*n*12
avatar(s) 140, 166, 181

Baker, Graham 14, 17, 58, 65, 82, 86–7, 119, 123–4, 139–40, 144, 152–3, 155, 161, 169, 182, 185, 196*n*5, 198*n*2, 204
Bakshi, Ralph 180
Baldr, Balder 83, 103, 108, 112–18
Bale (demon god in 1999 *Beowulf*) 150–1
Banderas, Antonio 60
Barthes, Roland 8–9
Bataille, Georges 88
Bazin, André 28, 34
Bear 25, 61, 63, 68, 85, 92, 132, 144, 151, 179, 192*n*7
Beatrice (character in *No Such Thing*) 23–4, 59, 73–6, 129–30, 172, 174, 182–3
Beauty and the Beast (fairy tale) 136, 182
Beaw 102–3, 197*n*21
Bede (the Venerable) 85–6, 89, 94, 114, 195*n*3
Beheoldan 37–38
Benton, Walter 122
Beorn's Hall (Tolkien artwork) 31
Beowulf (1998 animated film) 3, 141, 177
Beowulf (1999 film) 1–2, 14, 16, 20, 58, 65, 82, 86–9, 91, 97–8, 113, 119–20, 123–4, 128–9, 139–40, 144–5, 150–55, 158, 161, 165, 169–70, 175, 177, 178–9, 181–5, 196*n*4, 204
Beowulf (2007 film) 1–2, 14, 16–17, 19–20, 71, 73, 77–9, 87, 91, 97–8, 113, 119–20, 122–4, 139–41, 143, 145, 146, 158, 161–6, 175, 177, 179–84, 195*n*4, 204
Beowulf and Grendel (2005 film) 16, 21–4, 26, 71, 84, 87, 91–7, 113, 120, 123–6, 133, 138–9, 143, 145, 157–8, 172–5, 177, 179, 181–7, 195*n*13, 204
Beowulf: Prince of the Geats (film) 167–9, 177, 204
Bergman, Ingmar 198*n*1, 204
Berserkr(s), berserker(s) 132, 157

205

Beyond the Pleasure Principle 10–11
Bildungsroman 188
The Birds (film) 160
Bjorn (character in *Hrolfs Saga Kraki*) 151
body horror 152–5, 162
Bonjour, Andrien 101
Book of Enoch 87
Bowra, C.M. 167, 170–2
Brecca 50, 172, 188
Brewer, Derek 3
Bricolage 187
The Brood (film) 165, 204
Bruce, Alexander M. 197n21, 197n22, 197n23, 197n26
Bullvie (character in *The 13th Warrior*) 17
Butler, Gerald 94
Byron, Lord George Gordon 182

Cacus 46
Cain 16, 61, 87–8, 96, 102–3, 132, 150, 194n35, 196n8
cannibals, cannibalism 60–2, 83–5, 89–91, 137, 143, 157–9, 179
Carpenter, John 154, 158, 199n2, 204
Carrie (film) 160
Carroll, Noël 156–9, 198–9n4
Catabasis, catabases 36, 63, 163
cave paintings 63
La Chienne (film) 193n27, 204
child sacrifice *see* sacrifice
children's literature 71
Chora (Kristeva term) 161, 165
Christ 6, 82, 90, 94–5, 101–2, 112–4, 117–8, 194n28, 196n10, 196n12
Christian coloring 61
Chronicon AEthelweardi 102
Chrysophylax 136
cinémedievalism *see* movie medievalism
Civilization and Its Discontents 11–13
Clinton, William J. 162–3
close up 33, 39–40, 51–2, 59, 100, 171
Cohen, Jeffrey Jerome 148, 158–9, 198n30
Coleridge, Samuel Taylor 122
colonialism, colonialist, colonization 129, 139–40, 168, 185, 196n8
comic book(s) 5, 19, 24, 120, 128, 136, 151, 168, 196n4
commodification 66–70, 80
commoditization 66–80
commodity fetishism 70, 79
Computer Graphics Imaging (CGI) 31, 65, 98, 165, 181–2, 192n9, 195n4
A Connecticut Yankee in King Arthur's Court 61
Conrad, Joseph 6–8, 13–14
Corman, Roger 144, 204
Cosmatos, George 155

courage 66, 75, 77, 79–80, 107, 113, 121–3, 124, 127, 130, 139, 141, 167–76, 194n1, 195n8, 199n2
Craven, Wes 198n1
Creature from the Black Lagoon (film) 143–4, 178, 204
Creed, Barbara 159–60
Crichton, Michael 21, 57, 60–4, 83–5, 91, 123, 127, 132–3, 137, 157–8, 179, 181, 194n31, 195n2, 199n1
Cronenberg, David 165, 204
Cronos 83
cross-cutting 36, 49–50, 92, 188
cultural criticism 2, 22, 122, 134–5
cummings, e.e. 122
Cupiditas 82

Danes 12, 14, 16, 21, 36, 38, 48–53, 56, 58, 62, 64, 69, 71–2, 81, 86–90, 93, 95–100, 102–3, 106–9, 111, 117, 124–5, 139, 146, 158, 172, 179, 188, 197n29, 198n1
Daniel (Old English poem) 106
Dante 23–4, 75
Darwin, Charles 19, 91
death instinct 10
deconstruction 5, 8, 36, 112, 117, 171
deep focus 28, 34–6, 52, 59–60, 64, 181; *see also* depth of field
Deleuze, Giles 28, 81, 98–100, 148, 155, 191n2, 197n18
Denethor 98, 182
depth of field 30–1, 34, 37, 59, 193n14; *see also* deep focus
Derrida, Jacques 8
deterritorialization 81
Dom 6, 13, 42, 134, 169
Don Quixote 5
Donne, John 122
The Doors of Durin and Moria Gate I (Tolkien artwork) 31
Doppelgänger 148–50, 165
Double 85, 148–50, 165, 184, 198n1
Douglas, Mary 156, 198–99n4
Dragon 3, 20, 31, 40, 42, 47, 55, 57, 60, 62–3, 70–1, 74, 78, 87, 91, 97–9, 107–8, 113–6, 123, 132–42, 146, 150, 152, 154, 157, 160–6, 178–86, 193n20, 195n6, 195n8, 195n11, 197n27, 197n29, 198n1, 198n2; *see also* Fafnir
drama of proof, drama of investigation 156–8; *see also* Carroll, Noël
Dream of the Rood 114, 194n28
Driver, Martha 2
Druidh 91
Dryht 6, 35, 78
Dunharrow (Tolkien artwork) 31

Index

Earl, James 50, 195*n*3
Eastwood, Clint 87
Eaters of the Dead (novel) *see* Crichton, Michael
Ecclesiastical History of the English People see Bede (the Venerable)
Eco, Umberto 84, 191*n*1
editing (in film) 51, 57, 147
Ego 12–3, 21, 148–9, 156
The Ego and the Id 11
Einstein, Albert 7–9
Eisenstein, Sergei 28, 34–5, 52
Ekphrasis 32, 65, 194*n*39
Elene (Old English poem) 89–90
Eliot, T.S. 7, 13
Elsner, Jas 64–5, 194*n*39
The Elvenking's Gate II (Tolkien artwork) 31
Eormenric 103
Eówyn 183
Epiphany 113, 193*n*23, 199*n*3
Eros 10–13, 17–25; *see also* pleasure principle
eroticization of capital 82, 161
ethnogenesis 94, 103
euhemerism 60, 95–7, 108
Eve 61
evolution 60–4, 91, 105, 157–8, 179, 187, 194*n*33, 194*n*35
Excalibur (film) 98, 204
Exodus (Old English poem) 105–6
eye-line match 48, 59, 63

Fælsian 54, 111
Fafnir 135–6, 141, 195*n*6; *see also* Dragon
fairy stories, fairy tales 32, 71, 80, 81, 136, 192*n*5, 193*n*26, 195*n*10
Farmer Giles of Ham 136, 138
Fate's arrow (topos) 112–8
Faust, Faustian bargain 164, 182
The Fellowship of the Ring (film) 31, 180, 204
feminism 3, 14–21, 24–5, 62, 78, 119–31; *see also* second wave feminism
Femme fatale 16, 163
Fenrir 112
fetish, fetishizing 66–80, 111, 121, 195*n*5
feud 14–6, 44, 54, 61–2, 78, 84, 93, 109–10, 122, 128, 138, 145, 149–50, 158, 172, 185, 195*n*6
Figura 114
final girl (horror theme) 144, 155
Finn (character in 2007 *Beowulf*) 14, 164–5
Finnsburg (episode in *Beowulf*) 189
Fisher King 98
Flyting 72–4, 110
The Fog (film) 158

form cut 58, 181
Forni, Kathleen 87, 196*n*4
Fortuna 163
Foucault, Michel 101
Frank, Roberta 100–1
Frankenstein 157–8
Franks Casket 29
Frazer, Sir James George 105
Freawaru 14–16, 121, 122, 170, 189
French New Wave 28
Freoðu-webbe 138
Freud, Sigmund 3–4, 7–13, 17–21, 24, 88, 91, 98, 100, 105, 119, 121–2, 142, 152–3, 161, 166, 170
Freya (character in *Outlander*) 143, 157, 183
Friday the 13th 198*n*1, 204
Friday the 13th, Part 2 143
Frodo 31, 194*n*30
The Front Gate (Tolkien artwork) 31
Fulk, R.D. 193*n*17, 196*n*11, 197*n*25

Gabrielle (character in *Xena*) 180
Galadriel 45, 180
Gardner, John 21–2, 57, 71, 78, 91, 96, 126, 133, 138, 160–1, 170, 177–8, 181–2, 191*n*2, 199*n*1
Geats 17, 37–8, 44, 49–53, 56, 70, 72–3, 75, 93, 95–7, 106, 110, 118, 146, 167, 176, 195*n*6, 195*n*8, 196*n*8, 197*n*24
genealogy 61, 102–3, 106, 145, 150
Genesis (Old English poem) 106
Genesis, The Book of 33
genocide 17, 26, 150, 159
Germanic heroism 95, 122; *see also* heroism
Germanic paganism 33, 60, 81, 101, 106
Germanic theory of courage 123; *see also* courage; Tolkien, J.R.R.
giants 43, 45, 52–7, 63, 108, 110, 112, 117, 155, 169, 188, 194*n*35
gigantism 196*n*13
gift 43, 66, 69, 71–5, 97, 111–2, 183, 187; *see also* Giftstol
Giftstol 97, 154, 189
Gilgamesh 10
Gilmore, David D. 149
Girard, René 82–5, 91, 95–100, 105, 112–3, 117–8, 150, 158, 183, 195*n*1, 197*n*17, 198*n*30, 198*n*32
Glaurung Sets Forth to Seek Túrin (Tolkien artwork) 31
Glof (Grendel's "glove") 110–112
Gollum 180
Gondolin and the Vale of Tumladen (Tolkien artwork) 31
Gorgon(s) 152, 178
Gothic 86, 144–5, 159, 161, 196*n*4
Gregory the Great (Pope) 89, 118–9

Index

Grendel 3, 6, 12, 14, 16, 18, 19–22, 25, 33–6, 38, 40, 42, 44, 46–50, 52, 54–9, 62–4, 71, 74, 78–9, 82, 86–9, 91–100, 102, 107, 109–12, 115, 119–26, 128, 132–41, 143, 145–6, 148–51, 154–5, 157–66, 168–70, 172, 175, 178–80, 182–5, 188–9, 191n3, 193n20, 195n11, 195n13, 196n6, 196n8, 196n11, 196–197n13, 197n24, 197n27, 197n29, 198n31, 198n1, 198n2, 199n5
Grendel (film) 20, 71, 78, 87, 97–100, 113, 145, 157, 159, 167, 169, 177, 179, 181, 185, 204
Grendel (novel) see Gardner, John
Grendel Grendel Grendel (film) 177–8, 191n2, 204
Grendel's mother 3, 14, 16, 18–20, 22, 38–47, 54, 58–9, 78–9, 96, 119–25, 128, 139–40, 149, 151–61, 169–72, 178, 193n20, 197n27
Grettis Saga, Grettir's Saga 61, 63, 158, 186, 188–9
Grindl (character in *Xena*) 180–1
Grinhilda (character in *Xena*) 180–1
Grotesque 112, 128, 132, 135–7, 141, 152
Guattari, Felix 98–100, 197n18
Gunnarsson, Sturla 21, 93, 123–4, 157–8, 179–85, 204

Hæðcyn 114–6
Haggard, H. Rider 158
Hakon 103–5
The Hall at Bag End, Residence of B. Baggins Esquire (Tolkien artwork) 31
Halloween (film franchise) 198n1
Hamlet 95, 100, 115
Handscio 34, 95–6, 149
Hanks, Tom 120
Harry Potter (novels) 74
Hartley, Hal 22, 58–9, 65, 73, 75, 123, 136, 182–3, 204
Harty, Kevin 2, 177, 191n2
Heaney, Seamus 66–7, 70, 77, 86, 185, 199n2
The Heart of Darkness 6–9, 13, 19, 24–6
Heart of light 6–9, 19
Heathen, hæðen 88, 105, 111, 117–8, 197n29; see also pagan
Hefner, Hugh 122
Helm's Deep and the Hornburg (Tolkien artwork) 31
Heorot 16, 25, 33, 36, 38, 47–8, 54–6, 86–7, 96–7, 100, 111–2, 139, 146, 148–9, 155, 164, 170, 172, 182, 185, 189, 196n6, 196n11, 199n2
Herebeald 114, 116
Heremod 102–9, 116, 197n21

heroism 2, 9, 13, 18, 22, 75, 120, 122, 142, 171
Heros 4–5
Herzog, Werner 143
Higd see Hygd
Highlander (film) 86, 204
Hildeburh 14–5, 120, 122, 189, 197n27
Hill, John M. 101, 195n8, 198n31
Hitchcock, Alfred 31, 144, 204
The Hobbit (film trilogy) 177, 189
The Hobbit (novel) 135
Hod 115–6
Hodapp, William 196n6, 197n14, 197n15
Holofernus 89–90
Holy Grail 6, 94
homology 106, 114
Horace 28
horror (theory) 147–66
horror films 20, 54, 143–66
Hound of the Baskervilles (novel) 158
House of Usher 144, 204
Hrethric 35
Hrolfs Saga Kraki 61, 151
Hrothgar (or Hroðgar) 12, 14–16, 20–1, 35–6, 47–9, 52, 54, 57–8, 69, 71, 74, 78–9, 86–8, 91–5, 97–100, 102–3, 108, 112–6, 121, 123, 125, 128, 138–40, 145, 148–55, 158–9, 162–6, 169–70, 179–85, 189, 194n29, 196n11
Hrothmund 35
Hrothwulf 35
Hrunting (sword) 55, 72, 163–4
The Human Beast (*La Bête Humaine*, film) 28, 34, 193–4n27, 204
The Hunger (film) 151, 204
hybridity, hybrid(s) 119, 150–8, 165
Hyde, Mr. 165
Hygd 14, 17, 121
Hygelac 15, 17, 47, 69, 71–2, 74–5, 110, 121–2, 194n2
Hyndluljóð 108
hysterical feminine 155

I Spit on Your Grave (film) 198n1, 204
Iceland 23–4, 59, 71, 75–6, 91, 107–8, 119, 129, 158–9, 172, 182–3
iconoclasm 183
Id 13, 17, 21, 119–31
idols, idolatry 64, 88–90, 95–6, 106, 111–3
illusion of depth 30, 61; *see also* depth of field
image-in-the-mirror, mirror image 38, 40, 42, 44, 150, 182
Imaginary (Lacan) 164
Imperialism 88, 137, 186–7
impression of depth 30–2, 59, 192n7

infantile sexuality 9–10; *see also* Freud, Sigmund
Interview with the Vampire (film) 152, 204
Iraq 163
irony 5, 8, 53, 56, 59, 81, 89, 99, 110
Isaac 105–9, 113–4, 117
Isildur 180
Italian Neorealism 28

Jackson, Peter 31, 65, 180–2, 189, 194n30, 199n2, 204
Joan of Arc 178
Johnson, Samuel 80
Jolie, Angelina 20, 78–9, 113, 127, 161–6, 182
Jong, Erica 122
Jouissance 155, 163–6
Journey to Russia 82–4; *see also* Ahmed ibn Fadlan
Joy, Eileen A. 185, 191n1
Judith (Old English poem) 89–90, 108, 196n11
Juliana (Old English poem) 89–90, 108
jump cut 41, 49, 51, 56, 58, 188
Jung, C.G. 88
Jurassic Park (film) 157, 185

Kainan (character in *Outlander*) 150, 159, 184
Kearney, Richard 149, 196n8, 197n16
Kennedy, John F. 162–3
Ker, W.P. 171–2
King Arthur (film) 93
Kingdom of Heaven (film) 138
Klaeber, Frederick J. 40, 47, 88, 193n17, 193n20, 195n7
Kolbítr 66
Kouretes 83, 117
Kracauer, Siegfried 28
Kristeva, Julia 88, 91, 158–60, 163, 165, 194n 38, 196n7
Kulakov, Yuri 3
Kyra (character in *Beowulf* 1999 film) 16, 124, 128, 150–1, 154–5, 170, 183

Labartu 153
Lac 109–12
Lacan, Jacques 31, 88, 134, 142, 148, 150, 158, 161, 164, 166, 191n2, 198n30
Lack 76, 102, 152, 161–2
Lambert, Christopher 58, 86–7, 150
Lamia 153, 184
Laocoön 28
Lapidge, Michael 147–9
Lazarillo de Tormes 5
Leaf by Niggle 32
A League of Their Own (film) 120, 204

Leitmotif 38
Leoni, Sergio 87
Lerer, Seth 110–2, 185, 199n2
Lessing, Gotthold Ephraim 28–9
Leviathan (film) 155, 204
Lewinski, Monica 162
Leyerle, John 28–9, 37
libido 10, 20, 123–4, 129, 140, 169, 174
Libro de Buen Amor 5
Life of Alfred see Alfred the Great, King
Lilith 153–5, 178
Lindisfarne 186
Lindisfarne Gospels 29
Lof 6, 13, 42, 134, 169
Lord of the Rings (animated film 1977) 177, 180
Lord of the Rings (film trilogy) 26, 30, 65, 135, 177–8, 180, 194n30, 199n2, 204
Lord of the Rings (novel) 168, 178–9, 181, 192n5

Magennis, Hugh 64, 195n2
Manichean 56–7, 62, 93, 150
Marx, Marxism 69–70, 121, 161, 195n5
match cut 52
Matriarchal 62, 127, 137, 159, 194n36, 194n38
McCain, Howard 184–6, 204
McTiernan, John 60, 64–5, 82–3, 91, 93, 123, 137, 157, 204
The Medieval Hero on Screen 2
medievalism 1–2, 26, 27, 34, 65, 82–4, 93, 119, 134–5, 142, 157, 159, 191n1, 191–2n2, 196n8
Medusa 152–3, 155
Melancholia (film) 188, 204
Mere-wif 40–1, 46, 55, 97, 125, 143, 193n20
metamorphosis 135
Milton, John 182
mimetic rivalry, mimetic escalation 105, 113, 118, 150
Minos, King 179
Minotaur 155, 178–9
Mirren, Helen 183
mirror image *see* image-in-the-mirror
miscegenation 130–2, 151, 155
Mise en abyme 8
Mise en scène 28, 33, 37–9, 46, 51, 53–4, 143, 180
The Mist (film) 158
Misty Mountains (Tolkien) 157
Mitchell, W.T.J. 28, 192n3
Mitra, Rhona 183
modernism, modernist 5, 8, 28
Modthryth *see* Thryth
monotheism 106, 108, 117, 127

monster(s) 3, 6, 12–24, 34, 39–40, 50, 54–62, 69, 71–3, 75–8, 84–8, 91–103, 109–113, 117–130, 132–42, 143–66, 167–70, 172–5, 178–88, 191n1, 193n20, 195n11, 195n12, 196n8, 196n12, 198n2, 199n5
monster theory 148–9, 158
monsterization 159, 184
monstrous feminine 97, 155, 159–66
montage 28–9, 34, 36–7, 46, 49, 52, 58, 187–8
Monty Python 93
Monty Python and the Holy Grail 94, 204
Moorwen 159
Moria Gate I (Tolkien artwork) 31
Moses 102, 105–9, 113–4, 117
Mother Goddess 126
movie medievalism 1, 26, 27, 65, 82, 134, 157, 159, 191
Myers, Tony 166
Myles, Sophia 183
myth, myth criticism 60, 81, 83–5, 91–2, 95–100, 102, 108, 112–3, 117, 137, 144, 149, 152–5, 157–8, 178–80, 183, 192n5, 192n6, 196n8, 197n25, 198n31
mythologization 83, 85, 95, 97, 100

Nachtmere 25
Nægling (sword) 42
Nasmith, Ted 192n5
Neanderthal 16, 60–4, 85, 133, 137, 144, 157, 194n33, 194n34, 194n35, 194n36
New York Times Bestseller List 67
New Zealand 180, 184
The Nibelungenlied 28
Nietzsche, Friedrich 31
Nightmare on Elm Street (film franchise) 149
nightmares 94, 147–9
Niles, John D. 57, 101, 193n15
No Such Thing (film) 2, 22–4, 26, 58–9, 65, 71, 73–7, 119–20, 123, 129–32, 136, 157, 172–4, 177, 182–4, 195n12, 204
Noah's Ark 105
Norway 184, 186

Obama, Barach 161
objective camera 36–9, 43–8, 54, 64, 82, 189
objective correlative 52, 144
Odin 25, 103–4, 108, 112, 179
Odysseus 5, 84
Oedipal complex, Oedipus complex 9, 98, 155
Oedipalization 91, 98, 100
Olga (character in *The 13th Warrior*) 16, 127, 174

Olsen, Karin 134–5
Olsen, Robert 134–5
oppression 21, 25, 148–51, 158
oral transmission, oral formulism 28, 61, 84, 186–7
Orchard, Andy 197n28
Osborn, Marijane 101
Other, Otherness, Othering 13, 19, 21–2, 25, 62, 78, 88, 100, 119, 124–8, 130, 132–42, 148–50, 155, 172–5, 191n3, 195n12, 198n1, 199n4
Our Man Flint (film) 173
Outlander 143–145, 150, 159, 177, 181, 183–6, 204
Overing, Gillian R. 28–9, 57

paganism, pagan 30, 33, 60, 77, 81–2, 85–91, 94, 101, 104–17, 125, 137, 195n6
painting 29–33, 63, 65, 156, 192n5, 192n9
pan shot 33, 36, 43, 55, 91
Panofsky, Erwin 28
parody 89, 95, 173–4, 179, 184, 186–7
pastiche 87, 179–80, 186–7, 196n4
patriarchy 127, 137, 148
Peirce, Charles Sanders 29
Performance Capture Technology (PCT) 19, 77, 123, 140, 163, 165, 181
Peripatetia 156
personification 38, 40, 42, 88
perspective 29–51, 54, 56, 59–61, 67, 69, 82, 84, 86, 91, 96, 101, 137, 144, 146, 149, 173, 193n21
Phallus 98, 121, 161–4
Phantasmagoric 19, 164, 184–5
Phantom of the Opera (film) 144, 204
Picaro 5
Piers the Plowman's pardon 53
The Pit and the Pendulum (film) 204
The Pit and the Pendulum (story by Poe) 144
The Pleasure of the Text see Barthes, Roland
pleasure principle 8–12
Poe, Edgar Allan 144
Pogo (comic strip) 142
point of view (POV) 22, 30, 33–43, 82, 125, 149, 189
political correctness (PC) 123, 159
Polley, Sarah 24, 59, 73, 76, 94, 182–4
Poseidon 152
postcolonialism 185–7
postmodernism 8, 186
Predator (film) 144, 185, 204
The Prey (novel) 158
Price, Vincent 159
pride 6, 52–3, 57, 70, 108, 115–6
Prose Edda see Sturluson, Snorri
Prospero 158

Index

Protagonist 5, 48, 127, 138, 170
proto-cinematic style 36, 55, 58, 185, 189
Psycho (Hitchcock film) 144, 160, 204
Purity and Danger see Douglas, Mary

quantum physics 74–5, 77, 79
quest 6–10, 128, 134, 138, 172, 183

racism, race 13, 21–2, 25, 37, 52, 57, 62, 64, 75, 87, 91, 95, 105, 107, 119, 122, 124, 126, 133–9, 155, 165, 169, 172–3, 186, 195n13, 199n2
rack focus 39, 54, 193n19
Raiders of the Lost Arc (film franchise) 63
Ragnarök 112, 117
Ramsey, Mary K. 185–6
Raw Meat (film) 143, 204
Ray, Sid 2
Reign of Fire (film) 182, 198n1
Renoir, Alain 28–9, 33–8, 57–8, 149, 192n4, 193n13
Renoir, Jean 28, 52, 59, 193n14, 193n27, 204
Renoir, Pierre-Auguste 28
repetition 10, 30, 37, 101, 106, 149
repression 12, 98, 148–51, 158
reproductive anxieties 162
reterritorialization 82
The Return of the King (film) 31, 183, 194n30, 204
Das Rheingold (Wagner opera) 179
Rhine maidens 180
Rich, Adrienne 122, 159
Riddle of the Sphinx 152–4
Riddle 33 (Mail Coat) 39–40
Ring Cycle (Wagner) 179–80
Risden, E.L. 186, 193n20, 193n23
Rivendell III (Tolkien artwork) 30
Road Warrior 86
Roberts, Layla 58, 151–4, 162
Robin Hood 178
Robinson, Fred C. 28–9, 37, 121
Roman Britain 185
Romney, Mitt 161
Rosenbaum, Jonathan 2
Rossetti, Christina 122
Rotoscope 180
The Rules of the Game (film) 28, 34–5, 52, 204

sacred violence see violence and the sacred
sacrifice, human sacrifice 13, 25, 62–4, 75, 81–118, 120, 128, 159, 179, 183, 187, 196n10, 196n12, 198n31, 198n32
sacrificial mechanism 97, 100, 112–3, 117–8, 183
Saga of Gunnlaug Serpent-Tongue 104

Saga of the Jómsvíkings 103–4
Sancho Panza 5
Sapientia et fortitudo 97
Satan 90, 133, 182
Sauron 180
Saussure, Ferdinand de 7
Saxo Grammaticus 103
Scandinavia 30, 81, 102, 116
scapegoat, scapegoating 83, 88, 91–2, 94–8, 101, 113, 117, 157–8, 179, 184, 187, 196n8, 197n17
Sceaf 102–6, 197n20, 197n21, 197n25
Schliemann, Heinrich 84
science fiction, sci-fi 4, 144, 150, 159, 167–9, 196n4
Scott, Ridley 162, 204
Scott, Walter 84
Scream (film franchise) 198n1
Scyld Scefing 38, 46, 57, 81, 86–8, 92–3, 98–112, 116–7, 195n3, 197n21, 197n24, 197n27
Scyldings 46, 49, 188
Seax 43–4
second-wave feminism 17–8, 21, 25
Selma (character in *Beowulf and Grendel*) 16, 21–2, 24, 94, 125, 184
Sermo Lupi ad Anglos see Wulfstan, Bishop
Seventh Seal (film) 198n1, 204
Shaw, Bernard 73
Sherif, Omar 60
Sherlock Holmes 158
ship burial 59–60, 82–5
Shippey, Tom 2, 32, 167–8, 194n1
Sigemund 50, 107–8
Sigurd 108
Silence of the Lambs (film) 143, 204
The Silmarillion 135, 168
simile 43, 46, 56, 58
single take 28, 39
Sir Gawain and the Green Knight 28, 192n6, 193n18
Sister-Arts Tradition 29, 33, 65
Skal, David J. 162
Skarsgård, Stellan 92
Sklar, Elizabeth S. 64
slasher film 144
Sleipnir 108
Smaug 135–6, 158
Sphinx 152–3, 155
Stam, Robert 2
Star of Eärendil 194n30
Star Trek: Voyager ("Monsters and Heroes" episode) 167, 177, 191n3, 199n5, 204
Stith, Alexander 178
Sturluson, Snorri 103
sub-creation 60, 62
subjective camera 33, 36, 47–50

Index

subjectivity 88, 161
Succubus 151–5, 161–2, 182
Superego 11–3, 21, 166
superhero 24, 151, 168, 196n4
surplus repression 148
Sword (of the Giants), the hilt of that sword 45–9, 51–8, 63, 110–2, 121, 125, 146, 163, 193n24, 193n26
synecdoche 39, 56, 111

talisman 53, 110, 112, 123–4, 141, 193n23
Texas Chainsaw Massacre 144, 204
Thanatos 10–14, 17–25; *see also* death instinct
Theater of Cruelty *see* Artaud, Antonin
theory of courage *see* courage; Germanic theory of courage
Thetic break 160–1, 164
The Thing (film) 155, 204
Thirst (film) 194n3, 204
The 13th Warrior (film, alt. title: *The Thirteenth Warrior*) 2, 16, 21, 26, 59, 62–5, 71, 82–6, 89, 91, 93, 95, 97, 119–20, 123, 126–8, 132, 137, 144–5, 157, 172–5, 177–9, 181, 184, 187, 204
Thor 88, 110, 112
Three Cliffs Bay (Swansea, Wales) 31
Three Essays on the Theory of Sexuality 9–10
Thryth 18, 121, 197n24
Thunder Caves 60–3, 158
The Time Machine (novel) 61
Timeline (film) 157
Tiw (Old Norse *Týr*) 112, 198n31
Tolkien, J.R.R. 26, 28–33, 43, 57, 59–62, 70, 74, 98, 123, 133, 136, 138, 141, 145, 157, 167–8, 178–82, 187, 191n1, 192n5, 192n6, 192n7, 192n8, 193n11, 194n1, 194n30, 195n10
topos, topoi 54, 97, 115, 144
tracking shot 33, 36, 42, 181
Træf 89–91
Trier, Lars von 188, 204
trolls 16, 21, 41, 46, 54, 59, 61, 64, 91, 93–6, 120, 124–5, 133, 135–6, 138, 140–3, 157–8, 172, 181–4, 189, 195n13
Twain, Mark 51, 61; *see also Connecticut Yankee in King Arthur's Court*
Twilight (film franchise) 199n6
type figure, typology 105–7, 113–4

Uncanny 81, 96, 164, 179, 198n1; *see also Unheimlich*
understatement 15, 19
Unferth (or Hunferð) 35, 43, 50, 55, 72, 74, 94, 103, 165, 168
Unheimlich 36, 54, 98
Ut pictura poesis 28, 33

Valhalla 59, 82
Valkyries 179–81
vampire capitalism 161
vampires, vampirism 86, 152–3, 161, 164, 196n4, 199n6
vanishing mediator 155
Vertigo (film) 31, 204
video games 3, 24, 167
Vietnam 163
Viking Age 144, 159, 186
Vikings 61, 64, 85, 91, 143, 179, 185
violence and the sacred 113
Virgil *see Aeneid*
Virgin Spring see Bergman, Ingmar
Volsungasaga 135, 195n6

Die Walküre (Wagner opera) 180
Wall Street 175
The Waste Land see Eliot, T.S.
Wasteland 7–8, 13–14, 98
Watts, Murray 3
Wealhtheow (or Wealhþeow) 14–5, 35–6, 98–100, 120–4, 143, 157, 189
Welles, Orson 28
Wells, H.G. *see The Time Machine*
Wendol 16, 61–4, 85, 126–7, 137–8, 157, 173, 184
Weregild 16, 71
Widsið 102, 197n20
Wiglaf 20, 42, 78, 116–8, 123–4, 166, 180, 184, 195n8
Williams, William Carlos 122
Wilson, Eric 197n16, 198n32
Wizards (film) 180
The Wolf Man (film) 144, 157, 204
woman's time 163–4; *see also* Kristeva, Julia
Wood, Robin 147–51, 155–7
World War I 7
Wulfstan, Bishop 170
Wyrd 55, 81, 114

Xena 19
Xena Factor 19
Xena: Warrior Princess (television series) 177, 179–81, 204

Ynglinga Saga 104

Zeitgeist 2–3
Zemeckis, Robert 14, 17, 19–20, 73, 77–8, 87, 119, 122, 140, 143, 164, 169, 180–5, 195n4, 204
Zeus 83, 117
Žižek, Slavoj 158, 166, 191n2
zombie films, zombies 87, 144, 146
Zoom 31, 36, 39, 40, 42, 54

www.ingramcontent.com/pod-product-compliance
Ingram Content Group UK Ltd.
Pitfield, Milton Keynes, MK11 3LW, UK
UKHW041918140426
5217IPUK00013B/216